Pearson Edexcel GCSE (9-1)
History

Migrants in Britain, c800–present

Series Editor: Angela Leonard   Authors: Rosemary Rees   Tony Warner   Joshua Garry

Published by Pearson Education Limited, 80 Strand,
London, WC2R 0RL.

www.pearsonschoolsandfecolleges.co.uk

Copies of official specifications for all Pearson qualifications
may be found on the website: qualifications.pearson.com

Text © Pearson Education Limited 2020

Series editor: Angela Leonard
Produced by Florence Production Ltd, Devon, UK
Typeset by Florence Production Ltd, Devon, UK
Original illustrations © Pearson Education Limited
Illustrated by Florence Production Ltd

Cover photo © Keystone/Stringer/Getty Images

The right of Rosemary Rees, Tony Warner and Joshua Garry
to be identified as authors of this work has been asserted by
them in accordance with the Copyright, Designs and Patents
Act 1988.

First published 2021

24 23 22 21
10 9 8 7 6 5 4 3 2 1

British Library Cataloguing in Publication Data
A catalogue record for this book is available from the British
Library.
ISBN 978 1 292 39154 0

Copyright notice

Printed in the UK by Ashford Colour Press Ltd

A note from the publisher
1. While the publishers have made every attempt to ensure
that advice on the qualifications and assessment is accurate,
the official specification and associated guidance materials
are the only authoritative source of information and should
always be referred to for definitive guidance. Pearson
examiners have not contributed to any sections in this
resource relevant to examination papers for which they have
responsibility.

2. Pearson has robust editorial processes, including answer
and fact checks, to ensure the accuracy of the content in
this publication, and every effort is made to ensure this
publication is free of errors. We are, however, only human,
and occasionally errors do occur. Pearson is not liable for
any misunderstandings that arise as a result of errors in this
publication, but it is our priority to ensure that the content
is accurate. If you spot an error, please do contact us at
resourcescorrections@pearson.com so we can make sure it
is corrected.

Websites
Pearson Education Limited is not responsible for the content
of any external internet sites. It is essential for tutors to
preview each website before using it in class so as to ensure
that the URL is still accurate, relevant and appropriate.
We suggest that tutors bookmark useful websites and
consider enabling students to access them through the
school/college intranet.

Contents

How to use this book

What's covered?

This book covers the Thematic study on Migrants in Britain, c800 to present. These units make up 30% of your GCSE course, and will be examined in Paper 1.

Thematic studies cover a long period of history, and require you to know about change and continuity across different ages and aspects of society. You will need to know about key people, events and developments and make comparisons between the different periods studied.

Linked to the thematic study is a historic environment that examines a specific site and its relationship to historical events and developments.

Features

As well as a clear, detailed explanation of the key knowledge you will need, you will also find a number of features in the book.

- **Key terms** – where you see a word followed by an asterisk (e.g. Succession*), you will find a Key Terms box that explains what that word means.
- **Activities** – these are designed to help check and embed knowledge and get you to think about what you've studied.
- **Sources and interpretations** – this book contains numerous sources to show you what people from the period said or thought. You need to be comfortable examining sources for your Paper 1 exam. This book also includes extracts from historians, interpreting the events you've studied.
- **Extend your knowledge** – these contain useful additional information to add to your depth of knowledge.

- **Exam-style questions and tips** – these are to help you practise for the exams. The tip will help you with your answer.
- **Summaries and checkpoints** – at the end of each section, the main points are summarised to help embed your core knowledge. Checkpoints help you reflect on your learning. The strengthen section helps consolidate knowledge. The challenge section pushes you towards evaluating and analysing what you've studied.

Thinking historically

These activities are designed to help you develop a better understanding of how history is constructed, and are focused on the key areas of Evidence, Interpretations, Cause and consequence and Change and continuity. In the Thematic Study, you will come across activities on both Cause and Change, and in the Historical Environment on Evidence, as these are key areas of focus for these units.

The Thinking historically approach has been developed in conjunction with Dr Arthur Chapman and the Institute of Education, UCL. It is based on research into the misconceptions that can hold students back in history.

Preparing for your exams

In these sections you you'll advice on the demands of this paper. Written in consultation with Angela Leonard, this will help you prepare for and approach the exam with confidence. Each question type is explained through annotated sample answers at two levels, showing clearly how answers can be improved.

A note on language

The language used to discuss race has changed a great deal over time. Throughout history, words we rightly consider unacceptable today were often used to describe members of different ethnic communities. Many were also commonly used by members of the community they were describing, for example some mid-20th century black people described themselves as 'coloured'.

It is vital that racism should always be confronted. As education publishers, we want to support and promote discussions of anti-racism with students, both today and in the past. As such, we believe it is important, where we quote sources, that we reproduce the words actually used. This helps give a fuller insight into attitudes held at the time.

However, we have used asterisks (*) to strike out words that may cause readers particular distress.

About change

This course is about two things: it is about the history of migration, and it is about **change**. You are going to look at a long period of time – over 1,000 years. Migration is the theme you will follow through these years. Concentrating on just one part of British life means you can also focus on how and why things change (and sometimes how and why they don't).

This introduction is to help you understand the language and concepts historians use when they discuss change.

- **Change** – this is when things become different than they were before
- **Continuity** – this is the opposite of change, when things stay the same, sometimes for a very long time.
- Change isn't always the same as **progress** – which is when things get better.
- The **rate of change** – change doesn't always happen at the same pace – sometimes things change very quickly, but sometimes they change slowly. Historians are interested in why this is.
- A **trend** is when there are a number of similar and related changes, continuing in the same direction, over a period of time – for example, the fact that there were 57 million people with smartphones in the UK in 2019 is part of the trend in the growing use of mobile phones.
- A **turning point** is when a significant change happens – something that is different from what has happened before and which will affect the future. For example, it was a turning point when Michael Harrison made the first ever mobile phone call in Britain on 1 January 1985.

- Historians are very interested in the **factors** that affect change. Some of them can be quite obvious, but others are more surprising. For example:
  - Developments in science and technology, particularly around miniaturisation, have affected the development of the mobile phone.
  - People's attitudes have also affected the development of the mobile phone. For example, text messaging (SMS) was not originally designed to be used – it was built in to help scientists test the first networks and phones. But users found out about it, liked it, and it has now become part of our world.
  - Less surprisingly, governments have affected the development of mobile phones – with regulations about networks, laws about using them, and planning control of phone masts.

Look out for plenty more factors that affect change throughout the course.

Activities ?

1. Write your own definition of each of the words in bold above, and explain your own example of each one.

2. Make a table or graph to show change in your life over time. Show any trends or turning points and places where the rate of change increases. Explain what factors have influenced these changes.

Migration to England before c800

England was a country rich in resources. This made it very attractive for both migrants and invaders. The map below shows where these resources could be found, as well as indicating some of the earlier people to arrive in England.

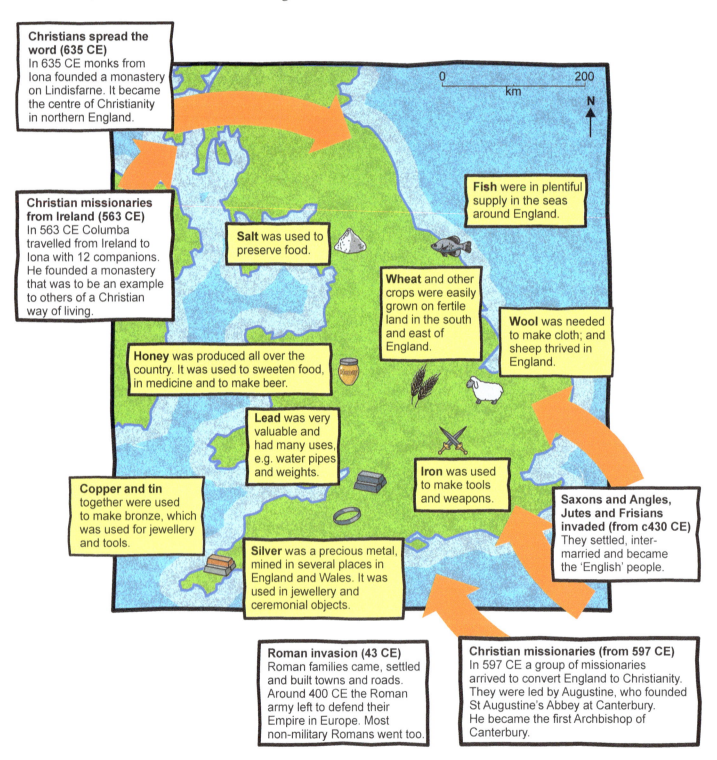

Christians spread the word (635 CE)
In 635 CE monks from Iona founded a monastery on Lindisfarne. It became the centre of Christianity in northern England.

Christian missionaries from Ireland (563 CE)
In 563 CE Columba travelled from Ireland to Iona with 12 companions. He founded a monastery that was to be an example to others of a Christian way of living.

Fish were in plentiful supply in the seas around England.

Salt was used to preserve food.

Wheat and other crops were easily grown on fertile land in the south and east of England.

Wool was needed to make cloth; and sheep thrived in England.

Honey was produced all over the country. It was used to sweeten food, in medicine and to make beer.

Lead was very valuable and had many uses, e.g. water pipes and weights.

Iron was used to make tools and weapons.

Copper and tin together were used to make bronze, which was used for jewellery and tools.

Saxons and Angles, Jutes and Frisians invaded (from c430 CE)
They settled, intermarried and became the 'English' people.

Silver was a precious metal, mined in several places in England and Wales. It was used in jewellery and ceremonial objects.

Roman invasion (43 CE)
Roman families came, settled and built towns and roads. Around 400 CE the Roman army left to defend their Empire in Europe. Most non-military Romans went too.

Christian missionaries (from 597 CE)
In 597 CE a group of missionaries arrived to convert England to Christianity. They were led by Augustine, who founded St Augustine's Abbey at Canterbury. He became the first Archbishop of Canterbury.

Factors affecting migration

Throughout this topic, there are four key themes that affect migration:

- Government
- Religion
- Economics and trade
- Attitudes in society.

In each chapter you will need to consider how these factors impact migration.

Factor	Impact on migration
Government c800–1500	
The Anglo-Saxon kingdoms were united in 927 as the Kingdom of England. The Witan was a council advising Anglo-Saxon rulers when they were asked. Many of these systems continued under the Normans. By 1500 England was governed by the monarch and his advisers (usually the barons) and a parliament of lords and commons. This was usually only called when the monarch needed money or to approve an important piece of legislation.	Arguments over who ruled England was central to invasion from the Vikings and Normans. The monarch invited migrants who would benefit them, e.g. Henry III invited Lombardy bankers and Flemish weavers to migrate to England. The government was able to make it easier for merchants to operate, by giving them a right to trade. They could also use their power against migrant groups, e.g. Edward I expelling all Jews.
Economics and trade	
Monarchs levied taxes. Over time, this needed to be agreed with parliament. England was rich in resources (see map opposite) and its trading links throughout Europe grew during this period. This made it more attractive for migrants either for conquest or settling for trade.	The Normans and Vikings were attracted to England by its resources and the land available. England's economic strength later attracted merchants looking to grow their trade network, while Flemish weavers developed the cloth trade. Economic growth needed money. Jewish migrants then Lombardy bankers helped provide this.
Religion	
Christianity had spread throughout England; people worshipped in churches and cathedrals; monks were supposed to lead godly lives in abbeys and monasteries. Monasteries looked after the poor and the sick. By 1500 England was a Catholic Christian country and an important part of Christendom.	The support of the Church was important to William I in his plans to conquer England. Being part of a shared European religion helped make England seem like a natural destination for European merchants and bankers.
Attitudes in society	
During this period England was a feudal country, with power concentrated in the hands of a small number of powerful barons and lords. Most English people had no say in making laws, lived in villages and worked on the land. Most people lived their whole lives in one small area and had very little contact with the outside world. Education was often limited.	Many were suspicious of 'outsiders'. Some were hostile to migrant merchants and weavers, feeling they were taking jobs and trade from Englishmen. Violence and arrests, particularly when England was at war, were common. As England was a Christian country, many people were hostile towards the Jewish community.

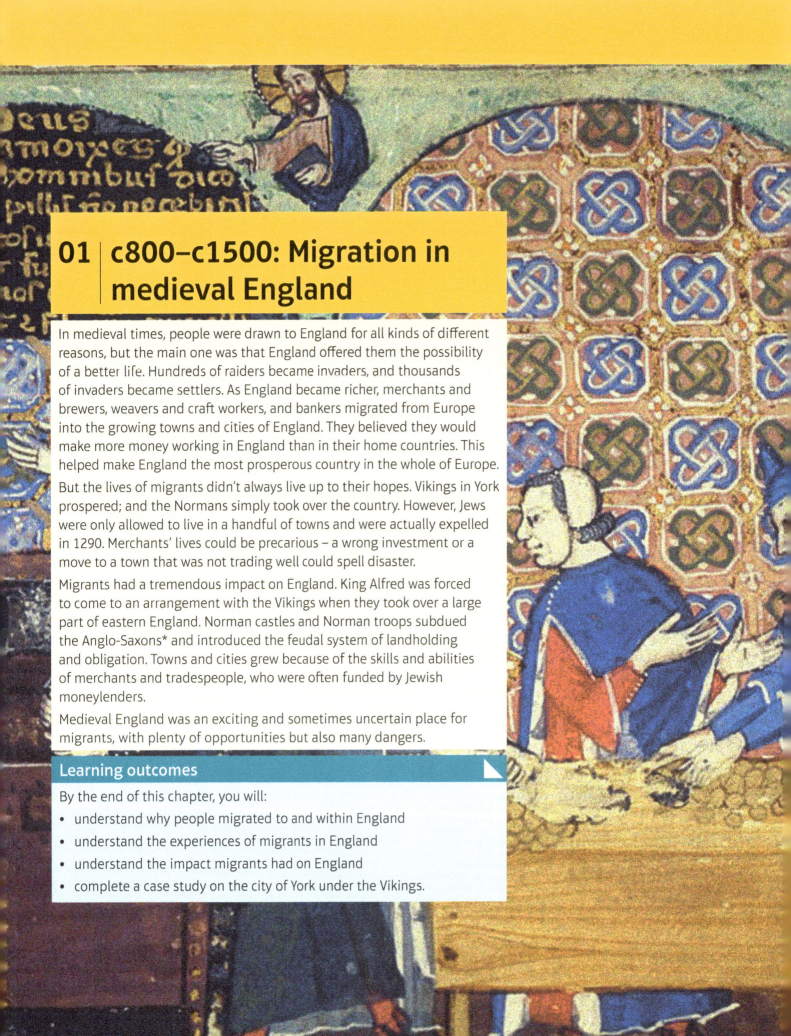

01 | c800–c1500: Migration in medieval England

In medieval times, people were drawn to England for all kinds of different reasons, but the main one was that England offered them the possibility of a better life. Hundreds of raiders became invaders, and thousands of invaders became settlers. As England became richer, merchants and brewers, weavers and craft workers, and bankers migrated from Europe into the growing towns and cities of England. They believed they would make more money working in England than in their home countries. This helped make England the most prosperous country in the whole of Europe.

But the lives of migrants didn't always live up to their hopes. Vikings in York prospered; and the Normans simply took over the country. However, Jews were only allowed to live in a handful of towns and were actually expelled in 1290. Merchants' lives could be precarious – a wrong investment or a move to a town that was not trading well could spell disaster.

Migrants had a tremendous impact on England. King Alfred was forced to come to an arrangement with the Vikings when they took over a large part of eastern England. Norman castles and Norman troops subdued the Anglo-Saxons* and introduced the feudal system of landholding and obligation. Towns and cities grew because of the skills and abilities of merchants and tradespeople, who were often funded by Jewish moneylenders.

Medieval England was an exciting and sometimes uncertain place for migrants, with plenty of opportunities but also many dangers.

Learning outcomes

By the end of this chapter, you will:

- understand why people migrated to and within England
- understand the experiences of migrants in England
- understand the impact migrants had on England
- complete a case study on the city of York under the Vikings.

1.1 The reasons why people migrated

The Vikings

Monks kept a record of events over hundreds of years in the *Anglo-Saxon Chronicle*. They recorded the first Viking* raid on England when, in 789, the Vikings attacked the kingdom of Wessex* on the south coast.

Source A

An extract from the *Anglo-Saxon Chronicle* for the year 789, describing the first Viking raid.

In this year there came three ships of Norwegians from Horthaland: and then the reeve [manager of the royal estates] rode thither and tried to compel them to go to the royal manor, for he did not know what they were: and then they slew him. These were the first ships of the Danes to come to England.

From raiding to invading

These three ships were the start of a terrifying wave of Viking raiders. They were searching for treasure – gold, silver and jewels – or anything that was valuable and easy to carry away on their ships. The rich, undefended monasteries and abbeys in the north, such as Lindisfarne, which was raided in 793, provided the richest pickings.

For over 70 years, Vikings terrorised, stole and slaughtered – mostly along England's north and eastern shores. Then things began to change.

- **850**: A raiding party spent the winter camped on the Isle of Thanet, Kent.
- **854**: Another raiding party spent the winter camped on the Isle of Sheppey, in the Thames estuary.
- **865**: The raiding stopped. The Vikings started to try to invade England. Why did they do this?

Key terms

Anglo-Saxon*
People who migrated from Europe and lived in England from the 5th century.

Viking*
People from the Scandinavian countries (Norway, Sweden and Denmark) who raided and finally invaded England in the 9th century.

Wessex*
An Anglo-Saxon kingdom established in southern England in 519.

Fertile*
Land that is able to support farming and the growing of food.

Agriculture: The land in eastern England was rich and fertile*. Vikings and their families could settle, farm the land and live well.

Trade: Many English towns were important trading centres with Europe. Taking over these towns and their trade could make Vikings rich.

Religion: Odin, the god of war and military victory, was the Vikings' most important god. To fight and to win meant that Odin would reward Viking warriors after death.

Figure 1.1 Why did the Vikings want to come to England?

From invading to conquest

In 865 the Viking army landed in East Anglia. Called the Great Army, it was in fact made up of several smaller armies, each with its own commander. The *Anglo-Saxon Chronicle* claimed there were tens of thousands of Vikings, though it was probably exaggerating. Even so, it was a huge invasion and must have been terrifying for the Anglo-Saxons.

In 866 the Vikings captured the heavily fortified* city of York. They used the city as a base to attack and conquer most of eastern England. They spent 14 years campaigning against the four Anglo-Saxon kingdoms.

By 878 the once great kingdoms of Northumbria, Mercia and East Anglia were gone for ever, their kings killed or fled abroad. The Vikings took over: they brought over their families and settled, as farmers, manufacturers, craft workers and traders. Only Wessex, the last Anglo-Saxon kingdom, remained unconquered.

Tackling Wessex

The Vikings had invaded Wessex earlier, in 871, and Alfred, King of Wessex, had paid them to leave. Now, seven years later and with the other Anglo-Saxon kingdoms gone for good, the Vikings finally turned their attention to Wessex. At first it looked good for the Vikings.

> The Vikings made a surprise attack against King Alfred and his Anglo-Saxon army at Chippenham in January 878. Alfred retreated into the Somerset marshes at Athelney. Most of Wiltshire and Hampshire surrendered to Guthrum, leader of the Viking army that attacked Wessex.

> Alfred rallied local leaders and won a great victory over the Vikings at the Battle of Edington four months later.

> Both sides agreed the Treaty of Wedmore. A boundary between Wessex and the Viking lands, called the Danelaw, was agreed.

> Guthrum was baptised a Christian and took his army into East Anglia to settle there.

> Wessex remained independent: the only Anglo-Saxon kingdom to be left after the Viking campaigns.

Figure 1.2 The Vikings and Wessex

It was over. The Vikings, who had started out as fearsome raiders, were now settled in a large part of England. To find out how successful they were, you will need to go to Sections 1.2 and 1.3.

Key term

Fortified*

Surrounded by defences against possible attacks.

Figure 1.3 The Anglo-Saxon kingdoms of England and the boundary of the Danelaw in 880

Timeline

Viking campaigns

865 Invaded East Anglia; the king agreed terms

867–68 Marched into Mercia, where the king agreed terms

866 Captured York and controlled the kingdom of Northumbria

869 Conquered East Anglia, killing its king

871 Marched into Wessex; King Alfred paid them to leave

873 Conquered Mercia; its king fled overseas

878 Defeated by King Alfred at the Battle of Edington; treaty agreed where Vikings controlled much of northern and eastern England and Wessex remained independent

Extend your knowledge

Archaeological evidence

Archaeologists excavated land at Torksey, in Lincolnshire, where the Viking army had spent the winter of 872–73. They found that it was not only warriors who had lived there, but also people involved in trade and manufacturing, as well as women and children.

Danegeld

A tax raised by Anglo-Saxon rulers and used to pay the Vikings to stop them devastating Saxon lands.

Activities ?

1 Read Source A.

  a What clues can you find there that the Vikings did not come peacefully to England?

  b Can the story this source tells be trusted?

2 Explain how the Vikings came to control most of northern and eastern England by the end of 878.

3 Start a mind map called 'Why was Britain attractive to migrants?'. Add in the reasons why the Vikings wanted to come to Britain. As you work through this section you will find out about other groups of migrants who moved into and within Britain. Add them in as you go along. By the end, you will have an excellent idea of why Britain was so attractive to migrants.

The Normans

Almost exactly 200 years after the Vikings invaded East Anglia, there was another invasion. This time it was by the Normans. They invaded England not from the east but from the south. Unlike the Vikings, they weren't looking for fertile land and trading centres; they were invading because of a promise, a promise that would bring power.

A succession* problem

On 5 January 1066 King Edward the Confessor died. He had been king of England for 24 years, and during this time England had been peaceful and prosperous. However he had no children to inherit the throne. What would happen next?

- The dying king had the right to say who should succeed him.
- The new king should ideally be a blood relative of the old king and an experienced warrior.

Edward had promised the throne to Harold Godwinson several times (probably even when on his deathbed). Godwinson was the most powerful noble in England. The Witan* agreed, and on 6 January Harold was crowned king of England.

Promises, promises, promises

William, Duke of Normandy*, believed that promises made to him by Edward and Harold meant that he was the rightful king of England. What were these promises?

In 1064 Harold Godwinson made me a solemn promise that I would be king of England when Edward died.

The Pope* supports me because Harold broke his word. With God and right on my side I can't lose.

Edward's mother was my great-aunt and so we have a blood connection.

In 1051 the Archbishop of Canterbury told me Edward made me his heir.

Decision made! I will invade England and turn it into a Norman country.

Figure 1.4 Promises made to William, Duke of Normandy, by Edward the Confessor and Harold Godwinson

Key terms

Succession* (to the throne)

The process that decided who should be the next king or queen and so 'succeed' to the throne.

Witan*

An Anglo-Saxon assembly of 'wise men' – nobles and clergy (churchmen) summoned by the king to advise him.

Normandy*

An independent dukedom in north-west France.

The Pope*

The leader of the Christian church. The Pope was based in Rome, Italy.

Source B

The Bayeux Tapestry was made in the 11th century, a few years after the Battle of Hastings. This part of the Bayeux Tapestry shows us a different sort of promise. On his deathbed, Edward is holding out his hand to Harold.

Invasion and victory

William prepared well for the invasion of England. He wanted to be crowned king of England and take over the whole country. He would fill it with Normans and run it his way.

The Normans who followed William were attracted by the opportunities for new land and wealth that England provided.

- William's army was superbly fit and well equipped.
- William ordered specially designed ships to be built and filled them with soldiers and horses.
- William brought castles with him. They were prepared in sections so they could be put together quickly. This meant that he could immediately establish Norman rule in England.

On 14 October 1066 the two armies faced each other. Harold Godwinson, King of England, was defending his country against foreign invaders. William, Duke of Normandy was fighting for the throne of England that he believed was rightly his.

William, Duke of Normandy, was crowned king of England in Westminster Abbey on Christmas Day 1066. During his coronation there was hand-to-hand fighting between Normans and Anglo-Saxons in the streets around the Abbey. This was not a good start to the Norman takeover. Would the Norman migration to England be successful? To find out, you will need to go to Sections 1.2 and 1.3.

Extend your knowledge

The Bayeux Tapestry

This is an embroidery approximately 70 metres long and 50 centimetres tall. Historians think it was probably stitched in England in the 1070s by women working in Kent. It is the earliest source of information we have about the Conquest. However, it tells the story of the Norman Conquest from the Norman point of view. There is nothing similar that tells the story from the Anglo-Saxon viewpoint.

The battle of Hastings took place on Senlac Hill, 7 miles from Hastings. It lasted all day and ended in a decisive Norman victory. Harold and his brothers were killed.

↓

William went to Hastings and waited for the Anglo-Saxon nobles to come and surrender to him. No one came.

↓

William sent troops to seize Winchester, where England's royal treasury was held.

↓

William marched towards London, burning farms and villages and destroying crops on the way. The terrified people of the towns and villages surrendered to the Normans.

↓

William reached Berkhamsted, north-west of London. England's leading nobles submitted to him and swore oaths of loyalty. They invited him to accept the crown of England.

Figure 1.5 William of Normandy: from Hastings to coronation

Activities

1 On slips of paper, write down the reasons William had for invading England. Now arrange them in order of importance.
   a Which was the most important? Which was the least important?
   b Compare your order with the person sitting next to you. Do you agree? If not, why not? Have either of you changed your mind?
   c Now write a paragraph explaining why the Normans went to England.

2 Remember to add to the mind map you started when you worked on the Viking invasion.

3 Think about the reasons why the Vikings and the Normans came to England. How similar were their reasons? Are there any differences?

Jewish migrants

Before the Norman conquest there were very few, if any, Jews in England. After about 1070 they arrived in ones and twos and then as whole families. They came because they were needed. How had that happened?

Religious beliefs and migration

Jews and Christians share many beliefs. However, there are some important differences and these set them apart from each other.

Table 1.1 Beliefs and important celebrations of Jews and Christians

Issue	Jews	Christians
God	Only one God	Only one God
Jesus	Not the Messiah	Son of God
The Bible	Old Testament* only	Both the Old Testament* and the New Testament
Important celebrations	Pesach (Passover)	Christmas
	Yom Kippur	Easter
	Rosh Hashanah	Whitsun

From about 70 CE, the Romans began driving Jews out of their traditional homelands in the Middle East.

Jewish people migrated far and wide, but they settled mostly in lands around the Mediterranean Sea. This is called the Jewish diaspora*. There are no records of any Jews coming to England. What happened, a thousand years later, that drew Jews to England?

Invitation, migration and settlement

William I planned to build stone castles and cathedrals to establish Norman control over England. This was going to be very expensive. William needed to borrow vast sums of money. The only people from whom he could borrow were Jews. Why was this?

England was a Christian Catholic country.

⬇

In medieval times, the Pope forbade Christians from charging interest on any loans. This was called usury*.

⬇

Jews were not Christians, so they did not follow the rules made by the Pope.

⬇

Many Jews became moneylenders. They could lend people money while also making money themselves from charging interest on these loans. This made Jews very useful members of medieval society.

⬇

William realised Jewish moneylenders could help him with his castle-building plans in England by lending him money.

Figure 1.6 Why William invited Jews to England

In 1070 William invited a group of Jewish merchants from Rouen, in Normandy, to come to England. William believed their commercial skills would help him to make England prosperous. The Jewish merchants would then share in this prosperity. William first asked the merchants to lend him money, which they did.

Key terms

Old Testament*
The first part of the Bible.

Diaspora*
The scattering of a population that had once lived in one place.

Usury*
Charging interest on a loan; in medieval times Christians were told by the Pope that this was a sin.

The first Jews from Rouen were followed by others. Jewish families did not settle outside London until after about 1135. But gradually, as towns and trade grew, they migrated, until there were Jewish communities in many English towns a hundred years later.

Source C

A modern photograph of the 'Jew's House' in Lincoln, which was built in 1170–80. The doorway was probably the entrance to a synagogue*, which stood behind the house.

Activities ?

1 Explain why Jewish people would want to migrate to England after 1070.

2 Look at Source C. What conclusions can you draw from the photograph about the Jewish community in Lincoln at the time?

3 Remember to carry on adding to your mind map. You should, by now, be able to make connections between the different reasons for migration.

Key term

Synagogue*
A building where Jewish people met for worship and teaching.

7

Migrants from the Low Countries and Lombardy

- The 'Low Countries' is the name given to modern Belgium, Luxembourg and the Netherlands. In medieval times the Low Countries were several small independent states, each with its own ruler.
- Lombardy is the name given to a collection of powerful city-states in the north of Italy. The main ones were Florence, Genoa, Lucca and Venice.

Both the Low Countries and Lombardy were generally prosperous regions, with skilled people working in many different occupations. However, in the years 1337 to 1453 a series of conflicts broke out in western Europe, later called the Hundred Years' War. Sometimes these disrupted people's work. But why would people want to emigrate to England?

Key term

Black Death*

A pandemic more accurately called bubonic plague. It reached England in 1348, killing between 30% and 60% of the population.

Skilled workers from the Low Countries

Most migrants from the Low Countries found work in south-east England, although many established themselves and their families further afield.

- Labouring work, whether in industries such as brickmaking or in farming, was easy to find, especially after the Black Death* of 1348–51 killed many workers.
- Many migrants were skilled craftsmen. The growing number of towns gave them many opportunities to work. Many saddlers, tailors, brewers and shoemakers either found work with established companies or set up on their own.

Weavers were a special group of migrants. English sheep produced excellent wool. This was exported to the Low Countries where it was woven into high-quality cloth.

Although English kings taxed every woolsack (literally a sack of wool) exported, they realised they would make more money if the weavers from the Low Countries were invited to weave cloth in England. There was more money to be made exporting high-quality cloth!

In 1270, King Henry III was the first monarch to invite weavers from the Low Countries to work in England.

Figure 1.7 The attraction of England for skilled workers from the Low Countries

Extend your knowledge

In the 1330s large numbers of weavers emigrated to England from the Low Countries. This was for two main reasons: Edward III allowed them to set up their own guild* if the English weavers proved difficult; and he temporarily banned the export of English wool so that weavers from the Low Countries would have to come to England if they wanted to carry on weaving high-quality cloth.

Key term

Guild*

An association of merchants or tradesmen who all work in the same trade. The guild works to create local rules for its members. You had to be a member of your trade's guild to sell your goods or services.

Bankers from Lombardy

Rich banking families from Lombardy began arriving in England in the 1220s, settling with their families. With towns and cities growing in size, many businesses needed to raise money to help them grow. This created excellent opportunities for the bankers.

They had heard about the success of the Jewish moneylenders. So they planned to take over from them, lending money to kings and businesses. In doing so, they intended to make huge profits because of the interest they would charge.

Source D

A picture of bankers from a medieval manuscript.

But there was a problem (see page 18). The Lombardy bankers were Christians and medieval popes banned usury. How had they got round this in Italy and what were they going to do in England?

The bankers simply used a loophole in the ruling that allowed them to pay a fine for charging interest on loans. The fine was far less than the interest they charged. Finally, in 1265, the Pope allowed Christians to charge interest. Lombardy bankers and their families looked forward to living very prosperous lives in England.

Activities

1. How could a weaver persuade his family that migrating to England would be a good idea? Write out the dialogue.
2. Update your mind map and don't forget to make connections.

Exam-style question, Section B

Explain **one** difference between the Viking and Norman invasions of England. **(4 marks)**

Exam tip

For this question you should identify one difference and add information from both the Viking and Norman periods to support it.

1.1 Summary

- England was a good place for migrants because they could settle and do well there.
- Vikings raided at first and eventually came to farm and trade.
- Normans came to run the country their way.
- Jews were invited to set up as moneylenders.
- European craftsmen came to set up their own businesses.

Checkpoint

Strengthen

S1 How did the Vikings gain control of eastern England?

S2 In what ways did King William I encourage migration to England?

S3 Why did many European weavers go to England after 1270?

Challenge

C1 Use the mind map you have made to explain why England was attractive to migrants in the years 800–1500.

1.2 The experiences of migrants

Learning outcomes

- Understand the ways in which migrants settled in England.
- Understand the relationship between migrants and the existing population in England.

Settling in the Danelaw

- Once the Vikings settled in eastern and north-eastern England, they were called Danes. It's usual, too, to call the Anglo-Saxons just Saxons from this point.
- Much of what we know about the ways in which the Danes settled comes from archaeological evidence because they left very few written records.

Five Danish armies settled with their families in Mercia. Derby, Leicester, Lincoln, Nottingham and Stamford became their fortified towns and, gradually, centres of political power. Each was run as a small kingdom, called a jarldom*.

Key terms

Jarldom*
A large area of land ruled by a jarl (a king or an earl).

Saga*
A story, usually told and sometimes written down, that mixes history and mythology.

Things*
Regional and local meetings held by important families where laws were made and criminal disputes were settled.

Villagers and townspeople bought and sold goods locally, nationally and overseas.

Villages and towns had workshops for a range of different craftworkers such as coppersmiths and blacksmiths, jewellery makers and silversmiths, woodworkers and weavers.

Danes had fun! They told long stories, called sagas*. These were a mix of history and imagination. They played chess and draughts, and made music with harps and fiddles, pipes and flutes.

Most families lived in longhouses hat were roughly 12 m x 5 m, with a central fire. They were made from wood or stone and were usually thatched.

Regional and local meetings, called *Things*, were held. Here they made laws, tried people accused of crimes and decided on punishments for the guilty.

Figure 1.8 Living and working in the Danelaw

This huge stone cross is in the graveyard of St Mary's Church, Gosforth, Cumbria. It is 4.4 m high and was made in about 940 CE.
At the top is a cross representing Christianity, but the carvings are of scenes from the Christian Bible and the Danish saga Ragnarök.

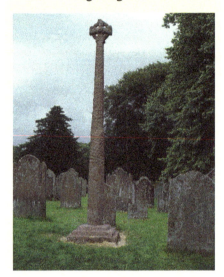

Many Saxons were already living in the Danelaw. They adapted quickly to the ways of the new settlers, and the Danes seemed flexible, too.

For example: at first the Danes didn't mint coins, but they allowed the Saxons in East Anglia to do so, and circulate them in the Danelaw. Many Danes became Christians like the Saxons. Most, however, worshipped the Christian god along with their own gods such as Thor, Odin, Loki and Freyr.

Extend your knowledge

The Cuerdale Hoard is the largest hoard of Viking silver ever found in western Europe. It was found in 1840 by workmen in Cuerdale, near Preston, Lancashire. It contained about 8,600 coins, armbands and brooches, chains and buckles. The date of some of the coins reveal it was buried between 905 and 910. You can see some of the items in the British Museum and the Ashmolean Museum in Oxford.

The Danelaw, Saxon takeover and a Danish king

The Treaty of Wedmore didn't mean the Saxons had given up. But neither had the Danes.

Alfred's son Edward and his grandson Athelstan fought a series of campaigns against the Danes for control of the Danelaw.

⬇

In 937 Athelstan won a tremendous victory over the Danes at the Battle of Brunanburh and England was brought under Saxon control with Saxon kings.

⬇

England prospered and was peaceful during the reign (959–75) of King Edgar.

⬇

Vikings began raiding in order to regain the old Danelaw. King Ethelred paid them large amounts of money, called Danegeld*, to stay away. This didn't work and the raiding continued.

⬇

King Ethelred worried that the Danes living peacefully in England's towns and villages might decide to join up with the Viking raiders. He decided to massacre them before they could do this.

⬇

King Ethelred ordered the massacre of all Danes living in English territory. It took place on St Brice's Day, 13 November 1002.

⬇

Viking attacks increased in response to the massacre. By 1013 Ethelred and his sons had been driven out of England. The Dane, Cnut, became king of England in 1016.

Figure 1.9 Saxon takeover and the Danes' revenge

Danegeld*

Money paid by the Saxons to the Danes in order to make them stay away.

The reign of King Cnut 1016–35

Saxons and Danes fought each other between 1013 and 1015 for control of England. Finally, the Saxons surrendered and in 1016, Cnut (or Canute) became king of England. The Danes, originally Viking raiders and invaders, then migrants and settlers, now ruled the country.

Cnut allowed Saxons to hold positions of power, and continued to use Anglo-Saxon laws. This brought peace and stability to England and the country prospered. Edward the Confessor later succeeded him and was king for 24 years. England prospered. Then (see page 4) England was threatened by Duke William of Normandy.

Source B

The skeletons of 35 young men who were killed in the 11th century.

They had been killed violently and archaeologists believe they were part of the St Brice's Day massacre of Danish migrants. The skeletons were discovered in Oxford.

Key term

Earldom*
A large area of land ruled by an earl.

> Became king of Denmark in 1018 and king of Norway in 1028, and so for a time England was part of the great empire that he ruled. This meant that trade between England, Norway and Denmark across the North Sea increased, leading to greater economic prosperity.

> Created four earldoms* – Mercia, Northumberland, East Anglia and Wessex. He put reliable Saxon nobles in charge of each one.

> Supported the leaders of the Christian church in England and visited the Pope in Rome to work with him in creating new English archbishops. England became a more important part of Christendom.

> Used Danegeld to pay off his Danish soldiers and by 1020 they were all out of England.

Figure 1.10 How well did Cnut rule England?

Activities ?

1 Make a timeline, starting with the Treaty of Wedmore and ending in 1035, with the death of King Cnut.
2 Find an important turning point that resulted in successful Danish settlement and explain why you think it is important.
3 Rudyard Kipling wrote a poem called 'Dane-geld'. Find it online or in your local or school library. Explain whether you agree with his lines '… once you have paid him the Dane-geld, / You never get rid of the Dane'.

The Norman takeover

Winning the Battle of Hastings was one thing. Establishing Norman control throughout England was quite another. Between 1067 and 1071, the Norman migrants struggled to control the land they had invaded.

Building castles

In less than ten years, the Normans had subdued Saxon England. But how could they keep control and prevent rebellions? One of the answers was building castles. William built hundreds of them throughout England. The first ones were built from wood and, although eventually most were replaced by stone, a well-constructed wooden castle could last for 200 years.

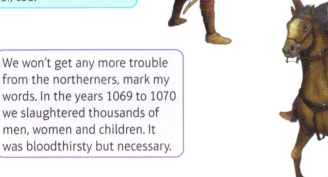

We didn't have much to do in East Anglia, did we? By the time we got to the Fens in 1071, the Danes had sailed away, paid off with Danegeld. The threat of us marching towards Ely was enough to frighten the monks into betraying the rebel Hereward and his Saxons. I wonder what happened to him?

In 1068 Exeter held out for 18 days, but we wore them down in the end.

We burned their crops and killed their animals so any people that were left would die of hunger. It was a hard winter, too.

Yes – and making Robert of Mortain the Earl of Cornwall in the same year turned Bristol and Gloucester over to us as well.

We won't get any more trouble from the northerners, mark my words. In the years 1069 to 1070 we slaughtered thousands of men, women and children. It was bloodthirsty but necessary.

The Saxons getting help from the Danes overseas and seizing York was a nightmare for King William, wasn't it? Paying Danegeld was a good move and we were able to throw the Saxons out of York in 1069.

Figure 1.11 We put down the Saxon rebellions!

Extend your knowledge

Harrying of the North

This is how historians describe the revenge taken by the Normans on the Saxons in the north of England in 1069–70. The Normans burned crops, destroyed seeds, killed livestock and destroyed Saxon homes. It was a punishment as well as a warning never to rebel again. It was meant to make it nearly impossible for any Danes or Saxons to use the north as a 'base' for attacking Norman rule in the future.

WHAT WERE CASTLES FOR?

A visible reminder of who was in charge.

Useful refuges for soldiers and a storage place for weapons and ammunition.

Controlling the surrounding countryside, river crossing, port or border. Some were built in the middle of towns, meaning hundreds of houses were torn down to make room.

Figure 1.12 What were castles for?

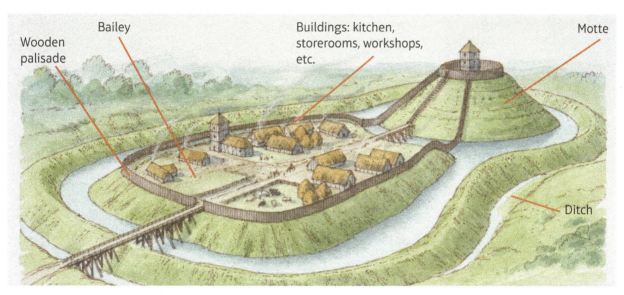

Figure 1.13 A typical Norman castle.

The feudal system

William knew he could not hold England by force for ever. He developed the feudal system. It worked like this: William owned all the land, but he would loan it to trusted Normans in return for their loyalty. In this way William had reliable support without giving anything away.

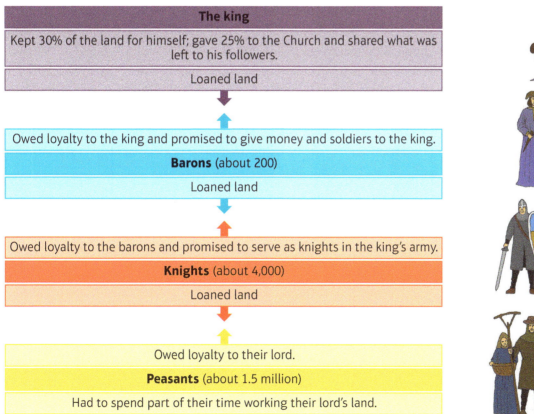

| **The king** |
| Kept 30% of the land for himself; gave 25% to the Church and shared what was left to his followers. |
| Loaned land |

Owed loyalty to the king and promised to give money and soldiers to the king.

| **Barons** (about 200) |
| Loaned land |

Owed loyalty to the barons and promised to serve as knights in the king's army.

| **Knights** (about 4,000) |
| Loaned land |

Owed loyalty to their lord.

| **Peasants** (about 1.5 million) |
| Had to spend part of their time working their lord's land. |

Figure 1.14 The feudal system

 Land ownership

 Value of estate

Taxation

Figure 1.15 What was the Domesday Book for?

Activities ?

1 Describe **two** ways in which the Norman invaders controlled England after 1066.

2 Look at Figure 1.13. Put yourself into the shoes of a Norman in charge of defending the castle. The Saxons are planning an attack. What are the weak points of your castle and how will you defend them?

3 Was William's castle-building programme a sign of weakness or strength? Discuss this in your class.

The Domesday Book

By 1085 some Norman landowners began arguing about who, exactly, owned what and where the boundaries were between their lands. In December 1085, William decided to hold a survey that would give an accurate record of the state of his land.

In 1086, royal commissioners travelled the country, questioning all the landowners, great and small. Their findings were written in a book, later called the Domesday Book. All landowners and their tenants were listed as well as all the other people who lived on the land.

The commissioners recorded buildings such as mills and barns; they noted how the land was used and they even counted the animals. Importantly, the commissioners asked how much tax was paid in the time of Edward the Confessor.

William wanted to raise money, but also show his subjects he was doing things in the same way as during Saxon times. But was he? You'll find out in Section 1.3. For now, it's important to remember that the Normans, like the Vikings, started out their migration to England as invaders. The Vikings ended up running the Danelaw, but the Normans ran the whole country.

THINKING HISTORICALLY   Cause and consequence (2a)

The web of multiple causes

Why did the Normans settle in England after William's coronation?

Study these causes. Which of them would help historians to explain why the Normans settled in England?

William won the Battle of Hastings and was crowned king.	William had the Pope's blessing for his invasion of England.	William granted land to his supporters.	William's feudal system rewarded loyalty to the king.
William built castles throughout England to control rebellions.	The Domesday Book gave William a full record who owned what land and how much tax they paid.	There was lots of land that could be seized and built on.	There were several rebellions that were put down, meaning more land for William's followers.

Work in pairs. Take an A3 sheet of paper. You will need to use all of it.

1 Write two of the causes on the paper with some space between them.

2 Think of anything that connects the causes. Draw a line between them and describe the connection by writing along the line.

3 Add the other causes in turn and make as many links as you can with other causes.

4 Now add the outcome 'Normans settled in England'. Think carefully about where this should come and how it should be linked to the diagram of causes.

Living in Jewries*

William I invited Jews to migrate to England because he needed their moneylending skills (see page 6). But they didn't only lend money to kings; Jewish money helped businesses and trade to flourish and so, for many years, Jews were accepted as members of society.

Jews settled in towns and cities. Some became very rich as moneylenders and financiers. Others made a reasonable living as, for example, cheesemakers and fishmongers. And some were poor, just like thousands of Saxons and Normans.

Jewish families often lived together in separate parts of towns and villages, called Jewries. They weren't forced to do this, but it was natural for people to want to live close to friends and relatives who shared their beliefs and customs. Jews set up their own kehilas*, mikvehs*, kosher* butchers and synagogues.

Key terms
Jewries*   Separate areas of towns and cities where Jews lived.
Kehila*   Jewish community council.
Mikveh*   Jewish bath house.
Kosher*   Food that is prepared according to Jewish laws.
Anti-Semitism*   Hostility to, and prejudice against, Jewish people.

Figure 1.16 A map showing the main Jewish communities in the years before 1290

The growth of anti-Semitism*

Gradually, however, prejudice against Jews began to grow and spread. Why?

- Jewish people were given a special status because they had been invited to England by William I and were useful to the Crown. In a crisis, Jews could pay to shelter in royal castles. However, many had to cover this cost by charging higher interest rates, causing resentment from people who borrowed money from them.
- Jews were regarded with suspicion as the only non-Christian group of people living in England, especially as the Christian church taught that Jewish leaders put Jesus Christ to death. This caused tensions between Jews and Christians which exploded into open hostility from time to time.

- The crusades* against Muslims started in 1095. The Church said that Muslims were 'unbelievers' and should be persecuted because they didn't believe in Christian teachings. Jews were 'unbelievers', too, so this was almost like giving permission for Jews in England to be persecuted. Gradually, anti-Semitism increased. On 3 September 1189, during the coronation of Richard I, mobs attacked the Jewish quarter of London, killing 30 Jews. More attacks followed over the next year, with hundreds of Jews killed.

1189 Important Jews attending Richard I's coronation in London were attacked and flogged.

1190 In York, 150 Jews fled for safety to part of the royal castle, now called Clifford's Tower. Besieged by the mob, some killed themselves and others were massacred as they tried to escape.

1218 Jews forced to wear a yellow cloth patch on their clothes.

1230s Jews expelled from many towns and, in others, were not allowed to own anything except their own houses.

1255 Henry III ordered the arrest of about 90 Jews and the hanging of those who protested, because he believed they were involved in the ritual killing of a boy in Lincoln. Rumours such as these had been around for over 100 years and were called 'blood libel' stories.

1275 The Statute of Jewry forbade Jews to charge interest on loans and those who owed money to Jews did not have to pay it back.

Figure 1.17 Increasing anti-Semitism in medieval England

The Church changes interest laws

In 1265, the Pope allowed Italian bankers to charge interest on loans. This was exactly what Henry III wanted. Now he didn't have to borrow money from Jewish moneylenders, and neither did anyone else.

Once the Italian bankers migrated to England, he could expel the Jewish people and put an end to mob riots. As the English kings became less dependent on Jews to support the royal income, they become less willing to protect them.

Persecution and expulsion

Throughout the 13th century, Jewish communities had been persecuted by the English kings and their government.

- In 1218 Jews were ordered to wear a distinctive badge, so they could be instantly recognised. This law was made stricter in 1253.
- In the 1230s Jews were expelled from several towns including Leicester, Bury St Edmunds and Newcastle.
- 'Blood libel' stories spread – there were many attacks, such as in 1265 when 500 Jews were killed in London.
- In 1275 Edward I made a law (the Statute of Jewry) banning Jews from collecting interest. This made many Jews almost penniless overnight. Some were forced to 'clip' coins (cut off the edges of coins and melt the metal down to be sold). In 1278 hundreds of Jews were arrested in London accused of this and 293 of them were hanged.

In 1290, Edward I finally ordered all Jews to convert to Christianity or leave England for ever. Some converted, but most refused (perhaps as many as 3,000) and chose to go. They were forced to walk to the south coast where they were shipped to Europe as refugees. It was nearly 400 years before Jews were allowed back into England.

Activities ?

1 Describe the ways in which Jewish migrants affected English society.

2 Explain how **(a)** the monarchy and **(b)** the Church stirred up anti-Jewish feelings in the years to 1290.

3 Why do you think Edward I wanted to expel Jews from England in 1290?

Settling successfully from Europe

Migrants from the Low Countries settled quickly in England, first in the south-east then across most of England. They had skills many people needed and were ready to pay for (see pages 8–10) and played a valuable role in helping England develop its trade and industry.

Some migrants worked with English people, teaching them new techniques and helping them earn more money. For example, Flemish brickmakers taught English brickmakers their method of making bricks, and how to set them in a different way when building a wall. Dutch brewers (who were mainly women) showed English brewers how to make beer with hops instead of with barley.

Weavers

Weavers were the most successful migrants from the Low Countries. They were welcomed to England by the king because they were skilled workers who made the cloth industry more profitable. In 1331, Edward III invited Flemish weavers to settle and work in London.

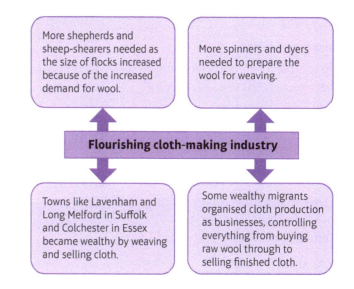

Figure 1.18 Flemish weavers and prosperity

Bankers

Henry III sent letters to important banking families in Lombardy promising them royal protection if they moved to England. This worked. In the 1220s powerful families such as the Bardi family from Florence and the Ricciardi family from Lucca moved to London.

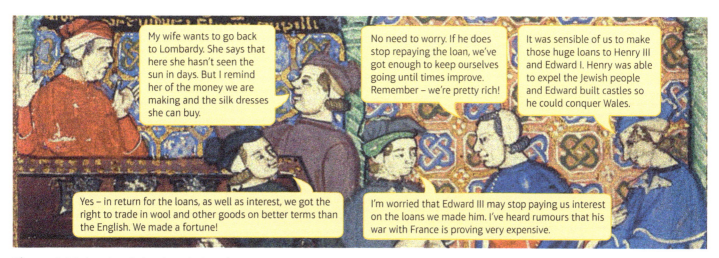

Figure 1.19 Lombardy bankers in London

Key terms

Hanseatic League*

An organisation of north German towns and German merchant communities that traded in northern Europe. The League dominated commercial activity in northern Europe from the 13th to the 15th century.

Customs tariff*

A tax placed on goods that are imported or exported in or out of a country.

Craft guilds*

Craftsmen such as weavers and bakers, goldsmiths and candlemakers, had their own guilds. These were organisations that set prices, wages and standards of work.

Peasants' Revolt*

In 1381, thousands of English peasants rebelled, demanding freedom from their lords and higher wages.

Edward III did, in fact, stop repaying loans from the Lombardy bankers, but they stayed on and worked hard, making London an important financial centre, as you'll see on pages 26–27.

Merchants

Merchants belonging to the German trading group, the Hanseatic League*, were called Hansa merchants. They established a base in central London called the Steelyard. This was a large, walled, self-contained community containing warehouses with direct access to the river Thames, offices, a chapel, a wine cellar, kitchens and houses for the merchants.

Edward I gave the League the right to trade as merchants in 1303. They traded in timber, furs and certain foods (such as honey and wheat). They were given royal protection as well as paying lower tax rates and customs tariffs* than other merchants. By the mid-1400s, German merchants controlled most of the English cloth industry.

Difficult times

It wasn't always easy, being a migrant from Europe. In difficult times, the English turned on immigrants.

- Craft guilds* believed migrants were taking their jobs and selling goods like cloth at lower prices than they did. This led to hostility between English and Flemish cloth workers. Edward III allowed Flemish weavers to set up their own guild that reached agreement with local craft guilds.
- During the Peasants' Revolt* of 1381, about 150 foreign weavers and merchants were murdered. People resented the special privileges the king had given them.
- During the Revolt in 1381 and again in 1492, the English attacked the Steelyard, burning buildings and destroying goods. They believed the merchants were only interested in making money for themselves.
- During wars, migrants could have their goods confiscated and sometimes they were expelled. People were suspicious of foreigners and worried that they could be a danger to the country. In 1325, for example, Edward II ordered the arrest of all foreigners near the south coast when he feared a French invasion.

However, no matter how tricky life was for migrants, in general they settled well and had an enormous impact on England, as you will see in the next section.

Activities

1 Explain how Flemish weavers created prosperity for hundreds of people who weren't weavers.

2 Why might some English people **(a)** welcome and **(b)** resent the arrival of Lombardy bankers and Hansa merchants? You could work in pairs to think this through and take part in a class discussion afterwards.

3 What common reasons encouraged European migrants to arrive in England? How were these different from the Vikings and Normans?

Exam-style question, Section B

Explain why many migrants to Britain from Europe during the 13th century settled successfully.

You may use the following in your answer:

- weavers from the Low Countries
- bankers from Lombardy.

You **must** use information of your own. **(12 marks)**

Exam tip

The question is asking you to explain **why** migration to Britain from Europe during the 13th century was successful. Instead of just describing what happened, explain why migrants from Europe were successful. For example, the bankers were successful because they were supported by the king. Remember to use your own knowledge about other migrants, not just the weavers and bankers.

1.2 Summary

- Danes established their own towns and villages, customs and laws, crafts and trades in the Danelaw. They lost control to the Saxons in 937 but regained it in 1016 when Cnut became king.
- Normans established themselves by using violence against the Saxons and building castles to control them. They kept control of England by establishing the feudal system.
- Jews lived in their own parts of towns and cities, called Jewries, following their own way of life. Although at first Jews had the protection of the monarchs, they were expelled from England in 1290.
- Bankers from Lombardy took the place of Jewish moneylenders. Weavers from the Low Countries developed the English cloth industry and German merchants controlled it by the 15th century.

Checkpoint

Strengthen

S1 What was Danegeld? Describe **two** ways in which it was used.

S2 Describe how the Normans controlled England after 1066.

S3 Why were Jews expelled from England in 1290?

Challenge

C1 Explain how the English cloth industry became so successful.

1.3 The impact of migrants on England

All migrants, whether they stay for a short or a long time, leave something of themselves in the communities where they live. It may be something big and obvious, like a castle or a cathedral; or something that affects how land is owned and used; or something cultural, like language. It may be a combination of all of these things.

The impact of the Vikings

The Vikings didn't leave any written accounts of the Danelaw. Archaeology can tell us a great deal. But there is more we can find out about their impact on England if we look and think.

Names, places and words

Vikings spoke a language we now call Old Norse. The English language we speak today is similar in grammar and word structure to Old Norse. Modern English also contains a lot of Old Norse words.

Government and the law

- Viking assemblies, called '*Things*', were public meetings of free men where laws were decided by voting.
- *Things* were also courts, where alleged criminals were tried by *Thing* members. Any punishments were discussed and agreed on by the *Thing*. The basis of Viking lawmaking was 'do not kill' and 'do not steal'.

Figure 1.20 Names, places and words

- Vikings divided the area of the Danelaw (now Yorkshire) into three administrative areas. The Old Norse name for a third was *thrithjungr*. This gradually changed into the name 'riding'. East Riding, West Riding and North Riding were the names of the administrative areas of Yorkshire until 1974.
- Women had almost equal rights with men. They could own and inherit land and could speak at *Things*.

The ways in which the Vikings organised their society had a significant impact on the development of England. Parliamentary democracy and trial by jury, for example, can be traced back to the Vikings.

The Normans

William I wanted to show people he was the true heir to Edward the Confessor. This meant he didn't want to be seen changing too much. He had to make sure there was more continuity than change in the way the Normans governed England.

Activities   **?**

1 Using a map of England, find **(a)** six places ending -by and **(b)** six places ending -thorpe. As a group build up a picture of where the Vikings lived. What conclusions can you make?

2 What, in your opinion, was the most significant impact the Vikings had on England? Discuss this in your class, and then write a paragraph beginning 'The most significant impact the Vikings had on England was…' There is no right answer – but you must explain why you have made your choice.

Key terms

Geld*

This land tax was the most important tax in Saxon England.

Shire*

A division of land in Saxon England.

Hundred*

In Saxon England, shires were divided into smaller areas called hundreds.

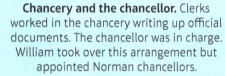

Chancery and the chancellor. Clerks worked in the chancery writing up official documents. The chancellor was in charge. William took over this arrangement but appointed Norman chancellors.

The geld* and taxation. Every year Edward and his advisers met to decide how much geld each shire should pay in taxation. The system worked and so William didn't change it. But he did use the findings of the Domesday Book to help increase taxes.

Keeping continuity in government

Shires* and sheriffs. England was divided into shires for the purpose of running the country. A sheriff was in charge of each shire*. William kept the arrangement but appointed Norman sheriffs.

Shire courts and hundred* courts. Shire courts heard the most serious criminal cases. Each shire was divided into areas of land called a 'hundred'. Hundred courts dealt with day-to-day disputes. Landowners made decisions in all the courts. Before long, all landowners would be Normans, so William didn't need to make any changes.

Figure 1.21 Norman continuity in government

Key term

Hierarchy*

A system where members are ranked according to their status or authority.

Changes to society

The Norman did make changes to the ways people lived their lives. Some of these were meant to help the Normans increase their control of the country. Some were huge and affected almost everyone. Some were small and affected only a few people.

By trying to balance continuity and change, William aimed to bring peace and stability to the land the Normans had taken and occupied by force.

The **landscape** changed. Huge castles dominated the countryside and the centre of some cities. Stone-built cathedrals and churches, monasteries and abbeys could be seen. In large areas of northern England villages had been destroyed and nothing grew in the burnt fields.

Land ownership changed when William introduced the feudal system. Everyone owed an obligation or duty to the person above them in the system and they were given protection in return. By 1087, only two of the great landowners were English; all the rest were Norman. The new landowners created deer parks and planted vineyards. Slavery was abolished after the Domesday Book revealed that 10% of those working on the land were slaves.

The **Church** changed when William replaced all but one of the 16 Saxon bishops with Norman ones. A hierarchy* was constructed, much like the feudal system, with archbishops at the top and parish priests at the bottom. By 1200, all the wooden Saxon churches had been replaced by stone ones. Links with Christendom grew as members of religious orders migrated to England to found monasteries and abbeys.

Language changed. The Norman rulers spoke a language, now called Old French, which only they understood. For some time, the rulers and the ruled spoke in separate languages. Gradually the languages came together. New words like 'pork' and 'beef' were used to describe meat from pigs and cows. Norman first names such as Robert, Richard and William began to be used for children.

Laws changed what people could do.

(i) **Forest Laws** protected William's hunting. Many English forests were made 'royal forests'. William created the 'New Forest' in Hampshire, destroying several villages to do so. Only the king and his friends could hunt in these forests. Ordinary people could not and there were severe punishments for poaching.

(ii) **Murdrum** was a fine enforced by law. It was imposed on any hundred where a Norman was killed and the murderer had not been caught.

Figure 1.22 What did the Norman conquest change?

Activities ?

1. In 1100 most English people were peasants living in villages and working the land. Write a paragraph to explain how the changes made by the Normans would have changed their lives.
2. Look at Figure 1.21. Pick out one part of keeping continuity in government that you think was the most important and explain why.
3. Using Figure 1.22, make a list of the changes made by the Normans. Rate each change on a scale of 0 to 10 for the importance of its impact on English society (0 = no impact and 10 = tremendous impact). Now explain why you have rated the changes in this order.

Jewish migrants

Lending money to monarchs

From William I onwards, English monarchs often borrowed money from Jews. This meant they didn't have to raise taxes or demand money from the barons to get the money they needed for day-to-day living or special projects and events.

However, not all the money was willingly loaned. Sometimes there were threats if loans were not granted. Some loans were never repaid.

Monarchs also taxed Jews heavily. For example, the war with France (1202–4) bankrupted the country and King John imposed huge taxes on Jews. Penalties for non-payment of loans or taxes were severe: confiscation of goods, heavy fines and the imprisonment of whole communities.

William I (1066–87) used Jewish money to help build 84 castles, including the Tower of London and the castles at York, Durham, Dover and Chepstow. Jewish money paid soldiers' wages.

William II (1087–1100) used Jewish money to build Norwich cathedral.

Stephen (1135–54) used Jewish money during his civil war with Matilda, as did Matilda. The money was used for weapons and to reward supporters.

In 1192, **Richard I (1189–99)** was kidnapped on his way home from the third crusade. Jewish money was used to pay his ransom* as well as to help fund the crusade.

John (1199–1216) used Jewish money to provide a royal dowry* for his daughter, Joan.

Henry III (1216–72) used Jewish money to rebuild Westminster Abbey.

Figure 1.23 Some of the ways English monarchs used Jewish money

Extend your knowledge

By the end of the 12th century, the Jewish community made up less than 0.25% of the total population, but was providing 8% of the total income of the royal treasury.

Change: supporting communities and creating wealth

Jews did far more than loan money to monarchs. As businessmen who could read and write, and who knew how money worked, they played a vital part in the economic life of England.

- In towns and cities, Jews lent money to local people to help them get their businesses started.
- Jews lent money to merchants to expand their trading overseas. Many Jews also became merchants, creating wealth for themselves and the people from whom they bought goods. Aaron of Lincoln, for example, was so wealthy that when he died in 1186, a special royal department had to be set up to sort out his financial affairs.
- The Jewish community in York lent a lot of money to Cistercian monks to build Fountains Abbey.
- One of the oldest Jewish communities was in Oxford, and Jews played a significant part in establishing the university there:
  - Merton College was founded in the 1260s with the help of money from a wealthy local Jew, called Jacob of Oxford.
  - Poor students pawned their books to Jewish pawnbrokers* to cover their expenses.
  - Jews worked as tutors to students studying Hebrew texts.

Despite this, Jews were ruthlessly expelled from England in 1290.

Key terms

Ransom*
A sum of money demanded for the release of a captive.

Dowry*
The money, land and/or goods that a woman's family gives to her husband's family when she marries.

Pawnbroker*
A person who lends money in exchange for an article.

Migrants change the economy

Weavers, merchants and bankers arriving in England in the 14th and 15th centuries had a huge and lasting impact on the country's economy.

Migrants from Europe helped transform England from a primary economy to a secondary one.

- A primary economy is based mainly on raw materials, such as from farming, hunting, fishing and mining.
- A secondary economy changes raw materials into manufactured goods, e.g. using wool to make cloth.

The Crown also grew rich because of income from taxes on the import and export of goods. The English economy prospered because of the hard work of the migrants.

Activities ?

1 Two students are discussing the impact Jews had on medieval England. These are their conclusions:

Student 1: The most important thing Jewish communities did was supply money to kings. This meant they weren't dependent on the barons for money. The barons could easily turn against a monarch if he made too many demands for money.

Student 2: I disagree. It was far more important that Jewish communities supported businesses, trade and education. That's the only way to make a country prosperous, regardless of what monarchs did or didn't do.

a A third student had a different view. What do you think it could be?

b What was the most important impact Jewish communities had on medieval England? Write a paragraph to explain your view.

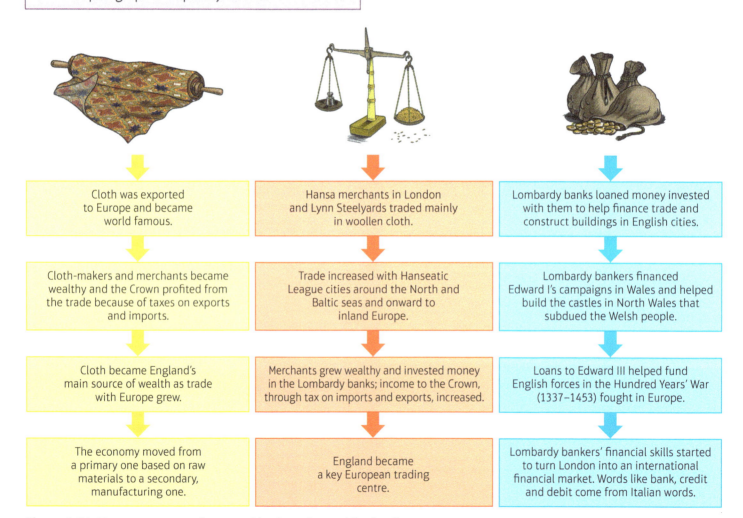

Cloth was exported to Europe and became world famous.	Hansa merchants in London and Lynn Steelyards traded mainly in woollen cloth.	Lombardy banks loaned money invested with them to help finance trade and construct buildings in English cities.
Cloth-makers and merchants became wealthy and the Crown profited from the trade because of taxes on exports and imports.	Trade increased with Hanseatic League cities around the North and Baltic seas and onward to inland Europe.	Lombardy bankers financed Edward I's campaigns in Wales and helped build the castles in North Wales that subdued the Welsh people.
Cloth became England's main source of wealth as trade with Europe grew.	Merchants grew wealthy and invested money in the Lombardy banks; income to the Crown, through tax on imports and exports, increased.	Loans to Edward III helped fund English forces in the Hundred Years' War (1337–1453) fought in Europe.
The economy moved from a primary one based on raw materials to a secondary, manufacturing one.	England became a key European trading centre.	Lombardy bankers' financial skills started to turn London into an international financial market. Words like bank, credit and debit come from Italian words.

Figure 1.24 How weavers, merchants and bankers changed England's economy

Figure 1.25 The Establishment of Flemish Weavers in Manchester AD 1353. This painting shows the visit to Manchester of Queen Philippa, the Flemish wife of King Edward III. It was painted in 1882 by Ford Madox Brown and can be seen today in Manchester's Town Hall.

Exam-style question, Section B

'The impact on land ownership was the most important consequence of migration to England during the years 800–1500.'

How far do you agree? Explain your answer.

You may use the following in your answer:

• the feudal system

• government.

You **must** also use information of your own.

Total for spelling, punctuation, grammar and use of specialist terminology **(4 marks)**

Total for question **(20 marks)**

Exam tip

The question is focusing on consequences – on the outcomes of events. Don't waste time writing about the events connected to migration, but look at what happened as a result of the different groups migrating to England at this time. Plan your answer: jot down the outcomes, and then decide which was the most important – and why.

1.3 Summary

• The Vikings impacted place names and language. Their system of government provided the basis of modern parliamentary democracy.

• The Normans impacted on language, landscape and landownership. Although they kept the Saxon system of government, they put Normans in charge.

• Jewish loans and taxes supported monarchs; their loans helped local businesses to grow and develop. The Jewish people's impact on society was positive, though it ended in 1290.

• Migrant weavers and merchants changed England's economy from being based on raw materials to manufacturing. Lombardy bankers began to change London into an international financial centre.

Checkpoint

Strengthen

S1 What was democratic about the Viking *Things*?

S2 How did the Normans change land ownership?

S3 Give three ways in which Jews in England changed society.

Challenge

C1 Explain how the English economy changed from an economy based on raw materials to one based on manufacturing.

1.4 Case study: the city of York under the Vikings

Learning outcomes

- Understand why the Vikings created a settlement at York.
- Know about how York developed as a trading port.
- Understand the relationship the Vikings had with the Church and the surrounding area.

The conquest of York

York was the largest town in Britain, north of the Thames. It was the centre of Anglo-Saxon government, trade and the Church in the north. Its church, York Minster, was one of the largest in the country. York also had the only mint* in the north of England.

York was built at the point where the rivers Foss and Ouse meet. The river Ouse flows out to the Humber and the North Sea. The town was also at the centre of a large network of Roman roads.

Key term

Mint*
A place that legally produces coins.

Because of its wealth, Viking raids had often targeted Northumbria (see pages 1 and 12). The Vikings conquered most of Northumbria, capturing York in 866. Northumbria became the Viking kingdom of York (or Jorvik). York itself was very important to the Vikings:

- Its roads and rivers made it easier to move quickly around Northumbria – and control it.
- York was connected to much of the known world and became an important trading city.
- The rivers meant there was lots of rich, fertile soil that could be used for farming.

The Viking settlement at York

- York grew under the Vikings. Historians estimate 10,000–15,000 people may have migrated to York between 866 and 950. Before the Vikings, York's population may have been as small as 1,000.
- York became a multicultural city. Many Northumbrians still lived there. Alongside them, Vikings mixed with migrants and merchants from Germany, modern-day Holland, Ireland and Scotland.
- The Vikings built small homes and workshops with thatched roofs and wattle walls (a timber frame with dried mud and straw plastered onto it). Later buildings were made from timber.

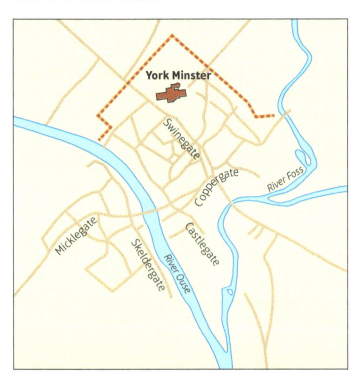

Figure 1.26 Map of Viking York

Street name	Translation	What could be found there
Coppergate	Cup-maker's street	Woodwork, especially to make wooden cups and bowls.
Skeldergate	Shield-makers' street	Shield-making and making other weapons, such as axes and swords. Metalworking was an important trade.
Swinegate	Swine street	Where pigs were kept – connected to farming and food.

Trades in York

You can see the huge range of trades in Viking York just by looking at the street names in the city today. 'Gate' is Norse for street. Some of the main Viking streets show us the sort of trades that could be found in York.

Specialist workers

Archaeologists have discovered a lot of skilled craftwork in York. These goods helped increase York's trading power in England and across the world. York attracted workers from across the country, such as potters from Lincolnshire.

Hunting and farming was also carried out on the rich lands around York. The city gave the Vikings an opportunity to build up land and wealth for their families.

Source A

A hoard of Viking goods found in Yorkshire. The hoard contains several examples of jewellery, craftsmanship and coins from York.

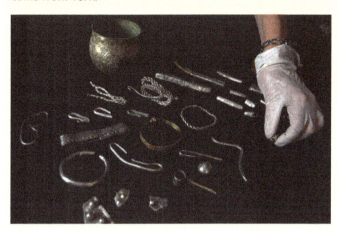

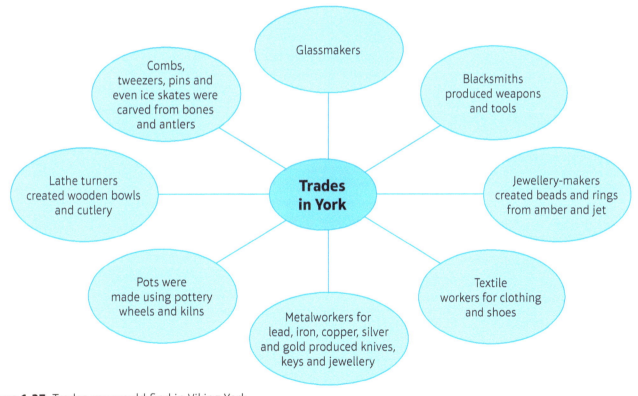

Figure 1.27 Trades you would find in Viking York

Coin production

Vikings started using coins – melting down their silver from trade and raiding. The kings of York used the mint to make coins with their names on them.

Extend your knowledge

As the Viking community did not keep any written records, much of what we know about the reigns (and even the names) of Viking kings is based on coins. As many hoards contain coins, **not** lumps of silver and gold, we can tell the Vikings had started using coins.

Trade: York connects to the rest of the world

The Vikings were great sailors. They turned York into a rich trading port.

- Viking traders travelled as far as the Black Sea, Caspian Sea, Iceland, Greenland and Newfoundland.
- Among the imports to York were walrus ivory, amber, German wine, and Arabian spices, oils and perfumes.
- Furs from Russia and fine silks from Byzantium were imported to create clothing.

York also had excellent road connections to the rest of England, with particularly strong links to Viking-controlled areas in the Pennines, Chester and the west coast (where ships travelled to Viking Ireland).

Timber, wool, iron ore and deer antlers were all brought into the city on roads. They were used to create craftwork traded from the city's port. Food, such as wheat, barley, oats, fruit and meat (from sheep and pigs) was also bought into the city for trading.

Viking York and the Church

The Church was an important landowner in York. The Vikings had to work with it. Because there are few written records, it is hard to know how much influence the Church had.

Source B

This coin from Viking York shows a sword, which can represent both a Viking symbol and the sword of St Peter.

Evidence the Church had influence

- The Church was active in Viking York. Other churches appeared in Viking settlements outside York.
- Many Viking kings converted to Christianity. King Guthram was buried in York Minster (895).
- Archbishops such as Wulfstan I (Archbishop 931–56) were involved in negotiations with other kingdoms and may even have helped choose Viking kings.
- Most of the coins created in York after 900 carried Christian symbols on them.

Evidence the Church did not have influence

- The Church in York was financially poor. It lost land to the Vikings.
- There is no record of an Archbishop in York from 904 to 928 – if there was one, he can't have been important.
- Many coins with Christian symbols had Latin spelling errors, and some also showed pagan symbols on the other side – if the Church was very influential in making them, how could this have happened?

Figure 1.28 Influence of the Church in Viking York

Viking York and Anglo-Saxon England

Viking coins have been found across England. This suggests that there was trade between York and the rest of England.

However, there was often fighting between the Viking kings of York and the Anglo-Saxon rulers in the south (see page 2).

Anglo-Saxon conquest of York

In 927 Athelstan, the grandson of Alfred the Great, conquered large parts of the Viking kingdom of York, including the city of York. The city was ruled by the Anglo-Saxons until 939. Despite this, it seems life in Viking York didn't change a great deal. Athelstan was willing to work with the Viking landowners and traders.

After Athelstan's death in 939, the Northumbrians wanted a 'northern' leader. After almost 60 years of living in the Danelaw, many felt the Vikings were more 'northern' than Athelstan's heirs.

In 939, an agreement to set a border between land controlled by the Vikings and the Anglo-Saxons was made (Archbishop Wulfstan of York negotiated this deal).

However, wars continued for the next 15 years until the last Viking king of York was driven out by the Anglo-Saxons. After this point, although York was often ruled by Anglo-Saxon lords, it continued to have a strong Danish influence.

Source C

The influence of the Vikings in York was still being felt later that century when Byrhtferth of Ramsay wrote his *Life of St Oswald* in the 990s.

There is a city called York, the metropolis of all the Northumbrians, which was once splendidly constructed and stoutly provided with walls. It is now decrepit with age; yet it boasts a large population – no fewer than thirty thousand men and women are counted as the populace of the city. It is... filled and enriched by the treasures of merchants, who come from everywhere, and most of all from the people of Denmark.

1.4 Summary

- York was very attractive as a settlement for Vikings because it was positioned at the centre of a road and river network, which made it perfect for trading.
- Thousands of merchants and migrants travelled to the growing city, which became a rich trading port full of exotic goods. Many skilled craftsmen worked in York.
- York mint created its own coins, which helped establish the city's importance.
- The Church continued to practise in York and many Vikings converted to Christianity.
- Despite conflict with the Anglo-Saxon kingdoms, the migrants continued to live and work in York.

Checkpoint

Strengthen

S1 Why do you think York became such an important trading port?

S2 Look at the Yorkshire hoard in Source A – what items can you see there? What might this tell us about life in York?

Challenge

C1 Look at the evidence for and against whether the Church was influential or not in York. Which do you think makes the more compelling argument? How might the influence of the church have affected Danish migrants? Discuss with a partner.

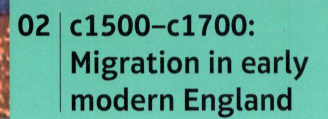

02 | c1500–c1700: Migration in early modern England

Between c1500 and c1700 there were wide-ranging religious, political and social changes in England. These changes meant that different groups of people migrated to England.

- England left the Catholic church and became a Protestant country. Protestants in Europe saw England as a place of safety.

- The English Civil War was in the mid-17th century. As a result, England became a republic for several years, ruled by Oliver Cromwell. The Jewish people returned during this time.

- Companies were set up to trade with West Africa and India. Africans in England were joined by new migrants from West Africa and some Indians, mainly sailors and servants, migrated to England.

- Migrants were accepted and even welcomed when they could contribute to the economy and help make the country prosperous. Where English people believed certain groups of migrants could not help to make England a prosperous country, they were treated very differently.

Learning outcomes

By the end of this chapter, you will:

- understand why some people migrated to England because they wanted to, while others were forced to do so
- know about the different experiences migrants had in England and understand why these experiences were different
- understand the impact migrants had on England
- know about the impact Flemish and Walloon migrants had on Sandwich and Canterbury in the 16th century
- understand the experience of Huguenots in 17th-century England.

2.1 The reasons why people migrated

What was England like in the 16th and 17th centuries?

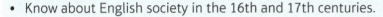

The period c1500–c1700 was a time of great upheaval in England. All these changes had a huge impact on migration to England.

- Leaving the Catholic church completely changed the country's relationship with Europe. Many migrants travelled to England to escape religious persecution.
- Enormous changes in government involved a civil war and the overthrow of the monarchy. New governments welcomed different migrant groups.
- England started to engage with the wider world through developing trading links and making new ones. This helped make England more attractive for many migrants, especially for economic reasons.

Changes in government

During the 1500s, Parliament was called more regularly and started to have a greater say in ruling the country. This led to power struggles between the king and Parliament in the 1600s. Some of the changes made it easier for migrants to enter England.

> **Key term**
>
> **Protestant***
> Christians who disagreed with the Catholic church's interpretation of Christianity.

Changes	Impact on migration
Between 1642 and 1651 a civil war was fought in England between the king and Parliament over who should control the government.	Government was closely linked to religion. Migrants were often either welcomed or rejected according to the religion of the government.
Charles I was executed in 1649 and Oliver Cromwell ruled England as a republic for 11 years.	
In 1660 Parliament invited Charles I's son to reign as King Charles II but limited his powers.	Protestant governments, keen for allies, often welcomed European Protestants.
Charles II was followed by his brother, James II (1685), a Catholic. This was very unpopular in Protestant* England. Parliament invited the Protestant Duke William of Orange (1688) to 'invade' England and become joint monarch with his wife Mary, who was James' daughter.	

Changes in religion

Religion in England changed a great deal in this period. This often had an impact on migration, as many non-Catholics started to see England as a place where they could be safe from prosecution. Later, changes after the civil war led to a return of Jewish communities to England.

Changes	Impact on migration
In 1500 England was a Catholic country.	Religion had a huge impact on migration in this period. European Protestants, like the Huguenots, migrated to England to avoid persecution. As one of the few Protestant powers in Europe, England was seen as a place of safety.
In 1534 Henry VIII made himself head of the Church of England instead of the Pope.	
Under Edward VI (1547–53) laws were passed that made England a Protestant country.	
Edward's sister, Queen Mary I (1553–58), returned England to Catholicism.	
Under Queen Elizabeth I (1558–1603) England became a fully Protestant country.	
Religion remained a dangerous issue. Parliament had feared Charles I was a secret Catholic (Charles had married a Catholic); it later removed the Catholic James II.	

Key term

Charter*

Written permission from the monarch giving rights and privileges to certain groups and individuals.

Activity ?

All these changes contributed to an increase in migration. Attitudes in society varied a great deal from group to group. Start a mind map and, as you read this chapter, add to it showing how English society reacted to each migrant group.

Economic growth

Inspired by the success of the Hanseatic League (see page 20), England and its merchants developed new trading links with the rest of the world. This helped to increase migration – although some of this, like slavery, was forced.

- In 1600 Elizabeth I issued a Charter* to set up the East India Company. The company developed trade links with the East, especially India. They traded in cotton, silk, dyes and spices.
- In 1660 Charles II issued a Charter to set up the Company of Royal Adventurers Trading to Africa. The company traded with West Africa in gold, silver and, significantly, slaves. This was the start of the slave trade that grew until, by 1730, Britain was the world's major slave trader (see page 75).

Economic and trade growth led to merchants and sailors migrating from areas England had had little contact with before, such as India. England's growing empire also led to an increase in forced migration, such as slavery.

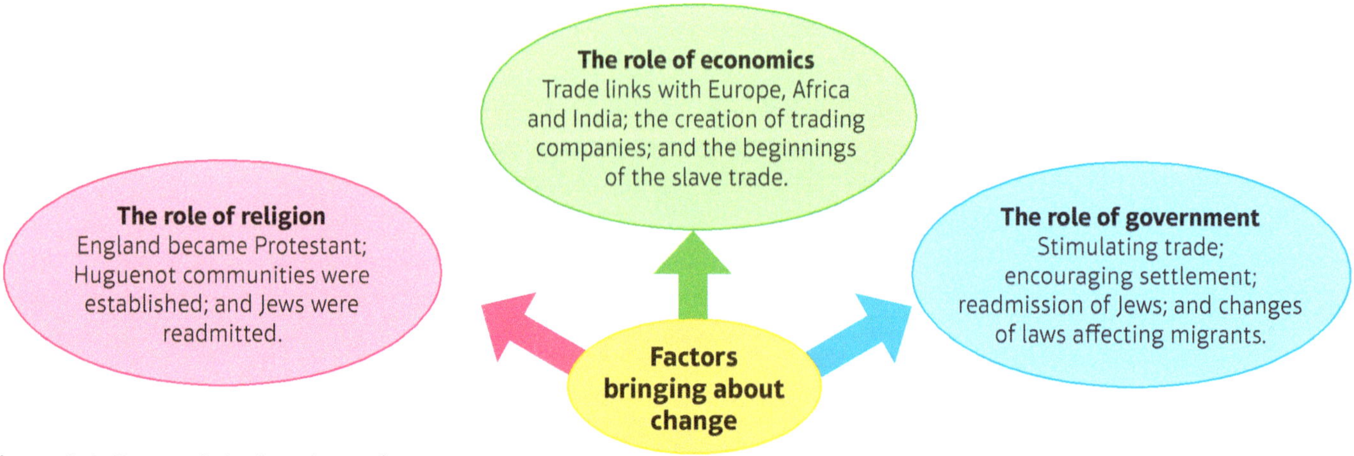

The role of economics
Trade links with Europe, Africa and India; the creation of trading companies; and the beginnings of the slave trade.

The role of religion
England became Protestant; Huguenot communities were established; and Jews were readmitted.

The role of government
Stimulating trade; encouraging settlement; readmission of Jews; and changes of laws affecting migrants.

Factors bringing about change

Figure 2.1 Factors bringing about change

Protestant migrants: Huguenots and Palatines

In England, as well as in Europe, the religion of the ruler was very important. Everyone had to follow their ruler's religion, and there were severe penalties for those who chose not to.

There were some exceptions: the Jewish people, for example, could follow their own faith. But for centuries most people in England and Europe were Catholic because that was the religion of their rulers. Gradually, however, change was coming.

Huguenot migrants from France

Huguenots were French Protestants. From the middle of the 16th century, they saw England as a place of safety. The first arrivals came from northern France and were welcomed by the Protestant King Edward VI. He issued a Charter on 24 July 1550 allowing a French Protestant church to be founded in London. More Huguenots arrived after the St Bartholomew's Day Massacre in 1572.

However, by far the greatest number of Huguenots (around 50,000) arrived between 1670 and 1710. In 1681, King Charles II offered them denizen* status. This gave them the right to live in England with certain rights of citizenship.

In Europe, growing criticism of the Catholic church after 1517, led by Martin Luther, resulted in the Reformation*. Followers of Luther were called Protestants.

'The Catholic church is too rich and corrupt. We want change now!'

Rulers in Italy, France and Spain held on to their Catholic faith. The Netherlands and some German states became Protestant.

'Don't persecute us for being Protestants!'

Until 1534, England was a Catholic country. People who questioned the Catholic church could be punished for heresy.

'It's just as well we're good, law-abiding Catholics.'

In 1534 King Henry VIII took England out of the Catholic church because the Pope refused his request for a divorce.

'I'm head of the Church of England. You will be punished if you continue to follow the Pope and the teachings of the Catholic church.'

In 1559 Queen Elizabeth introduced a religious settlement that established England as a Protestant country.

'We defeated the Spanish Armada in 1588. No other Catholic country will threaten us now. All Protestants are welcome here!'

Key terms

Reformation*

A European movement, headed by Martin Luther, that started by criticising what they saw as the corruption and power of priests, bishops and the Pope. They argued that only by going back to the teachings of the Bible that people could find true faith. Luther and his followers created a split in the Catholic church. His followers were called Protestants.

Denizen*

Certain rights allowed to migrants in their new country.

Figure 2.2 Religious changes in the 16th century

1572 The massacre of Huguenot leaders took place in Paris on St Bartholmew's Day. Slaughter spread throughout France. Over 10,000 were killed.

1685 King Louis XIV of France made it illegal for French people to be Protestants. Huguenot church services were banned, businesses were attacked, and Protestants were forced to become Catholics.

1570s The first Huguenot refugees arrived in England.

1680s 40,000–50,000 Huguenot refugees arrived in England.

Figure 2.3 Huguenots migrated to England

Extend your knowledge

St Bartholomew's Day Massacre, 24 August 1572

King Charles IX of France ordered the killing of Huguenot leaders in Paris celebrating the marriage of their leader, Henry of Navarre, to Charles' sister Margaret. It is believed about 3,000 Huguenots were killed in Paris and about 70,000 in the rest of France.

The Edict of Nantes 1598 (withdrawn 1685)

The Edict of Nantes of 1598 gave French Protestants religious freedom. In 1685 it was revoked (withdrawn). Protestant services were banned and Protestant businesses attacked.

Activities **?**

1. Use Interpretations 1 and 2, and Source A (on the facing page). Write down one thing you can learn from each about the Huguenot migrants.

2. Why were the Huguenot migrants so determined to get to England? Use your own knowledge and the answer you wrote above in your explanation.

Huguenots migrated to England because they couldn't work at their trades and businesses in France, and because they couldn't follow their religion there. Most people welcomed them into England. They were skilled migrants.

Many Huguenots, particularly after 1670, came to join relatives and friends who had been running successful businesses in England for years. Others had no such connections. Churches collected money for poorer refugees and food kitchens fed them until they could settle and find work.

Interpretation 1

From *Bloody Foreigners: the story of immigration to Britain* by Robert Winder, published in 2004. Here he describes some of the ways in which the Huguenots travelled to England in the 1670s.

They hid in bales of straw, casks of wine, empty vats or heaps of coal; they were disguised by neighbours or sheltered by friends, and crept across borders or out to sea. The journey to England was hazardous, especially for those forced to make the long detour through Gibraltar. Many were captured and enslaved by Spanish pirates; others were intercepted by French patrols and sent as slaves to the galleys of the French fleet.

Interpretation 2

A 19th-century engraving by C. Durand showing Huguenot refugees arriving in Dover shortly after 1685.

The Minet family

Ambroise and Susanna Minet, together with their nine children, were a Protestant family from Calais. Ambroise was a shop owner, selling groceries, medicines, alcohol and tobacco. He died in 1679 and his son Isaac took over the business. In 1685, after the Edict of Nantes was revoked, the Minet family knew it was time to go. Emigration from France was forbidden but Isaac and his brother Stephen (who was a merchant in Dover) had a plan.

On their first attempt to leave France they were spotted and captured. But in 1686 the family managed to escape on a boat sent by Stephen. Isaac set up a new shop in London, selling alcohol and perfumes. When Stephen died in 1690, Isaac moved to Dover and took over his brother's business. He turned the business into an insurance firm that continued successfully into the 20th century.

Palatine migrants from Germany

In 1709, the government passed the Foreign Protestants Naturalisation Act. This allowed European Protestants to live in England, with full civil rights providing they swore loyalty to the Crown. It was meant to attract wealthy entrepreneurs and skilled craftspeople from France and Holland.

Later that year a huge refugee camp appeared on the outskirts of London. Thousands of people lived in tents provided by the British government.

Most came from a part of Germany called the Palatinate. Most were poor farmers and their families who, after a run of bad harvests and a series of wars between German states, were looking for a better life.

Some were hoping to migrate to a better life in America: the British-owned Carolina Company had advertised in Germany for migrants to settle in America.

Between May and June 1709, almost 12,000 Palatines and other German Protestants migrated to England. At first, the public were generous in their support. Londoners alone raised £20,000 and MPs donated to a charitable fund opened by Queen Anne. But gradually, as you will see in Section 2.2, attitudes changed.

> Although Palatine migration took place post-1700, it has been included here because of its close links to Huguenot migration.

Activity   ?

Compare the Huguenots and the Palatines. Find one similarity and two differences between them. Share what you have found with the rest of your class and build up a complete list of similarities and differences. Which do you think was the most important difference?

A contemporary picture of the refugee camp on Blackheath, then outside London, for migrants from the Palatinate.

The return of Jewish people

Jews were officially expelled from England in 1290 (see page 19). Some managed to remain in the country, either by converting to Christianity or by practising their faith in secret. But England remained hostile to Jews.

However, by the 1650s the situation had changed dramatically. England was not only a Protestant country but also a republic* with Oliver Cromwell as its leader. Persecution of Jews in Europe was increasing. In 1655, a rabbi* from Amsterdam, Menasseh ben Israel, visited Cromwell to argue for Jews to be allowed back into England (see Figures 2.4 and 2.5).

Cromwell's council came up with a solution.

- The expulsion order in 1290 had been issued by royal prerogative* and not passed by Parliament.
- The law only applied to Jews living in England at the time. It didn't affect any Jews after this time.

So there was no need for debates or a grand announcement that might frighten people. All that was necessary was to quietly let Jewish people come back if they wanted to.

In March 1656, a small group of Jews settled in the London suburb of Aldgate. They were permitted to follow their religion privately 'in their houses for prayer'. By the end of the year Cromwell's council allowed them to build a synagogue. More and more Jews arrived, and Aldgate became a thriving Jewish community.

Key terms

Republic*
A country where the head of state is not a monarch.

Rabbi*
A Jewish religious leader and teacher.

Royal prerogative*
The right of a monarch to make decisions without reference to Parliament.

Activities

1 Menasseh ben Israel gave Cromwell several reasons why Jews should be allowed back into England. Explain which one you think was the best.
2 Explain why Jews came back to England.

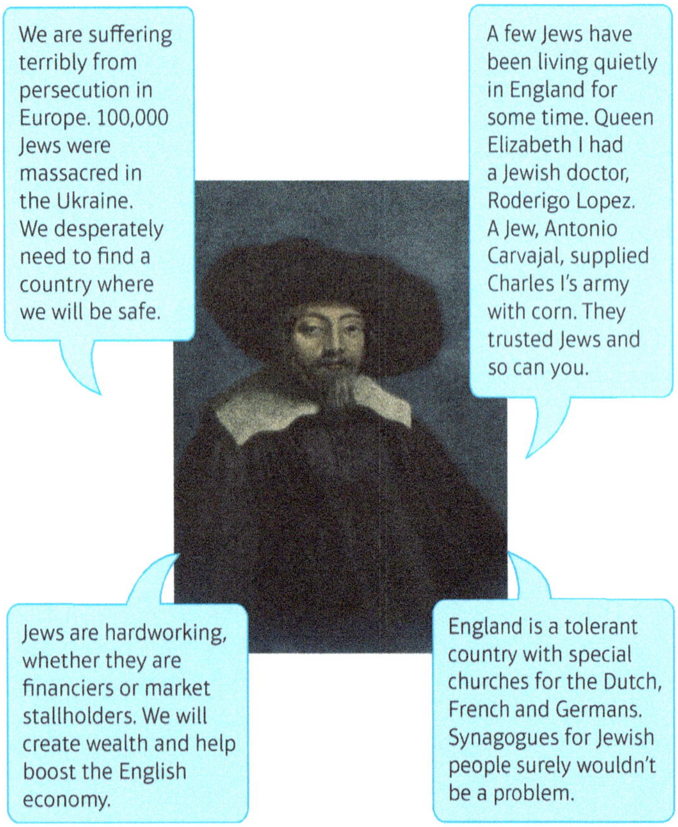

We are suffering terribly from persecution in Europe. 100,000 Jews were massacred in the Ukraine. We desperately need to find a country where we will be safe.

A few Jews have been living quietly in England for some time. Queen Elizabeth I had a Jewish doctor, Roderigo Lopez. A Jew, Antonio Carvajal, supplied Charles I's army with corn. They trusted Jews and so can you.

Jews are hardworking, whether they are financiers or market stallholders. We will create wealth and help boost the English economy.

England is a tolerant country with special churches for the Dutch, French and Germans. Synagogues for Jewish people surely wouldn't be a problem.

Figure 2.4 Menasseh ben Israel puts his case to Oliver Cromwell

Because of my religious beliefs, I think Jesus Christ will only come to Earth again if we can convert Jews to Christianity. This will be easier if they are in England.

As far as I can tell, there isn't any obvious anti-Semitism in England. But can I risk it breaking out again, as it has done in Europe?

The economy is weak. We badly need the skills Jewish people can bring to England.

I've asked my council for a quick decision. But they have set up a committee to discuss the whole issue and they are taking far too long!

Figure 2.5 Cromwell decides what to do

Africans

Black people have lived in England since Roman times. By the 16th and 17th centuries there were Africans in the royal court and working in the households of important people such as Catherine of Aragon, the Earl of Leicester and Sir Walter Raleigh.

Black Africans were also found in ordinary households. They carried out a wide range of skilled jobs and were paid the same wages as others. Although some employers treated **all** their servants as if they owned them, Africans in Britain were not slaves under the law. They were respected and equal members of society: for example, court records show Africans testifying against suspected criminals.

Parish registers* show Africans marrying local people and being baptised and buried in parishes up and down the country (mainly in London and the south of England). It's impossible to know how many there were, but clearly Africans were part of everyday life. How and why did they migrate to England?

In the 1440s Portuguese merchants captured my great grandparents and took them to Europe as slaves. I don't believe all our exciting family stories about escapes, but by 1500 they were in England. Thank goodness slavery is illegal here.

An English merchant bought me from a Portuguese slave trader. He wanted to teach me English so I could work as an interpreter.

I was born in England. My grandmother was a servant to Catherine of Aragon. That was in 1501. She hated leaving Spain but really settled here once she got married.

My family were forced out of Spain in 1568 because they were part of the Muslim rebellion against the Catholic Spanish government. We came here as refugees.

Figure 2.6 Why did we come to England?

Extend your knowledge

Sir John Hawkins (1532–95) was a talented English admiral. He was also the first Englishman involved in the transatlantic slave trade. In 1562, he took three ships to Guinea in West Africa where he filled their holds with around 300 Africans. He sailed across the Atlantic to Hispaniola*, where he traded them for pearls, sugar and animal skins. English involvement in the transatlantic slave trade didn't take off for another 70 years, but Hawkins' involvement in the trade was an indication of what was to come.

Interpretation 3

From *Black Tudors: the untold story* by Miranda Kaufmann, published in 2017.

Social class governed society. Everyone, from the King, through the aristocracy, to the gentry, yeomen and husbandmen, down to the lowliest vagrant, occupied a particular place in the 'Great Chain of Being'*. When Africans arrived in England as ambassadors, they were treated as such. But when they arrived on board a captured ship, they found themselves at the bottom of the pile. Those who had skills, such as musicians, sailors or craftsmen, fared better. In many ways, their lives were no worse than the vast majority of Tudors,… this was the result of having no social standing, not of having dark skin.

Key terms

Parish registers*

These were introduced in September 1538. Every Church of England parish had to keep registers of all baptisms, marriages and burials that happened there. The parish priest had to keep them up-to-date.

Great Chain of Being*

Tudors believed that God set everything out in order of importance. This was called the Great Chain of Being. It started with God at the top and ended with rocks and minerals at the bottom.

Hispaniola*

The first Caribbean island to be settled (which was by the Spanish at the end of the 15th century).

Source B

Sketch for the coat of arms of Sir John Hawkins, 1586. Hawkins had an image of a slave in shackles* added to this.

1585 Queen Elizabeth sent Ralph Fitch to the court of the Emperor Akbar to find out whether it was worth trying to trade with India. He reported back that it was.

1600 Queen Elizabeth issued a Charter to a group of merchants allowing them to have a monopoly* of trade with 'the East'. They set up the East India Company.

1608 The first East India Company ships set sail for India.

The East India Company set up trading posts, called factories, in India. The most important factories were at Surat (1613), Chennai (1641), Mumbai (1668) and Kolkata (1690).

Figure 2.7 Starting trade with India

Key terms

Shackles*
Metal cuffs connected by a chain that fasten a person's ankles or wrists together.

Monopoly*
Exclusive control of trade.

Indians

India was a thriving, multi-faith society of about 100 million people, ruled over by Mughal emperors and a number of princes. It was rich in silks, spices and sugar. In England in 1500, only a handful of merchants and explorers knew this. Travel to India, either overland or by sea, was dangerous and took several weeks. How did trade with India start, making it possible for Indian people to migrate to England?

As the East India Company expanded its trading activities, more and more officials were needed in India to run the Company's affairs. Traders and merchants, administrators and officials, officers and soldiers (the Company had its own army) went out from England to try to make their fortunes. A few settled permanently in India. It was the returning Englishmen that made it possible, in these years, for Indian people to migrate to England.

Source C

A contemporary picture of the East India Company's factory (trading station) at Surat.

Activities ?

1   Using the information on page 39, write three statements about black Africans. Now compare your three statements with a partner's. Keep comparing until you have a class list of different, but correct, statements.

2   Look carefully at Source C. What does this tell you about trading with India at the time? Explain your answer.

I was working as an ayah* for my employer's children. My employer liked the way I looked after their children and brought me back to England with them. I don't know what I'll do when the children grow up. How many people would employ an Indian nanny?

My husband is an Englishman working for the East India Company. We got married in Bengal and have three children. We all came back to England together. It's not easy, adapting to a different way of life.

When my master and his family returned to England from Madras, he brought all his servants with him. I could have refused, but it would be difficult to get such a good job if I had stayed in India.

I worked as a lascar* on an East India Company ship. The work was hard, and I didn't go back when we reached London. I'm working on the Thames barges now.

Figure 2.8 Why did we come to England?

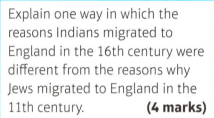

Key terms

Ayah*
Indian word for a nanny – a woman who looks after children.

Lascar*
The name given to Indian sailors working on ships owned by the East India Company.

Exam-style question, Section B

Explain one way in which the reasons Indians migrated to England in the 16th century were different from the reasons why Jews migrated to England in the 11th century. **(4 marks)**

Exam tip

The question tests knowledge and difference over time. Remember to **explain** one difference – don't just describe it, explain why it was different.

2.1 Summary

- Huguenot migrants were French Protestants who were persecuted in Catholic France. They were generally skilled workers with colleagues, friends and relatives in England.
- Palatine migrants were poor farmers mainly from the Palatinate but also from other German states.
- Jewish people came quietly back to England after 1656.
- Africans had been living in England since before 1500. Some had escaped from slavery; others were driven out of Spain.
- Most Indian migrants were brought to England by the families with whom they had worked in India. Others were sailors (lascars) who had jumped ship when arriving in England.

Checkpoint

Strengthen

S1 What were the main differences between the Protestant migrants in England?

S2 Why were Jews allowed back into England?

S3 Give two reasons why Africans came to live in England.

Challenge

C1 Explain how religion and trade made England an attractive country for migrants.

2.2 The experiences of migrants

Learning outcomes

• Understand the ways in which, and how successfully, migrants settled in England.

• Understand the relationship between migrants and the existing population.

Protestants: success and failure

Huguenots and Palatines were Protestants who migrated to Protestant England. At first, they were welcomed (see pages 35–37) but soon the attitudes of English people changed. This meant that Huguenots and Palatines ended up having very different experiences.

Huguenots: a success story

Huguenots had a range of skills and expertise that meant that most were able to find work. Many joined businesses that friends or relatives were already running, and some set up businesses of their own.

Figure 2.9 What skills did Huguenots bring to England?

Some Huguenots were desperately poor, and others took to petty crime. In this they were no different from thousands of English people. However, most Huguenots prospered in England and, as you'll see in Section 2.3, they contributed in a huge way to the economy of the country.

Case study

Henri de Portal, 1690–1747

In 1705, the young Henri de Portal, a Protestant refugee from France, landed at Southampton with his family. They found help and shelter from the Huguenots there. Henri worked at a paper mill at South Stoneham, just outside Southampton. The French Protestant owner, Gerard de Vaux, taught Henri the craft of papermaking so well that, in 1718, Henri opened his own mill at Laverstoke in north Hampshire. Henri was so skilled that in 1724 he won the monopoly for manufacturing the special paper the Bank of England needed for banknotes. By hard work and skill, Henri de Portal turned his mill into one of the most successful paper mills in England.

Palatines: a story of desperation

It was different for the Palatines. They did not have the Huguenot's skills, nor did they have family and friends already established in England. They were poor and they were desperate.

Figure 2.10 Problems faced by Palatines

42

A few Palatines found work in Liverpool unloading ships, and others joined the army. But thousands were stuck in London, with no work, no homes and nowhere to go.

They faced a life of poverty and starvation as well as anger from English people who feared the Palatines would take jobs away from English people. Then the government came up with a solution.

Deportation!

Around 3,000 Palatines were deported to Ireland in September 1709. The government assumed that, because the Palatines were mainly agricultural labourers, they would be able to farm the land. They were wrong.

- Some land was very poor quality and the Palatines couldn't grow enough to support their families.
- They were hated by the Catholic Irish majority who were suffering under English rule. The Palatines were seen as being there to strengthen English Protestantism.
- Almost two-thirds of those deported drifted back to England.
- Some landowners, for example Sir Thomas Southwell, used their own money to support the Palatines. By 1714 he had settled about 130 families on his estates in Limerick. Descendants of the original Palatine settlers still live in the area. Landowner Abel Ram settled 30 families in Wexford.

Suffering and afraid, over 3,000 Palatines set sail for New York. Many died on the voyage. Once in New York, hundreds died from typhoid or were killed by immigrant-hating mobs. The survivors made the best living they could, and their descendants are still living in the Hudson River Valley.

Activities

1. Read the case study about Henri de Portal. What does it tell you about Huguenot migrants? Write down as many things as you can.
2. Look at Figure 2.10 'Problems faced by Palatines'. Explain which problems you think affected them the most.

Exam-style question, Section B

Explain why the Huguenots settled successfully in England.

You may use the following in your answer:

- manufacturing skills
- the poor harvest of 1709.

You **must** also use information of your own.

(12 marks)

Exam tip

The question asks you to explain why the Huguenots settled successfully. Don't just describe what happened, but instead focus on **explaining** why these things happened.

Jews: settling quietly

Gradually Jews from other countries joined the community in London. By 1701 a larger synagogue was built that could seat 400 men and 160 women. The London authorities gave permission for this. This was the Bevis Marks synagogue, the oldest British synagogue still in constant use.

Every year, from 1679 to 1780, Sephardic* Jews from the Bevis Marks synagogue presented the mayor of London with a beautiful silver dish filled with sweetmeats*. Other minority communities, like the Dutch and French Protestants, did the same. They needed to be sure the mayor would support them in time of trouble.

Key terms

Sephardic Jews*

Jews coming mainly from communities in Spain and Portugal.

Sweetmeats*

Food rich in sugar, such as candied or crystalised fruit.

The London Jewish community included merchants and bankers, dealers in precious stones and doctors, as well as rabbis and kosher butchers. Some did very well indeed. In 1657 Solomon Dormido was the first Jew to trade on the Royal Exchange*. The Mendes da Costa family were successful bankers with houses in Highgate, Surrey and Hertfordshire.

However, some did not do as well. In 1700 half of the nearly 1,000 Jews in London depended on help from richer members of the community.

While the London community of mainly talented Sephardic Jews grew slowly, Ashkenazi* Jews from central and eastern Europe arrived in increasing numbers. They settled in the trading ports of Hull, Liverpool, Portsmouth and Plymouth as well as London.

Some Jews set up as dealers in the seaports, selling marine stores and supplies to shipowners and captains or worked as dockers and warehousemen. There was plenty of work for tailors, shopkeepers and pawnbrokers.

Others, though, became pedlars, moving between towns and villages, selling lace and ribbons, pins and needles, brushes and buckets. The Jewish community, like every other community, had poor, hungry and sometimes destitute men, women and children.

- Synagogues raised collections to look after Jewish people fallen on hard times. There are reports that the Jewish relief system* was so good, some non-Jews pretended to be Jewish to claim help.

- In 1644 the Gates of Hope, a boys' school for poor Jewish boys, was founded in London and paid for out of synagogue funds. At first, only religious and Hebrew studies were taught. Later, maths and reading and writing of English were added. Every boy had to arrive washed with combed hair and also wash his feet once a week.

- In 1730 Villa Real, a similar school for educating poor Jewish girls, was opened in London.

Key terms

Royal Exchange*

A centre of commerce for the City of London.

Ashkenazi Jews*

Jews coming mainly from Germany, Poland and Russia.

Relief system*

A system whereby food, clothing and money was given to poor people who were either out of work or earning too little to be able to look after themselves and their families.

Source A

The Bevis Marks synagogue, London.

Anti-Semitism

After 1656 English people were much more willing to accept Jews living and working in England than they had been in medieval times. There was still, however, a lot of evidence of anti-Semitism.

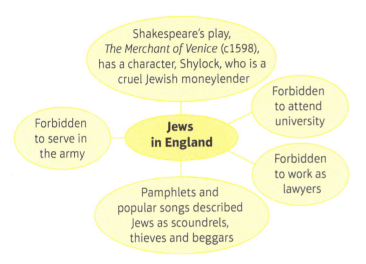

Figure 2.11 Anti-Semitism in England c1700

Gypsies: unwelcome migrants

Gypsies came and went. They set up their tents wherever they chose, usually on common land or in forests, and moved on whenever they wanted. Sometimes they worked as farm labourers or entertainers at fairs; they mended pots and pans, sold herbs, or bought and sold animals. The authorities regarded them as vagrants – wanderers and beggars – a danger to peace and order, who didn't bring any economic benefit to England. The answer was to get rid of them.

Many were persecuted by the law, but still the Gypsies stayed on – in fact more travelled over from Europe. In the 1650s, the government began the forced transportation of gypsies into slavery in North America and the Caribbean. Even so, gypsies continued to live in England in the years to 1700 and beyond, but always as a persecuted minority.

Timeline

Persecution of Gypsy communities

1530 Henry VIII ordered all Gypsies to leave the country within 16 days. If they didn't, they would be imprisoned or deported

1554 Queen Mary I allowed Gypsies to remain in England, but only if they stayed in one place. They didn't! English people were forbidden to travel with Gypsies

1562 Queen Elizabeth I said Gypsies could become English subjects if they stayed in one place. If they refused and were caught, they would be hanged

1577 Six people were hanged in Aylesbury, Hertfordshire, for mixing with Gypsies

1592 Five Gypsies were hanged in Durham

1595 Nine Gypsies were hanged in York

Activities ?

1   Draw a pair of scales. On one side write all the positive things that happened as a result of Jews settling back in England. On the other side, write all the negative things. Do they balance? Remember that balance comes not from numbers but from the weight of their importance.

2   'The resettlement of Jews in England was a complete success.' How far do you agree with this statement? Use your scales to help you plan what you will write.

3   Imagine you are a Gypsy brought in front of a local magistrate, simply for being a Gypsy. What will you say to persuade the magistrate not to throw you into prison or, worse, hang you? Remember to put in as many relevant facts as you can.

Africans: part of society

You read on page 39 that Africans were part of English society throughout the 16th and 17th centuries. They led lives that were no different from those around them. Figure 2.12 shows what some of them did.

In the 1590s **Edward Swarthye** was a porter at Sir Edward Wynter's house, White Cross Manor, in Gloucestershire. Wynter ordered him to whip a white Englishman, John Guye, who was suspected of theft.

Jacques Francis was a diver who helped salvage goods from the *Mary Rose*, Henry VIII's flagship, when it sank in Portsmouth harbour in 1545.

John Anthony was a sailor based in Dover, Kent, at the beginning of the 17th century. He worked on the ship, *The Silver Falcon*, and had earlier been involved in piracy under Henry Mainwaring.

Cattelina was an independent single woman living in Almondsbury, outside Bristol, who owned a cow. She died in 1625.

Reasonable Blackman was a silk weaver living in Southwark, London, in the 1580s and 1590s. He had three children, two of whom died in the plague of 1592.

John Moore paid for the Freedom of the City of York in 1687. He was a wealthy citizen; paying for the Freedom meant he could enjoy a lot of privileges, for example the right to fish in the city's rivers.

Mingoe worked as a servant for Sir William Batten. Batten was a naval officer and an MP who owned Harwich lighthouse. When he died in 1667, he left his lighthouse and £20 a year to Mingoe.

John Blanke was trumpeter for Henry VIII.

Figure 2.12 African workers in England in the 16th and 17th centuries

Runaways

Not all Africans were happy in the work they were doing, as Sources B and C show. *(Note: These sources contain racist words and imagery unacceptable today. They appear to accurately reflect the writer's attitudes.)*

Source B

From the newspaper *Flying Post*, 10 August 1700. A periwig was a fashionable wig worn in the 17th and 18th centuries and livery was a uniform.

Last week ran away from his master, J. Bromley Esq., of Bookham in Surrey, his Negro Man Prinpey, alias Harry Johnson, aged about 35 Years, tall of stature, sometimes wears a Periwig, speaks English well, in a blue livery with brass buttons, and has taken with him several of his master's goods. Whoever secures him, and gives notice to his Master or to Mr Richard Sheppard in Lothbury, London, shall have a Guinea reward.

Source C

From the *London Gazette*, 21 June 1703. Stuff was a woollen cloth and breeches short trousers.

Run away from his master, a Negro Boy about 15 years old, speaks pretty good English, tall for his Age, with long slender legs, very thick Lips, and has lost a bit of the lower part of his left ear, had a Stuff coat, dark coloured Cloth Waistcoat, a pair of Stuff Breeches with Pewter Buttons, supposed to be gone on board some ship. Whoever secures him, so that he may be had again, or brings him to Mr Stephen Peters in Birchin Lane near the Royal Exchange, shall have 20s Reward and reasonable Charges.

Child servants

Most children worked in the 16th and 17th centuries. They worked in streets and fields, along the rivers and back alleys, and in stables and cowsheds. If they were lucky, they worked in the houses of people richer than their parents, scrubbing and sweeping, washing and brushing, chopping and peeling.

It was different for many African children. In the late 1600s, it became fashionable to have a black servant, especially a child.

Source D

A portrait of Louise de Keroualle, Duchess of Portsmouth, who was Charles II's mistress. It was painted in 1682 by Pierre Mignard while the Duchess was visiting Paris. The black child is a status symbol, and to be shown presenting Louise de Keroualle with precious coral and pearls in a shell further emphasises the Duchess's wealth and social standing.

Source E

From the *London Gazette*, June 1694. A London-based journal, the *Gazette* carried notices about missing people as well as national news.

(Note: This source contains racist words unacceptable today. They appear to accurately reflect the writer's attitudes.)

A GUINEA NEGRO BOY, ABOUT 8 YEARS OLD, NAMED JACK, STRAIGHT LIMB, NO MARK ON HIS FACE HAS STRAYED AWAY FROM MR PETER PAGGERTS IN CROSS-LANE, ON ST MARY'S HILL NEAR BILLINGSGATE. WHOEVER SHALL BRING THE SAID NEGRO BOY OR DISCOVERS WHERE HE IS SO HE MAY BE HAD AGAIN, SHALL HAVE 20 SHILLINGS REWARD.

Activities ?

1 Read Sources B and C. What can you learn from these two advertisements about **(a)** African servants in England and **(b)** attitudes towards Africans in England in the early 18th century?

2 Look at Source D. What can you learn from the picture about the African child servant?

3 Now read the information about Source D. What do you think are the reasons for the differences in the experiences of the African child in this source and the African child in Source E?

On 22 December 1616, at St Dionis Backchurch in London, in the presence of members of the Privy Council, the lord mayor and aldermen, and the governors of the East India Company, an Indian youth brought to Britain two years' previously was publicly baptised. The church was packed and a crowd of curious onlookers gathered outside. The Archbishop of Canterbury had given his approval, while the name given in baptism [Peter] was chosen by King James I. This is the first known record of a baptism of an Indian brought to Britain.

The Company's chaplain in India had taught him to read and write English and was instrumental in bringing him to England. The Company voted '30 marks per annum' for his schooling in England, so that he could be instructed in religion and sent back as a missionary to convert his own people.

Extend your knowledge

In 1662 Charles II married Catherine of Braganza, a Portuguese princess. As part of the marriage settlement, Charles was given the city of Bombay (modern-day Mumbai), which was part of the Portuguese Empire.

Indians: sailors and servants

Some Indians (see page 40) came to England because they were sailors, called lascars, on East India Company ships. Others, as you read (pages 40–41) were brought to England by merchants and those working for the East India Company. What happened to them in a country so different from India?

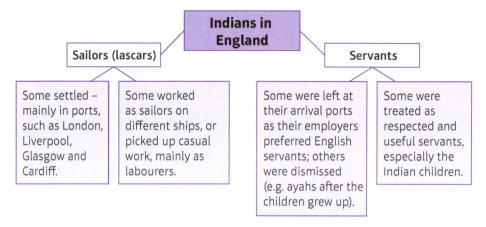

Figure 2.13 Indians in England

Indian child servants were used in much the same way as African child servants – as status symbols that indicated their employers' connections with the fabulous, exotic and mysterious India.

Source F

A painting of Lady Charlotte Fitzroy, the illegitimate daughter of King Charles II, with her Indian pageboy. It was painted by Sir Peter Lely, who was Charles II's principal artist, in 1674. Lady Charlotte was aged eight and her pageboy was about the same age.

Activities

1 Compare Source D and Source F. What similarities can you find in the two paintings? Are there any differences? What does this tell you about how migrant child servants were treated?

2 Read the case study about a baptism. This was clearly an important occasion for everyone involved. Why do you think this was?

Exam-style question, Section B

Explain one way in which job opportunities for Jewish migrants were different from job opportunities for Indian migrants. **(4 marks)**

Exam tip

The question tests knowledge of similarity and difference over time. Remember to give one way in which job opportunities for Jewish migrants were different from those for Indian migrants and then add details to show the differences.

THINKING HISTORICALLY ▶ Cause and consequence (1a)

The language of causation

There are many useful words and phrases you can use when writing about cause and consequence. Some of these words and phrases can be used to describe short-term causes. Other words are used to describe long-term causes that develop over a longer period of time.

Look at the table below. The first example has been completed for you.

Word/phrase	Meaning	Short term or long term
Triggered	*The final factor that caused change.*	*Short term. Suggests the change happened immediately afterwards.*
Influenced		
Led to		
Developed		

1 Copy the table above and complete it by filling in the blanks.

2 Complete the sentences below by using the above words and phrases from the first column of the table.

The visit of Menasseh ben Israel to England _____ the decision to allow Jews to return.

Many Huguenots settling in England _____ successful businesses.

The desire for status symbols _____ rich people having African and Indian children as servants.

3 The phrases below can be used to describe the importance of a particular cause. Write them out in a list, starting with the one that means 'most important' and ending with the one that means 'least important'.

| necessary | contributed to | added to | marginal |
| fundamental | influenced | supported | negligible |

2.2 Summary

- Huguenots settled successfully because they had a range of useful skills. They joined businesses already in existence in England, being run by family and friends, and some set up their own businesses.
- Palatines had few useful skills so they were eventually transported to Ireland and America.
- Jews were quietly settled in England and worked at a range of jobs from selling rags to banking.
- Gypsies were feared and hated; laws were passed to try to keep them out of England.
- Africans and Indians more often worked as servants.

Checkpoint

Strengthen

S1 Give two differences between the Huguenots and the Palatines.

S2 Give one reason why gypsies were unwelcome migrants.

S3 Describe the work done for rich people by their African and Indian child servants.

Challenge

C1 Explain the importance of trade in making it possible for migrants to settle successfully in England.

2.3 The impact of migrants on England

Learning outcomes

- Understand the impact of migrants on industry, trade and agriculture.
- Understand the impact of migrants on English society and culture.

Migrant communities in England played an important part in starting Britain's move towards being an industrial nation. Migrants used their skills in industry, trade, banking and agriculture to help make the country more prosperous. Migrants also helped encourage art, science and religious tolerance.

Industry, trade and banking: the Huguenots

The Huguenots had a huge economic impact on England.

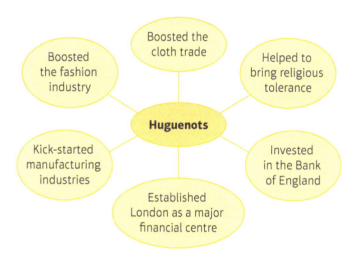

Figure 2.14 Huguenot impact on England

How did the Huguenots change England?

- **Boosted the cloth trade**. Huguenots were skilled silk weavers. Between 1650 and 1700 there was a twenty-fold increase in England's silk production, a lot of which was exported – mainly to France! Huguenots brought new techniques to England for weaving velvet, taffeta* and brocade* and these were quickly learned by the English weavers of cotton, woollen and worsted* cloth.
- **Boosted the fashion industry**. The new fabrics, especially silk, were in great demand by rich women for their dresses. Dress designers and dressmakers were kept very busy.

- **Kick-started manufacturing industries**. Huguenot ironworkers helped develop the steel industry in Sheffield and Shotley Bridge. Huguenots started the English paper industry – by 1714 there were 200 paper mills in England.
- **Invested in the Bank of England**. When the Bank of England was founded in 1694, 10% of its capital (£104,000 out of £1.2 million) was provided by 123 Huguenots. Seven of the 25 directors were Huguenots, as was the first governor, Sir James Houblon.
- **Established London as a major financial centre**. The Huguenots knew about investment and the importance of a National Debt* (which enabled the government to borrow money). A lot of that money was used to expand the British Empire.
- **Helped to bring religious tolerance**. Huguenots were allowed their own churches. This helped make society more open to religious differences.

Key terms

Taffeta*
A fine, shiny silk fabric

Brocade*
A richly decorated heavy silk fabric, sometimes with gold and silver thread woven into it.

Worsted*
A finely woven woollen fabric.

National Debt*
The amount of money a government has borrowed.

Activities

1 Make a spidergram showing how all the different ways in which the Huguenots impacted England were linked.
2 Which one do you think is the key? Explain why.

Jewish financiers and merchants

Although many Jews made important contributions to the English economy, they were not allowed to attend universities, serve in the army or work as lawyers. This meant the greatest impact was as financiers and merchants.

Case study

The Hart family

Moses Hart was a Jewish merchant who migrated from Germany towards the end of the 16th century. He was one of the 12 'Jew brokers' allowed to trade on the Royal Exchange, and he made a fortune. In 1692 he helped finance the first 'Great' synagogue, built in Aldgate, London, for Ashkenazi Jews. His brother Aaron was the Chief Rabbi.

Moses bought a huge house in Twickenham, which he filled with paintings by Christian artists such as Rubens and Van Dyke. Like many Jews, Moses felt he had to lose some of his Jewish identity to be fully accepted by the English. He trimmed his beard and refused to wear a head covering.

Moses' daughter Bilhah married Aaron Franks, uniting two of the most important Jewish families in London. The Franks were merchants, dealing mainly in diamonds and coral. They also had government contracts to supply the British army with equipment. The married couple moved to a mansion next door to Moses. They were renowned for their lavish entertainments involving concerts and balls.

The Harts and Franks lived lives of luxury, but their lifestyle meant that they provided employment for vast numbers of people such as maids, cooks and butlers, gardeners and stable boys, builders, decorators and furniture-makers, musicians and singers. Moses Hart never forgot the poorer Ashkenazi Jews who remained in Europe.

Key term

Glorious Revolution*

Took place 1688–89 and involved the overthrow of the Catholic King James II and his replacement by the Protestant William, Duke of Orange, and his wife Mary. Mary was James' daughter by his first wife.

Source A

A portrait of Moses Hart, painted by an unknown artist in 1722.

Many successful Jewish businessmen supported monarchs and noblemen.

- Lopes Suasso funded William III's 'Glorious Revolution'*. He encouraged several Jewish bankers to move to London. One of these was Isaac Pereira who became Commissary-General for Shipping and Supplies, a very important post.
- Solomon de Medina financed the Duke of Marlborough's campaigns. He travelled with him and saw he had sufficient supplies and funded him with about £6,000 a year. He was rewarded with a knighthood, the first Jew to receive one.

Activities

1   Make a list of all that Jews did to make an impact from 1656 to the early years of the 18th century.
2   Which do you think had the most important impact on (a) the Jewish community and (b) the British economy? Explain your answer.
3   How did the experiences of Jews in the 18th century differ from their experiences in 1066 to 1290?

Agriculture: the Dutch

In the 1630s and 1640s gangs of Dutch workmen descended on the Fens and were kept busy there for years. They were making great changes that would have a lasting impact. Land drainage work in the Netherlands had made many Dutch engineers valuable experts.

In 1630 Cornelius Vermuyden, a Dutch drainage and embankment engineer, was invited by Charles I to drain the Fens in East Anglia. If the land was properly drained, vast areas of fertile farmland would be created.

For over 20 years Dutch workmen, managers and engineers, partly funded by Dutch money, worked hard in the Fens. They straightened rivers and dug ditches, built embankments and sluices*, created washes* and dams, and built windmills and pumps. By 1642 about 40,000 acres had been drained and turned into agricultural land.

Key terms

Sluices*
Channels for water which are controlled by gates.

Washes*
Reservoirs to store floodwaters.

Extend your knowledge

The Fen Tigers

There was fierce opposition from local fenmen who had lost their livelihoods. They could no longer cut reeds, catch eels and trap wildfowl. Called the Fen Tigers, they tried to sabotage the drainage works. They smashed dams and embankments, pulled down windmills, destroyed pumps and broke up the camps where the Dutch workers lived.

What were the Fens like?

Vast areas of marsh and wetlands, criss-crossed by shifting ditches and streams. Wild, dangerous places, though with areas of solid ground, such as the Isle of Ely. In the summer the Fens were often dry, but in the winter, when the easterly winds combined with the high tides, huge areas flooded.

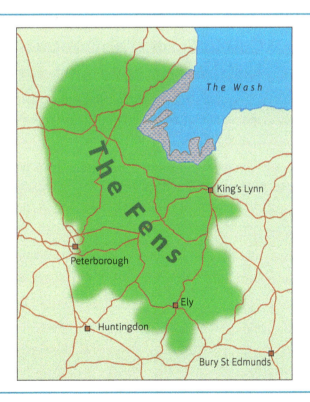

Who lived and worked on the Fens?

It was not an easy life. Most people lived in isolated settlements. In the dryer summer months, some looked after the cows and sheep that grazed the Fens. However, the main occupations were catching eels, fish and wild birds, cutting peat for fuel, and cutting sedge and reeds for thatching.

Figure 2.15 The Fens before the great changes

Key terms

Coleseed*

The 17th-century name for rapeseed.

Woad*

A plant used to make a blue dye.

Interpretation 1

From *England's Apprenticeship 1603–1763* by Charles Wilson, published in 1965.

No longer a backwater, the Fens were becoming a centre of agricultural enterprise.

Activities ?

1. Explain how far the work of Dutch migrants improved the economy of East Anglia.

2. Use the list you have made to design a 17th-century poster inviting people to come and work in the Fens. You could focus on specific occupations or make a more general employment.

3. Explain, with examples, what Charles Wilson (Interpretation 1) meant by 'agricultural enterprise'.

Key term

Stationer*

Person who supplies paper and writing materials.

How did the Dutch work in the Fens change England?

- The landscape changed. Straight waterways, windmills and pumps, ditches and sluices appeared.

- Farming changed. The reclaimed land was used to grow oats and coleseed*. Cattle and sheep grazed there too. Flocks of geese were introduced, not only for their eggs and meat, but for their feathers, which were in high demand by the makers of quill pens.

- Crops changed. Coleseed was crushed to make oil for lamps and for preparing wool; the straw was made into cakes of fuel, and the leftover seed was used to feed sheep.

- Oil mills were built to crush the coleseed and separate out the straw and the seeds.

- New crops were planted: hemp for making ropes and canvas, and flax for making linen, as well as onions, mustard and woad*.

- New lakes were created and filled with pike and eel for wealthy Londoners would order in advance. Their cooks could then prepare the fish, which was transported to London using large tanks on specially designed carts.

The changes that came about as a result of the Dutch draining the Fens completely altered the ways in which the Fens were used.

Culture: migrant impact on language, fashion, history and art

In the years 1500–1700 cultural changes mainly affected the rich. Most people in England lived in the countryside and were incredibly poor. Changes in fashion and art were unknown to them.

Even new words and names were used only in the areas where, for example, Jews and Huguenots lived and worked. It wasn't until communications improved that cultural changes began to affect everyone, as you'll see in Chapters 3 and 4.

One very important way communication improved was through printing. In most villages, there was often only one person who could read (usually, but not always, the parish priest). That person would read out pamphlets and show printed pictures to villagers. Slowly, reading became important and more people learned how to do it.

Until the 15th century, all books were written and copied out by monks. They were written in Latin and were beautifully illustrated. This meant the Church controlled what was read. Once books were printed, and printed in English or other European languages, the Church lost this control, leading to the sharing of many new ideas.

In 1500 there were only five printers in England, and they were all Europeans. Henry VII appointed Peter of Savoy as his stationer*, and for about 40 years European books brought new words and ideas to England.

By 1535 about two-thirds of those working in the book trade in England were Europeans. Then Henry VIII imposed restrictions on foreign printers and stationers to encourage English craftsmen and booksellers.

Words, words, words

- Huguenots brought many new words with them. 'Brocade' and 'shot silk' described the new fabrics they were working with; road names such as Threadneedle Street, Turnagain Lane and Petticoat Lane became familiar to Londoners; and the word 'vending' came from the French 'vendre', meaning 'to sell'. Huguenot surnames such as Tyzack and Henzey became familiar, and some were anglicised: for example, Andrieu became Andrews and Delacroix became Cross.

- Jewish words, familiar before 1290, became familiar again. As Jewish communities grew and spread, words such as synagogue, rabbi and kosher became well known.

Fashion

You read on page 51 how the Huguenot silk industry made silk popular as a dressmaking fabric among the rich. Source B is a portrait by Peter Lely (himself a migrant), which shows how silk dresses captured the light and could fold softly around the wearer. Silk was used for men's shirts, too. Look at Source E – the young Charles II's tunic and breeches are made from golden silk.

A portrait of Margaret Brooke, Lady Denham, painted by Peter Lely in about 1665. Lely was the most important artist at the court of Charles II.

Writing history

Polydore Vergil (1470–1555) was born in Italy and trained as a priest. The Pope sent him to England in 1502, where he held various church appointments. He wrote 26 books about English history. In 1582 the Privy Council ordered these books became compulsory reading in English schools. Vergil's books had a huge impact on later historians because they started with what Vergil had written, believing he was correct.

But this wasn't always the case: a lot of what he wrote was incredibly biased. Vergil's histories also influenced William Shakespeare when he wrote his history plays, especially Richard III. Because Vergil was writing for the Tudors, he had described Richard III as a tyrant and a monster. This was because Henry Tudor (later King Henry VII) had defeated Richard III at the Battle of Bosworth in 1485.

Artists

Hans Holbein (1497–1543) was a German artist, specialising in painting portraits. He visited England in 1526–28, before settling there in 1532. He died from the plague 11 years later. Holbein painted pictures of Henry VIII and his wives, as well as members of the royal court and other important people. You can see his portrait of the Hansa merchant Georg Giese in Source C.

Holbein's portraits were among the first to show their subjects in natural poses. The portrait of Henry VIII (Source D), although more formal than Georg Giese's, captures the king's character. Only rich people would have seen Holbein's portraits. However, they made people with money and influence used to the idea that paintings could be informal and not just of kings and lords.

Source C

A portrait of Georg Giese, a merchant from Danzig who worked in the London Steelyard. It was painted by Hans Holbein in 1532 and is one of a series of paintings of wealthy merchants made by Holbein in the 1530s.

Source D

A portrait of Henry VIII, painted by Hans Holbein in 1540. The picture was completed before Henry's marriage to Anne of Cleves. Holbein managed to make the focus of the picture Henry's magnetic eyes.

Anthony van Dyck (1599–1641) was born in Antwerp in the Spanish Netherlands. He worked for James I in England until 1621 and then went back to Europe, painting in Flanders and Italy. In 1632 Charles I invited him to England, where he became the court portrait painter. Charles so admired van Dyck's work that he knighted him. He died in 1641 and was buried in St Paul's Cathedral.

Van Dyck's portraits were admired by the rich and his painting of Charles I's children (Source D) was copied many times. These led to the development of family portraits in the 18th and 19th centuries.

Source E

A portrait of Charles I's eldest children, painted by Anthony van Dyck between the end of November 1635 and March 1636.

Extend your knowledge

The portrait of Charles I's children

The painting was originally done for Queen Henrietta Maria to send to her sister Christina, Duchess of Savoy. However, when Charles I saw the portrait, he was horrified. Van Eyck had, correctly, painted his eldest son, also called Charles, wearing skirts. Charles was five years old at the time, and that was what boys his age wore. It's what Charles' younger brother James, standing next to him, is wearing. Van Dyck was instructed to change the portrait so that the future Charles II looked more grown up. Charles appears in the redone portrait wearing a golden silk jacket and breeches.

Peter Lely (1618–80) was born in Soest, now in Germany, to Dutch parents. Arriving in England in about 1643, his portraits were much admired. He was soon employed by the royal court, succeeding Anthony van Dyck as the favourite court painter. He was so good that he worked for Charles I, Oliver Cromwell and Charles II. You can see two of the portraits he painted on pages 48 and 55.

Extend your knowledge

Peter Lely

When Peter Lely (1618–80) was born his name was Pieter van der Faes. He anglicised his first name to Peter and changed his surname to Lely. This was sometimes spelled Lily or Lilley. He chose the surname as he liked the lily carved on the gable of the house in the Hague where his father was born.

Although at first only rich people would see the portraits painted by court painters, the pictures had a tremendous impact. The rich and the well-off began to want their own portraits painted, especially after prints were made of the royal children (Source E). Having portraits painted of your family and your animals became the thing to do. This fashion developed in the 18th century.

Impact of artists

As you have seen, some migrants became famous for their contribution to art and literature.

This not only helped to make migrants a strong part of England's culture. It also helped to start a process that would eventually make the country more diverse.

Activities

1. Choose one of the pictures painted by a court artist. Explain what impression the artist was trying to create. Why do you think monarchs wanted to have court artists? Discuss as a class.
2. Draw a spidergram showing the connection between printing and all the other aspects of culture described in this section.

○

Exam-style question, Section B

'Draining the Fens was the most significant consequence of migration to Britain during the period 1500–1700.'

How far do you agree? Explain your answer.

You may use the following in your answer:

- agriculture

- printing.

You **must** also use information of your own.

(20 marks)

Exam tip

The question is asking for consequences: what happened as a result? Don't describe what happened but focus your answer on **outcomes**. Remember, too, that the 20 marks contain 4 for punctuation, spelling and grammar – so be careful!

2.3 Summary

- The Huguenots' skills in silk weaving boosted the cloth trade; they invested in the Bank of England and helped establish London as a major financial centre.
- Jews were forbidden from entering many areas of work and so they concentrated on working as financiers and merchants.
- Dutch migrant workers drained the Fens, creating thousands of acres of fertile land.
- Individual migrants worked as artists in the royal courts, added words to the English language, wrote English history, printed books and changed fashions for rich people.

Checkpoint

Strengthen

S1 Describe two ways in which the Huguenots changed England.

S2 Give two reasons why rich Jews were only able to work as financiers or merchants.

S3 How did Dutch workers in the Fens help make England more prosperous?

Challenge

C1 Explain the importance of printing in bringing about change to England in the years 1500–1700. How far were migrants involved?

C2 With a partner, discuss the impact migrants had on trade. Was this the most important thing they did at this time?

2.4 Case study: Sandwich and Canterbury in the 16th century

Learning outcomes

- Know about the Flemish community in Sandwich.
- Know about the Walloon community in Canterbury.
- Understand the success and impact of these communities.

A town in decline

The town of Sandwich in Kent had been an important port in the middle ages. However, by the 16th century, the port had declined. This affected the whole economy of the town. With the town getting poorer, it needed help. The answer turned out to be inviting 'strangers' to the town.

Who were 'the strangers'?

These 'strangers' were Flemish weavers. They were Dutch Protestant migrants. Flemish weavers had been invited to live and work in England in the past by Edward III (see page 9).

Extend your knowledge

Why 'strangers'?

The Flemish and Walloon weavers (see page 61) were known as 'strangers'. This is because the French word for foreigners – 'étrangers' – sounded like 'strangers' to the people of Kent. The name stuck despite most Flemish weavers' native language actually being Flemish Dutch.

In 1561, Sandwich needed 'men of knowledge' to boost its economy. Flemish weavers could bring a new business to the town and help it to build its trade and economy.

The town asked Elizabeth I's council for permission to invite Flemish weavers to live and work in Sandwich. The council agreed. Everyone felt it was an excellent opportunity to use the skills of these migrants to improve life in the town.

Source A

In 1561 Elizabeth I allowed Flemish weavers to move to Sandwich but her council issued a decree they could only work in either cloth or fishing.

For the exercise there of making [cloth], which hath not been used to be made in this realme of England, or for fishing in the seas, not exceeding the nombre of twentie or five and twentie householders.

The Flemish community

In 1561, 25 Flemish households arrived to set up textile workshops in Sandwich. Each household could be no more than 12 people. Weavers such as Francis Bole arrived with his wife and nine children. Over the next few months 407 Flemish migrants arrived in Sandwich.

Source B

The Flemish weavers built their own homes in Sandwich. These homes used distinctive Dutch architecture, which you can see in the top half of this building in modern-day Sandwich, known as the 'Sandwich Weaver's House'.

The cloth trade

The Flemish weavers were very successful. Soon they were making a lot of money from their high-quality cloth and helping the town's market to prosper.

- Many of the original migrants to Sandwich were master weavers, who produced high quality goods.
- The Flemish weavers used raw wool to spin broadcloth, an expensive luxury item.
- Two markets were held in Sandwich every week for them to sell their goods.
- All cloth was given a 'grading' for its quality. There were fines for any cloth below the expected quality.

A successful community

By 1568 a third of the population of Sandwich had been born abroad. By 1582 there were nearly 1,600 Flemish migrants in Sandwich, over half the town's population.

The Flemish were given the use of St Peter's Church in Sandwich to worship. Flemish farmers introduced new crops, such as celery (the first time it was grown in England) and carrots, in the land east of the town.

Wealthy weavers built their own homes, with Dutch features such as gable walls and ornate brickwork. In 1572 the community took part in celebrations when Elizabeth I visited the town.

Source C

In 1563 Archbishop Matthew Parker of Canterbury visited Sandwich and gave his impression of the Flemish community there.

[They are] very Godly on the Sabbath day and busy in their work on weekdays, and their quietness such as the Mayor and his brethren had no [disagreements] between them coming before them... profitable and gentle strangers ought to be welcomed and not grudged at.

Too much success?

The Flemish were so successful, they started to set up businesses outside the cloth industry. In 1564 Lyven Symons opened a tailor's shop – but was told he could only employ Englishmen in it. The town started to worry about 'the strangers' taking jobs from the English people in the town.

1569 Town ordered migrants could only work as bricklayers, masons and carpenters if Englishmen had refused the work. Migrants also banned from making shoes.

1581 Town prevented migrants from running shops. Ordered them to only work in the cloth and fishing trades (as stated by Elizabeth I in 1561). Fined anyone breaking the laws.

1582 Flemish migrants appealed to Elizabeth's council. The council agreed Flemish migrants in Sandwich should work only in cloth and trade. But the council gave them permission to find other work elsewhere and protected them from being fined by the town.

Figure 2.16 Changes in reaction to the Flemish community in Sandwich

In 1582 almost 45 families left Sandwich to find opportunities elsewhere in England, such as London. Over the next 100 years, although some remained, more and more Flemish migrants left Sandwich.

Activities ?

1. What advantages could there be for Sandwich inviting 'the strangers' to the town? As a group draw up a list of all the reasons you can think of.

2. Reading the information in this section, why do you think the Flemish weavers were keen to migrate to Canterbury?

Canterbury and the Walloons

One of the migrant groups that had moved to Sandwich were Walloons. The Walloons were French-speaking Protestants from the Spanish Netherlands (modern-day Belgium and the Netherlands), fleeing persecution from the Catholic Spanish rulers.

In 1575 they were invited by the city of Canterbury to leave Sandwich and move there instead.

Canterbury sees an opportunity

Like Sandwich, Canterbury was declining. Before the Reformation, many pilgrims had travelled to Canterbury. After the Reformation (1530s), these pilgrimages ended, meaning the city suddenly had far fewer visitors and less trade.

Canterbury saw that the Flemish migrants had improved trade in Sandwich. In 1575, the city received permission from Elizabeth's council to invite Walloon migrants to fill 100 empty houses in the city.

Interpretation 1

In a 1987 article, historian Anne Oakley discusses the types of houses given to the Walloon migrants.

Generally speaking this was the poorer area of the city where there were many small houses built with narrow frontages to the street.

The Walloon community

Around 750 people moved into these houses. The Blackfriars monastery had been closed during the Reformation and the Walloons were allowed to use it.

- Part of the old monastery was converted into a church and a school.
- Another part became the Weavers' Hall and Market, which the Walloon weavers used to create and sell their goods. It also became the heart of the community.

Just as in Sandwich, the Walloons created a successful cloth and weaving market. By the end of the century, 800 looms were spinning fine cloth and silks. This helped create jobs in the city, as well as increasing its trade.

Unlike in Sandwich, the Walloon community developed new trades, such as silk dyeing, refining sugar and diamond cutting, that didn't previously exist in Canterbury. This meant there was less jealousy from the other inhabitants of the city about losing their jobs and businesses to 'strangers'.

The community had a group of 12 'elders' who set the rules for the community and kept order. They worked closely with the city authorities.

Source D

The city authorities were pleased with the impact the Walloons had. In an annual report from the 1580s, they stated how the community supported itself and others.

[The Walloons] not onely maintain their own poore at their owne charge without permitting any of them to beg... but also set many hundreds of the English poor on work.

Source E

Timber-framed buildings, like this one in Canterbury, were adapted to be used for the looms of Walloon weavers. The river was used to help finish the cloth, and mills on the river helped power the looms.

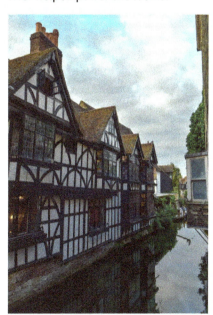

Extend your knowledge

Changing names

Many Walloon settlers started anglicising their names: Du Bois became Wood, De Bourges became Burgess and Blanc became White.

Activity **?**

What lessons might both **(a)** the local government of Canterbury and **(b)** the Walloon migrants have learned from what happened in Sandwich? Draw up your own list for each and then compare with a partner's. What do you agree on?

A success story

The community grew quickly:

- By 1582 there were 1,600 people in the Walloon congregation.
- This grew to 2,700 by 1592 and nearly 3,000 by 1595 – one-third of the city's population.

It was such a success that, just like in Sandwich, there were concerns too many 'strangers' were arriving. By 1585 new arrivals had to prove to the Walloon Congregation Elders that they had left their homes on religious grounds. They also needed to prove to the city authorities that their businesses would not complete with existing businesses in Canterbury.

The Walloon community was accepted as part of the city. In 1588 they helped prepare the defences against a possible Spanish invasion. Canterbury's Walloon (and later Huguenot) community continued to grow and prosper into the 17th century – by 1676 there were over 1,000 looms employing 2,700 migrants and non-migrants.

2.4 Summary

- Sandwich and Canterbury both recognised that skilled Flemish and Walloon weavers could help its economy and trade to improve and grow.
- Sandwich invited Flemish weavers. Later Canterbury invited Walloons.
- The communities were very successful and improved trade in the area. They were allowed to set up their own churches and allowed to organise themselves.
- There were some fears that business opportunities for Englishmen were being lost in Sandwich. To try to avoid this, in Canterbury the Walloons created their own trades.

Checkpoint

Strengthen

S1 Why do you think the people of Sandwich and Canterbury wanted to invite the Flemish and the Walloons to live and work there?

S2 Why do you think the Flemish and the Walloons were willing to take up this offer?

Challenge

C1 What problems did the migrant communities have to overcome to become accepted in these areas?

2.5 Case study: Huguenots in Soho and Spitalfields, London, in the 17th century

Learning outcomes

- Know about the ways in which the Huguenots lived and worked in Soho and Spitalfields.
- Understand the importance of the Huguenot contribution to the cloth trade.
- Understand how the Huguenots tried to retain their own culture.

Arriving in England

Huguenots arrived in England in two main time periods. The first was in the 1570s and the second, which was much larger, was 100 years later (see page 35). King Charles II offered 'denizen' status to these migrants, and William III went a step further.

William III supported the Huguenots for many years. His Declaration, made just months after becoming king, made it clear the Huguenots had royal support. It implied that he expected his new subjects to accept and welcome them. But this wasn't just kindness. He had other motives.

- William III and his wife Mary II were Protestants. They had been invited by Parliament to become monarchs in place of the Catholic James II. William knew that there was still sympathy in England for James and for Catholicism. He wanted to strengthen the Protestant population in his new country.
- William understood that the skills and expertise of the Huguenots would help make England prosperous. This helped fund his war with the French King Louis XIV who persecuted the Huguenots.

Extend your knowledge

Foreign Protestants Naturalisation Act 1708

This Act was supported by a majority in the House of Commons and in the House of Lords. It meant that all foreign Protestants could be naturalised, provided they swore allegiance to the government and received the sacrament* in any Protestant church. Once naturalised , the 'foreign Protestants' had the same legal rights as English people.

Settling in London

This second period of Huguenot migration was of 40,000 to 50,000 people. About half of them settled in London. Some arrived directly from France, some via Amsterdam, and some had worked in Canterbury before moving on to London.

Two important Huguenot communities developed in London in Soho and in Spitalfields. Many settled in Soho, although most went to Spitalfields, where food and housing were cheaper, and where there was more freedom from the controls of the London guilds*.

Source A

Part of a Declaration made by King William III in 1689.

We do hereby Declare, That all French Protestants that shall seek their Refuge in, and Transport themselves into this Our Kingdom, shall not only have Our Royal Protection for themselves, Families and Estates within this Our Realm, but we will also do Our Endeavour in all reasonable ways and means, so to Support, Aid and Assist them in their several and respective Trades and Ways of Livelihood so that their living and being in this Realm may be comfortable and easy to them.

Key terms

Sacrament*
A religious ceremony such as baptism.

Guild*
An association of craftspeople or merchants having considerable power over the quality of work produced and so over membership.

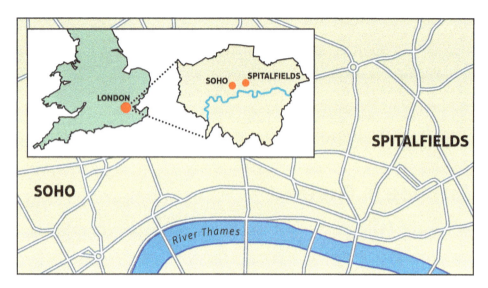

Figure 2.17 A sketch map of London to show Soho and Spitalfields

Most Huguenots brought with them manufacturing skills, particularly in silk weaving, and many brought money. Some, however, had escaped French persecution with nothing more than their lives, and they needed the sort of help described in William III's Declaration (Source A).

By the end of the 17th century, a relief committee set up as a result of the Declaration had raised £64,713 to help Huguenot resettlement. This was about £3.5 million in today's money. William and Mary donated about half that amount in the years 1689–93.

Gradually, as the silk weavers prospered, new, large houses were built. Some were workshops and others were the homes of the Huguenot master weavers who controlled the silk industry.

Source B

A modern photograph of surviving Huguenot houses in Spitalfields.

Interpretation 1

From *Bloody Foreigners: the story of immigration to Britain* by Robert Winder, published in 2004. Here he describes Spitalfields today.

Various street names in Spitalfields – Princelet Street, Fournier Street – bear witness to the prosperity of the Frenchmen [Huguenots] who settled there: the neat roads are lined by large, handsome houses. Some still have the big, glass-ceilinged workshops the Huguenots built at the back for their looms. You can easily imagine the ceaseless clacking of the machines punctuated by sudden chirrups of birdsong – the Huguenots liked birds, and often hung caged canaries in their lofts.

Spitalfields: weaver town

The Huguenots had a huge impact on Spitalfields – so much so that it was nicknamed 'weaver town'. The arrival of thousands of skilled silk weavers transformed the area's small weaving industry. The weavers' faith encouraged them to believe that it was their duty to work hard to be successful – this later became known as the 'Protestant work ethic'*.

- A lot of large workshops were established.
- The workshops employed hundreds of Huguenot workers and made their owners extremely wealthy.
- Spitalfields' workshops produced a wide variety of silks, especially figured silks (which had a raised pattern), taffetas, velvets and brocades.
- Several highly skilled Huguenot weavers were admitted to the Weavers' Company, an ancient guild that controlled weaving in the City of London.
- The demand for the new silks was excellent, especially in London. Between 1650 and 1700 there was a twenty-fold increase in silk production, most of it due to high levels of production from Spitalfields. Much of the silk was exported.

Huguenot churches

In 1550 Edward VI signed a Charter allowing the 'Church of the Strangers' to be built in London. This was the first Huguenot church in the country. It gave the earlier Huguenot refugees, in the 1570s, a place to worship. Built originally in Threadneedle Street, it burned down in the Great Fire of 1666 and was eventually rebuilt in Soho Square.

It was to this church, and the houses around it, that some Huguenot migrants came in the 1680s and 1690s. There was already a small Huguenot community in Soho, and the new migrants wanted to join people whose customs, culture and religious beliefs and ceremonies were the same as theirs.

The Huguenots who decided to live and work in Spitalfields had to ask permission to build their own churches as there were none there in 1685. By 1700 nine Huguenot churches had been built.

Key term

Protestant work ethic*
The value attached to hard work and efficiency.

Case study

James Leman: designer and master weaver (1688–1745)

Born in Tourcoing in northern France, James and his parents fled to Canterbury when he was a baby. By the time he was age 14, the family was living in Stewart Street, Spitalfields. James' father was a silk weaver. Unusually for weavers at the time, James trained as a designer as well as a weaver. By the time he was 18, James was producing beautiful designs.

In 1711 he was admitted as a 'foreign master' to the Weavers' Company. When his father died in 1712, James took over running the business. He continued producing brilliant designs, some with silver and gold thread running through them. James was so well regarded by other weavers that he became 'Renter Bailiff' (the second-in-command of the Weaver's Company) in 1731.

Source C

Some of James Leman's designs. He kept them in his album, which can now be seen in the Victoria & Albert Museum, London. New designs were essential if London-based silk weaving was to grow and flourish – which it did.

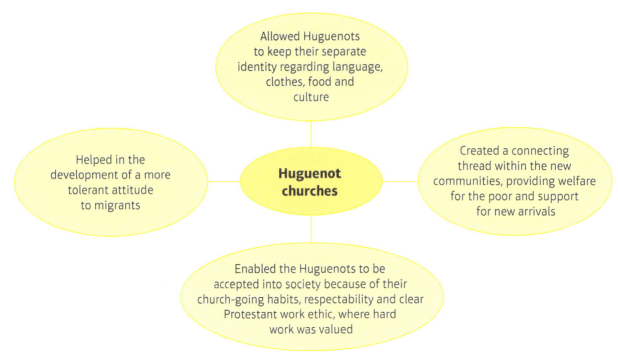

Figure 2.18 The importance of Huguenot churches

Extend your knowledge

A Huguenot church was built on the corner of Brick Lane in Spitalfields. It later became a Jewish synagogue and is now a Muslim mosque.

The reaction in London

Londoners were traditionally anti-Catholic and this, combined with propaganda about atrocities against Protestants in France, meant the Huguenots were generally welcomed in London.

There were minor disturbances in Spitalfields towards the end of the century when English weavers complained that the Huguenots were taking work from them. However, it quickly became clear the Huguenots were willing to teach their skills to the English, and that they were creating prosperity in the area. They taught the English weavers, for example, how to weave 'shot' silk where two colours are woven together to create a shimmering appearance.

Activities ?

1   Imagine you are a Huguenot who has settled in Spitalfields. Some of your family are still living in France. Write a letter to them explaining the advantages of living and working in London and encouraging them to join you.

2   'Huguenots were only welcome in London because of the skills they brought with them.' Explain how far you agree with this statement.

2.5 Summary

- Huguenots settled and worked in the Soho and Spitalfields areas of London.
- Huguenot silk-weaving skills created work and prosperity.
- Huguenot churches kept their culture alive, provided support and respectability.

Checkpoint

Strengthen

S1 Give two ways in which Huguenot migrants were supported when they arrived in London.

S2 Note down three ways in which Huguenot churches were important.

Challenge

C1 Why were the Huguenots so successful in London?

Activity ?

What were the most important factors bringing about change in migration during this period? You have a bag of 100 weights. Copy the table to distribute them between the factors, according to which you think was the most important.

Remember that your total number of weights can't go above 100, and you need to explain your thinking in the final column.

Factor to balance	Number of weights	Reason why
Government		
Religion		
Economic influences		
Attitudes in society		

03 | c1700–c1900: Migration in 18th- and 19th-century Britain

In the years 1700–1900 there were enormous changes in British society that affected the numbers of people migrating to Britain and the countries they came from. There were huge changes, too, in migration within the British Isles.

Britain became the first industrialised nation in the world. Factories offered thousands of new jobs as well as investment opportunities for entrepreneurs. Building houses, docks, mills, canals and railways all needed workers and many of them were migrants.

Britain built up the largest empire in the world. While there was migration to Britain of people from the Empire in order to work, one of the significant outcomes of Empire was the forced migration of thousands of black Africans as enslaved people to the sugar plantations of the West Indies. This deeply affected the lives of black people in Britain.

Migrants were accepted where they could be seen to be contributing to British life and prosperity. Thousands, however, lived lives of poverty and persecution, facing prejudice because of their race or country of origin.

Learning outcomes

By the end of this chapter, you will:

- understand how the changes in British society led to both voluntary and forced migration
- know about the different experiences migrants had in Britain and understand the reasons for these differences, especially the role played by the media
- understand the impact migrants had on Britain
- complete a case study on the role migrants played in 19th-century Liverpool
- complete a case study on the experiences of Jewish migrants in the East End of London in the late 19th century.

3.1 The reasons why people migrated

Learning outcomes

- Know about English society in the 18th and 19th centuries.
- Understand the reasons why different groups of people migrated to, and within, Britain.

What was Britain like in the 18th and 19th centuries?

The period 1700–1900 was one where great changes affected nearly everyone in the country. All of these impacted migration, as you will see in this chapter.

Government changes
Greater freedoms encouraged many migrants, especially from Europe; other groups, such as Jews, migrated to escape religious and social persecution

Industrialisation
Growing towns attracted migrants with job opportunities; factories needed labour, and building projects needed workers (such as Irish navvies)

Changes in British society in the 18th and 19th centuries

Growth of the British Empire
Britain became a major economic power, attracting migrants. Slavery led to increased forced migration

Improved transport links
Made travel to and around Britain much easier and increased opportunities for many migrants to make homes outside of ports and major cities

Figure 3.1 Changes in British society in the 18th and 19th centuries

Changes in Parliament

In the 19th century, laws were passed making Parliament more inclusive of men from different backgrounds and faiths. But there was also a large amount of continuity – and there were still no votes for women. Political change gave some migrants the chance of greater freedom in Britain.

Changes in Parliament	Impact on migration
Before 1832, only 5% of the population could vote. Few industrial towns had an MP. The 1832 Reform Act gave the vote to more men owning property or paying high rents and allowed larger towns two MPs. In 1867 and 1884 more working-class men were given the vote.	Greater rights for workers helped make industrial towns more attractive for migrants. Greater political freedoms also attracted many European migrants, particularly liberal and socialist thinkers.
In 1829 the Catholic Emancipation Act allowed Catholics almost all the civil rights of Protestants. Restrictions on Jews were lifted in the 1830s and they could become MPs from 1858.	Greater political freedoms encouraged the growth of Jewish migrant communities and helped Irish (largely Catholic) communities grow.
Britain's slave trade was abolished in 1807 and slavery in the British Empire was forbidden in 1833.	African and black American migrants saw Britain as a place offering greater freedoms.

Changes in industry

Between 1750 and 1850 Britain underwent the Industrial Revolution. There was worldwide demand for British manufactured goods. To meet this demand, factories increased production.

Thousands of people, from rural Britain (as machines meant fewer people were needed to work the land) and from Europe, migrated to work in expanding factories. Migrants, skilled and unskilled, were an essential part of this economic growth. Many migrated to urban areas to work in factories, which helped Britain produce more goods to trade with the rest of the world.

As growing industry changed Britain, towns and cities across the country grew in size. This is known as urbanisation.

Changes in industry	Impact on migration
Manufactured goods were produced in factories, powered first by water, then by steam. Weaving and spinning machines transformed the textile industry (especially cotton). Later, coal was mined on a very large scale in order to power factories.	Factories needed workers. This attracted migrant workers, while trade of the goods they produced bought more migrant merchants and sailors to Britain.
By the mid-1800s there were large industrial towns, such as Glasgow, Birmingham and Manchester. The urban population grew from 5 million in 1700 to 32.5 million in 1900.	Growing industrial towns made it easier for migrant communities to grow and develop, such as Chinatown in Liverpool.
New docks were built in Liverpool, London, Cardiff, Bristol, Hull and Glasgow. They became the busiest in the world, providing jobs for thousands of people.	The huge demand for labour – both in the docks and on ships – attracted thousands of migrants from across the world.

Changes in transport

Changes in transport were essential to get raw materials to factories and finished goods to markets. Improved transport made it easier to travel around Britain, meaning migrants could travel to a greater range of places.

Changes in transport	Impact on migration
Roads were improved. By 1840 a network of roads ran from London to all major cities.	The huge developments in transportation had a massive impact on migration.
Canals carried heavy goods in large quantities. In 1761 the Bridgewater canal linked the Worsley coal mines and Manchester. By the 1820s a canal network linked all the main manufacturing areas and Britain's main ports.	As modern ships made the world faster to move around, many migrants from Asia and Africa found it easier to make their homes in Britain.
The Liverpool to Manchester railway opened in 1830 – a faster and cheaper way of transporting goods than the Bridgewater canal. By 1900 five major railway companies operated 22,000 miles of rail track.	Improved transport helped encourage economic growth, creating new jobs and opportunities for migrants. It also made it easier for migrants to arrive in a port but then travel to other parts of the country to build communities.
Steam power transformed shipping, connecting Britain with ports around the world. In 1838 the *SS Great Western* travelled from Bristol to New York. In 1852 the *SS Great Britain* sailed from Liverpool for Australia.	

Changes to the British Empire

The growth of the British Empire meant that by 1900 Britain ruled one-fifth of the world's land and a quarter of the world's population. The growth of the British Empire increased Britain's contact with the rest of the world leading to increased migration.

- Britain used its Empire as a huge source of food and raw materials and as a market for its manufactured goods. This sometimes destroyed local industries, such as the Indian cotton industry.
- The American colonies became independent in 1783.
- In 1858 Britain took over control of India from the East India Company.
- In the years after 1885, European powers scrambled for territory in Africa. Britain acquired a lot of land, especially Southern Africa, Egypt and the Sudan.
- Sugar from the plantations in the British-owned West Indies made many merchants extremely rich and port cities (for example, Bristol and Liverpool) very prosperous. This was based on slave labour in the colonies and the transatlantic slave trade.

Attitudes in British society to migration

Just as in the period 1500–1700, the attitude in British society to migrants could change considerably, depending on who the migrants were and where they came from.

Migrants often faced prejudice on arrival, with some treating them with suspicion or prejudice:

- Many were worried migrants could take jobs from them. This was often despite many migrants, such as Irish navvies, taking on manual labour jobs others did not want.
- Migrants with cultures that seemed unusual to many British people were also seen suspiciously. For example, the Jewish communities in the East End of London were accused of being 'alien' or 'foreign'.
- Other migrants, such as lascars and ayahs, were often seen as being in Britain only 'to do a job' and expected to leave when it was completed.

Attitudes changed over time, as British society integrated these new communities. But, for many migrants, facing prejudice was a fact of life.

Activity   ?

1. Draw a mind map or spidergram to show the links between the factors that brought change to Britain. For example, the Empire's raw materials link to factories, which link to railways, which link to ports. Draw these to start your mind map and then add to them. How many other links can you find?

2. For each area of change, find three ways in which migration could be affected. Remember to think as well about internal migration.

Migration in Britain

The great changes you have just read about meant people moved about a lot. They moved mainly from the countryside to the towns, in search of higher wages and a better, more exciting, life.

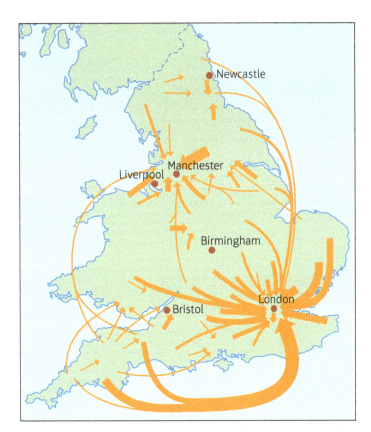

Figure 3.2 Internal migration in England between 1851 and 1861 (the thicker the lines, the greater the number of people migrating)

Interpretation 1

From *Joseph Ashby of Tysoe* by M. K. Ashby, published in 1961. This is an account of her father's life.

In 1892 the causes of removal were unemployment, low wages and bad cottages. The attraction of the towns was a myth; men were not so much drawn away as propelled out. There was an increased tendency for girls to leave the countryside for 'service' [working as a maid]… From one small area the migrants flowed to Birmingham and its neighbourhood, from another chiefly to Coventry and again to the railway works at Crewe and the breweries of Burton-on-Trent.

Extend your knowledge

Highland Clearances

Between 1750 and 1860, Scottish landowners introduced sheep farming in the Highlands. Sheep needed far fewer farm workers than arable farming* and wool was very profitable. Tens of thousands of tenant farmers and their families were evicted and forced to migrate to the rocky north coast where farming was almost impossible, or further afield to Canada, New Zealand, America and Australia.

Key terms

Census*

A census is a count of people living in a country on a specific day. In Britain a census is taken every ten years and the first official one was in 1841. The 1851 census was the first to give the place of birth of people being counted, and so it's a useful starting point for looking at migration.

Arable farming*

Growing crops such as oats, barley and wheat.

Activities ?

1 Look at the map in Figure 3.2.

    a Note down the names of the towns that were attracting migrants. For each town, use the internet to find out what it was producing at that time that made it such a draw for migrants.

    b Suggest why so many people left the south-west and the south-east to go to London. How could you check whether you were right?

2 Explain how far the map supports M. K. Ashby's account in Interpretation 1.

Irish migrants

Irish people had often travelled to England for seasonal work (such as helping with the harvest) then returning to Ireland. Then, in the 1800s, events caused thousands of Irish people to migrate from Ireland.

Interpretation 2

From *Bloody Foreigners: the story of immigration to Britain* by Robert Winder, published in 2004.

Those who fled east were not only desperate, they were angry and resentful at having to throw themselves on the mercy of the country that was largely responsible for the agricultural and political system that had ruined then in the first place.

Exam-style question, Section B

Explain one way in which opportunities for Irish migrants in the 19th century were similar to those for lascars in the 18th century. **(4 marks)**

Exam tip

The question is asking you to explain similarities, not describe them. You need to add some detail of your own to show you understand the nature of the similarity.

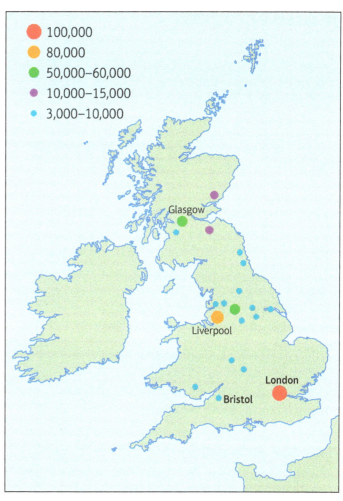

Figure 3.3 The main places where Irish migrants settled

Most land owned by wealthy English protestants. Most tenants Catholics.	Few landlords supported their tenants. High rents for poor land and bad housing.	Poverty, anger and resentment, particularly in Catholic community.
1815 Collapse in agricultural prices alongside rise in population.	Shortage of food and high food prices.	Increase in poverty; starvation for some.
Belfast only industrialised city. Main jobs weaving linen and enlarging the docks.	Few jobs available and mostly given to Protestants.	Increasing poverty, particularly among Irish Catholic population.
Most rural occupations (e.g. spinning and weaving) in small workshops.	English factories more efficient.	Irish rural industries collapsed: hundreds out of work.
Potatoes main food for millions of poor people. **1845** blight destroyed one-third of crop. **1846** blight destroyed whole crop.	British government export food (e.g. grain) from Ireland, believing it would create money to help Irish people.	Food prices rose. People could not feed their familes or pay rent. Many evicted.	About 1 million people died from starvation; 2 million forced to migrate to England.

Figure 3.4 Reasons for migration from Ireland

Jewish refugees

In the 18th and early 19th centuries the Jewish community in Britain grew to about 65,000 and many Jews prospered. Gradually, restrictions on Jews were lifted and, despite anti-Semitism, the situation of Jews in Britain improved.

This helped to make Britain more attractive to Jewish migrants.

Suddenly, in the 1880s, all this changed.

From 1880 to 1900, over 100,000 Jews arrived in Britain. Most went to established Jewish communities where they expected to find help and support. Many Jews in these communities were afraid the arrival of these poor refugees would damage their carefully won acceptance. The chief rabbi even wrote to Eastern European rabbis asking them to persuade Jewish refugees not to make the journey to England.

However, Jewish communities in general wanted to help, setting up soup kitchens and charities to support the poor. In London the Poor Jews' Temporary Shelter allowed Jewish immigrants to stay for a maximum of 14 days and gave them two meals a day while they looked for housing and work.

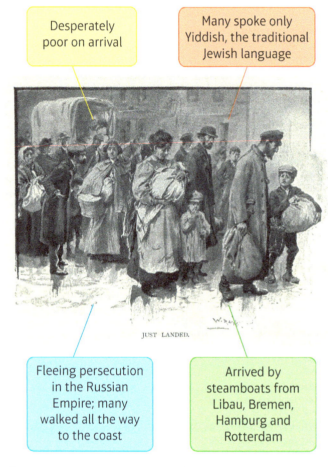

Desperately poor on arrival

Many spoke only Yiddish, the traditional Jewish language

JUST LANDED.

Fleeing persecution in the Russian Empire; many walked all the way to the coast

Arrived by steamboats from Libau, Bremen, Hamburg and Rotterdam

Figure 3.5 Eastern European Ashkenazi Jews migrate to Britain

Timeline

Changes to the status of Jews

1798 Nathan Rothschild founded London branch of Rothschild's bank

1802 Solomon Hirschell became Britain's chief rabbi after a ten year gap

1822 Jewish Free School opened with 107 pupils

1833 Jews were allowed to serve on juries and to become lawyers

1855 David Solomons became the first Jewish lord mayor of London

1856 Jews were allowed to study at Cambridge University (and at Oxford University in 1871)

1858 Lionel de Rothschild became the first Jewish MP

1860 In London, a Jew opened the first fish-and-chip shop

Activities ?

1 Read Interpretation 2. Explain why the Irish migrants were 'angry and resentful'. Use Figure 3.4 in your answer.

2 Draw a grid to represent the similarities and differences between Irish and Jewish migration. Work with a partner to identify these. Are there more similarities than differences, or is it the other way round?

Forced migration: Africans

Africans had been living and working in Britain since Roman times, some as servants to white masters (see page 39). But during this period, hundred of thousands of black Africans were forced to migrate from Africa.

This was the slave trade, whereby thousands of black Africans were forcibly taken from Africa to work as enslaved people in the plantations of British colonies in the West Indies and North America. This dreadful trade brought huge wealth to British merchants and adversely affected the lives of black Africans living in Britain, as you will see in Section 3.2.

The transatlantic slave trade

As well as Britain, Portugal and France, Spain, the Netherlands and Denmark all traded slaves. However, by 1750, Britain was the largest slave-trading nation. Historians have calculated British ships transported 3.1 million Africans across the Atlantic until 1807. People were ripped away from all that they knew, transported in terrible conditions, and then sold as slaves. The work they had to do was unbearably harsh.

> **Extend your knowledge**
>
> **The Royal African Company**
>
> The Royal African Company was founded by Charles II in 1660 and led by his brother, the future James II. From 1662 to 1731 it transported over 212,000 enslaved people – 44,000 died on the journey. Many powerful politicians and public figures invested in the company.

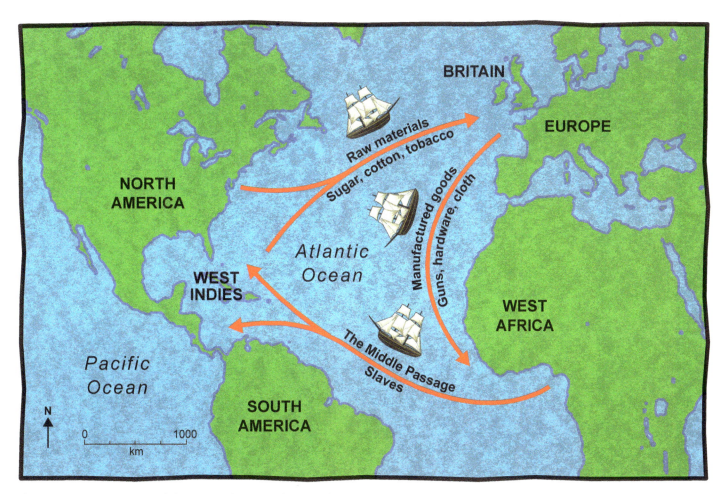

Figure 3.6 The operation of the transatlantic trade triangle

Asian migrants

British presence in India strengthened and trade increased, particularly after 1858 (see page 71) when the British government took over control of India from the East India Company. Thousands of Indians, Sikhs, Hindus and Muslims travelled to Britain. Some stayed for a short time, others for ever.

Indian students attended English and Scottish universities, especially after 1857. Law was a popular subject. Some newly qualified lawyers stayed on in Britain. (Education opportunities also attracted other migrants.)

Indian princes migrated with their riches. They had been forced out of their lands by the East India Company and, later, by the British government. They settled and never returned to India.

Indian servants migrated with their colonial families. Numbers increased after 1700 as Indian servants were cheaper than English ones and seen as a status symbol.

Lascars from China, Malaya, India, Somalia and Yemen were all recruited by the East India Company. Wages and working conditions were poor. Many refused offers to work on the return journey and 'disappeared' into dockland communities.

Figure 3.7 Why did Asian people migrate to Britain?

Migrants from Europe: Germans and Italians

In the second half of the 19th century thousands of people migrated to Britain from Germany and Italy. The figures below are from census data.

- In 1861 there were 28,644 Germans living in England and Wales; by 1911 this had risen to 53,324.
- In 1861 less than 5,000 Italians lived in England and Wales. By 1901 this had risen to 20,000.

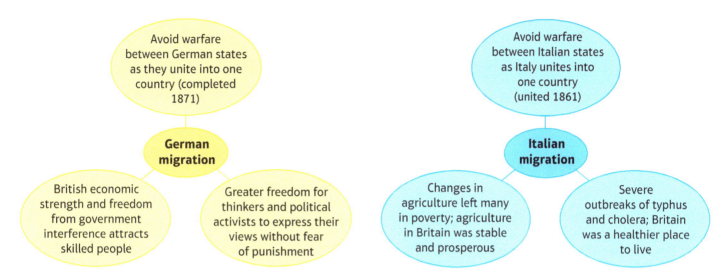

Figure 3.8 Migration from Germany and Italy

Activities ?

1 Copy out the grid you completed for your answer to Question 2 on page 74. Add more rows for African, Asian, German and Italian migrants. Then complete the table, looking for similarities and differences as before.

2 Are there more similarities than differences, or is it the other way round?

3.1 Summary

- Industrialisation resulted in internal migration from rural areas to towns.
- Many Catholics migrated from Ireland because of bad land management by absentee Protestant landlords. This mismanagement led to famine, starvation and death.
- By 1750 Britain was the dominant slave-trading nation, forcing the migration of over 3 million black Africans to slavery in the West Indies and North America.
- Jewish, Asian, German and Italian migrants chose to go to Britain because it was a country where they felt safer and more able to use their skills.

Checkpoint

Strengthen

S1 Name one 'push' factor that drove people to migrate, and one 'pull' factor attracting them to Britain.

S2 Name three groups of people who chose to migrate.

S3 What was the transatlantic slave trade and which country was the dominant slave-trading nation by 1750?

Challenge

C1 Why did the Industrial Revolution make Britain an attractive country for migrants?

3.2 The experiences of migrants

Learning outcomes

- Understand the ways in which, and how successfully, migrants settled in British towns and cities.
- Understand the differing relationships between migrants and the existing population.

Living in Britain's cities

Most migrants headed for Britain's cities. A sudden arrival of hundreds, or even thousands, of migrants put huge pressure on those cities' local government and services. Cities were used to supporting much smaller populations, and often not coping very well with that. Sometimes basic facilities broke down.

- People crowded into existing tenement* buildings or sub-standard newly built houses.
- Diseases spread quickly. Common 'killer' diseases were cholera and typhus, TB (tuberculosis) and measles, scarlet fever and whooping cough.
- Many people were desperately poor, and this put a huge strain on existing relief* offered by the poor law.

Thousands of people, including migrants, lived in buildings like those in Figure 3.9. These buildings were tightly packed around a courtyard. Other houses for the poor were built in terraces of 'back to back' houses, where they shared a back wall.

Source A

From a report about Manchester written by Dr James Kay Shuttleworth in 1832. He was a doctor who worked among poor people in the city, many of whom were migrants.

Frequently, two or more families are crowded into one small house and often one family lived in a damp cellar where twelve or sixteen persons were crowded. Children are ill-fed, dirty, ill-clothed, exposed to cold and neglect; in a consequence more than half of the children die before their fifth birthday.

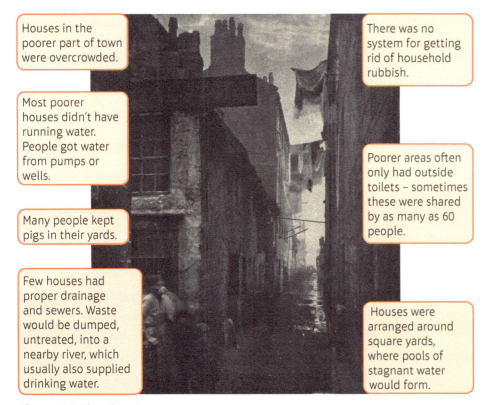

Houses in the poorer part of town were overcrowded.

There was no system for getting rid of household rubbish.

Most poorer houses didn't have running water. People got water from pumps or wells.

Poorer areas often only had outside toilets – sometimes these were shared by as many as 60 people.

Many people kept pigs in their yards.

Few houses had proper drainage and sewers. Waste would be dumped, untreated, into a nearby river, which usually also supplied drinking water.

Houses were arranged around square yards, where pools of stagnant water would form.

Figure 3.9 Slum housing

Key terms

Tenement*

A run-down and often overcrowded building, housing many people in poor conditions.

Relief*

Help given to poor people who could not support their families. It was sometimes given while they stayed in their own homes; or, more often after 1834, inside a workhouse, where parents and children were separated and conditions were worse than those of the poorest people living outside.

Irish: low paid and dangerous work

Most Irish migrants were poor tenant farmers and labourers. They had few of the specialist skills some jobs needed in British factories. Many of them took on hard labouring work in docks (see pages 95–97), mines and quarries. They worked as navvies*, digging out canals and building railways, blasting through solid rock to make tunnels and climbing high to build viaducts. The work was hard and dangerous. Many were killed or injured, forcing wives and children into even deeper poverty. Many Irish migrants joined the army: by 1868 there were 55,000 Irish soldiers in the British army.

Source B

Navvies building the Manchester Ship Canal in 1887. Around 16,000 navvies were employed for this work, most of whom were Irish.

Prejudice and hostility

The map on page 73 shows that Irish migrants settled mainly in the industrialising cities of Britain. Here they did hard, manual work that was dirty and often dangerous. Despite doing this useful work, many people were prejudiced against Irish people. Where did this prejudice come from?

Key term

Navvies*

The name given to the men who dug the canals and built the railways. The name came from the word 'navigator', which was the name given to the men who built the first canals.

Case study

The Cooper and Ferris families

Often, looking at local sources really brings a topic alive. You can find material online or from your local library or history society. If you live in an area that had a lot of migrants in the 19th century – give it a go!

This story begins with a gravestone in the churchyard of Settle parish church in North Yorkshire. It reads:

IN AFFECTIONATE REMEMBRANCE OF THOMAS COOPER OF NEWRY WHO DIED AT SETTLE FEB 22ND 1875 AGED 23 YEARS, ALSO THOMAS FERRIS OF NEWRY WHO DIED AT SETTLE APRIL 30TH 1873 AGED 28 YEARS. ALSO MARY JANE FERRIS WHO DIED AT SETTLE AGED 17 MONTHS. NOT LOST BUT GONE BEFORE.

Who were these people? Why did they come from Newry in Ireland and end up dying in North Yorkshire? Why were people with different surnames buried in the same grave? This is what happened.

In about 1872, Thomas Cooper moved from Newry to Settle with his family. Thomas was a 20-year-old stonemason. He and his father and brothers came to help build a railway. They worked on the 'Long Drag' a steep stretch of track from Settle to Dent Head. This was the first part of the Settle to Carlisle railway, built by 2,300 navvies. Conditions were hard, and Thomas died from TB and pneumonia on 22 February 1875, aged 23.

Thomas Cooper had a sister called Eliza Jane. She married Robert Ferris, also from Newry. Robert was a greengrocer, supplying the navvies. Robert's brother, Thomas Ferris, worked as a navvy. Thomas died on 28 April 1873, aged 28, from 'inflammation of the lungs' (probably TB). Robert was with him when he died.

Robert and Eliza had eight children, three of whom died before they were five years old. This was common in the 1800s. Robert and Eliza's first child to die was Mary Jane in 1875 when she was just 17 months old. Her parents buried her with her two uncles in Settle churchyard.

We have come full circle and have solved the mystery of the three burials. In doing so, we have found out quite a lot about Irish navvies.

Key term

Fenian*

A member of the Irish Republican Brotherhood, a revolutionary nationalist organisation. They staged an unsuccessful revolt against the British in 1867 and were responsible for acts of violence against the British authorities.

Activities

1 Read through the case study about the Cooper and Ferris families. Working with a partner, write everything it tells you about Irish navvies. Compare your list with those of the rest of your class until you have a complete list of everything you can learn from the story.

2 Look at Source A and think about the list you have for Question 1. A historian is trying to find out about Irish navvies working in England. How useful would they find Source A and the research into the Cooper and Ferris families?

3 Irish navvies did useful but dangerous work, yet many English people were prejudiced against them. Read the information in Figure 3.10 and use it to write a paragraph explaining why many English people felt this way.

Figure 3.10 Prejudice against Irish people

Jews: segregation and prejudice

About nine-tenths of Jewish migrants from Eastern Europe settled in London, mainly in the East End where there were established Jewish communities. This section looks at the experience of migrant Jews in London. You read (page 74) how the settled Jewish communities were afraid the arrival of thousands of poor Jews could affect the way English society viewed all of them.

Source C

An extract from the *Jewish Chronicle* 1881.

The foreign poor form a community within a community. This is most undesirable: it is more than a misfortune, it is a calamity. Our outside world is not capable of making minute discrimination between Jew and Jew, and forms its opinion of Jews as much, if not more, from them than from the Anglicised portion of the community.

Jewish leaders urged the new immigrants to learn English and adopt the English way of life while keeping their Jewish religion and rituals. Adults were taught English in evening classes, and children attended Jewish schools. It was a difficult balancing act and not many managed it in the early years of migration.

Extend your knowledge

The London Jewish Free School, located from 1822 in Bell Lane, Whitechapel, in the East End of London, was key to integrating Jewish children into English society. Between 1880 and 1900, one-third of all London's Jewish children were educated there. For 51 years the head teacher was Moses Angel. He was dedicated to helping his pupils integrate into English society while retaining their Jewish identity.

Living and working

The most urgent priority for the new immigrants was finding somewhere to live and work. Most wanted to stay in Spitalfields and Whitechapel, in the East End of London, but this area was already overcrowded.

- In 1871 there was an average of 9 inhabitants per house; by 1901 the average was 14.
- Many houses were multi-generational, holding parents, children and grandchildren as well as lodgers. Almost every Jewish home was cramped.
- It was common for eight or nine individuals to share two rooms, with children sleeping 'top to toe', three or four in the same bed.

Working

From 1881 to 1914, two-thirds of Jews in England worked in three main trades: clothing, shoemaking and furniture-making. All of these occupations could be done in part of a house, a shed or a disused building as no heavy, specialised equipment was needed.

However, in Whitechapel many Jews worked in clothing sweatshops*. Men and women worked long hours in terrible conditions for little money, sewing cheap clothes as fast as they could. Some of the sweatshops were set up in rooms in the grand houses once lived in by Huguenots.

Extend your knowledge

The Four Per Cent Industrial Dwellings Company was founded in 1885 by Lord Rothschild, a member of the famous banking family. He was heavily involved in charitable work among Jewish communities. In 1884 a Sanitary Committee reported 'the houses occupied by the Jewish poor are for the most part barely fit, and for the many utterly unfit, for human habitation'. The company worked to change this. It got its name because investors in the company were promised a 4% return on their investment. By 1899, the company had housed over 4,000 people and the death rate in their tenements was a third of the average.

Source D

A contemporary illustration of Petticoat Lane market, Spitalfields. This was where many Jewish migrants sold cheap clothes.

Key term

Sweatshop*

A place where people worked long hours in poor conditions for low wages. In Spitalfields and Whitechapel, many sweatshops were organised and run by Jews. Those not run by Jews also exploited their Jewish workers. Some of the more basic clothing was sold locally while fancier clothes were sold in shops elsewhere.

Extend your knowledge

Singer sewing machines

Singer sewing machines transformed the work of everyone involved in making clothes. Small and transportable, they speeded up sewing stitches and making buttonholes. In 1870 Singer opened its first factory in England and sold 170,000 machines.

Anti-Semitism

Despite the hard work done by established Jewish communities, dislike and resentment of the Jewish migrants was evident, particularly in Spitalfields and Whitechapel. You can see how this affected the hunt for Jack the Ripper (pages 99–102).

> They take lower wages! We've struggled for years for better pay and these Jews don't bother.

> When they set up sweatshops they only employ other Jews, not us.

> I just don't like them. Their food and clothes are different. They don't even speak English!

> Their holy day is Saturday, so they can work on Sunday when we Christians can't. They'll drive us out of business.

Figure 3.11 Prejudice against Jews

Africans: free or enslaved?

By the middle of the 18th century, there were about 10,000 black Africans living in Britain. Many were from families that had been in Britain for hundreds of years. Others, as you read on page 75, were more recent. Many were forced to come by their owners, and worked as servants. In theory they were free, but their legal status wasn't clear.

Activities ?

1 If living and working conditions in Spitalfields and Whitechapel were so bad, why did so many migrant Jews from Eastern Europe choose to live there?

2 Describe the ways in which the established Jewish community tried to help the new migrants.

Exam-style question, Section B

Why did prejudice against Jews in the East End of London increase during the 19th century?

You may use the following in your answer:

- sweatshops
- migration from Russia.

You **must** include information of your own.   **(12 marks)**

Exam tip

The question tests your understanding of key features and causation. Focus on the factors that help explain why prejudice increased and make links between them.

Case study

James Somerset

In 1771 James Somerset was forced to travel to Britain as an enslaved man by his master, an American called Charles Stewart. That year, Somerset ran away and hid among London's black community. Stewart tracked him down and put him in chains on a ship to Jamaica. Stewart told the ship's captain to keep Somerset locked up and, when they landed in Jamaica, to sell him.

Granville Sharp, a white abolitionist*, worked closely with the black community. Charles Stewart had behaved as if James Somerset was his slave while they were living in Britain. Granville Sharp wanted a judge to decide whether slavery was legal in Britain. The case was heard by Lord Justice Mansfield. On 22 June 1772, he gave his judgement: *'Slavery was never in use in this country. It is so odious that it cannot be supported on moral or political grounds.'* James Somerset was set free.

It's important to realise that Judge Mansfield didn't say that slavery was illegal in Britain, only that it did not legally exist and the only way to make it exist was to pass a law allowing it. That was very, very unlikely and many black Africans celebrated Mansfield's judgement.

Forgotten fighters for Empire

- During the American War of Independence (1775–83) many black African people fought for the British. In return, they were offered freedom. Britain was defeated, and the former enslaved people left America. Many came to Britain and couldn't find work, so ended up begging.

- In 1786 the 'Committee for the Relief of the Black Poor' was set up to provide food and clothing for black beggars until they could find work. Later the Committee tried a different solution: sending poor black people to Africa. To 'encourage' this, the Committee stopped helping people who wanted to stay in England.

- In April 1787 a ship sailed for the Sierra Leone with 401 former beggars on board. However, 133 of them died on the journey or within days of arriving.

Working in Britain

By 1800 around 15,000 Africans were living in London. During the 19th century, black communities began to grow in major cities such as Liverpool, Glasgow and Cardiff. Africans worked in many different occupations. Some earned a lot of money, other less and some were very poor – just like everyone else in British society. However, it was black Africans, horrified by the Triangular Trade (see page 75) who played a major part in its abolition. You can read about that in Section 3.3.

Activity ?

Think about the James Somerset case and explain why it might have created problems for some black Africans.

Key term

Abolitionists*
People who wanted to abolish the slave trade.

Asians: ayahs and lascars

In 1869 the Suez Canal opened, cutting over 5,090 miles off the journey between India and Britain. Communications were improved by steam-powered liners (see page 70) and regular passenger services. This greatly increased the opportunities for people from India, Malaya and China to travel to and from Britain.

Extend your knowledge

Mohammed Abdul Karin was an Indian servant of Queen Victoria. Called 'the Munshi', he worked for her from 1887 until she died in 1901. He taught her Hindustani , helped with her official and private letters and introduced her to curries. She was very fond of him and gave him titles and cottages. The Royal Court was jealous of him, and after her death he was sent back to India and all his papers were burned.

Ayahs

Ayahs (see pages 41 and 71) were like nannies and travelled to Britain with the families they had worked for in India. Many stayed with the families until the children had grown up and then found work with other English families, but some were left to fend for themselves. The Suez Canal made it easier for ayahs to travel to Britain.

- Travelling ayahs on the new ocean liners became popular. They would be hired for the voyage and looking after the children and family in general.

- On arrival in Britain, the travelling ayah's duties ended. A return ticket to India was generally part of the deal. However, some employers 'forgot' this, and ayahs were left stranded in a strange country.

- Many became destitute. In 1855, for example, 50 to 60 ayahs were found living in a run-down lodging house in London's East End, and a further 140 were living in dreadful conditions in a London slum.

- In the mid-19th century a group of English women set up a hostel for abandoned ayahs. Supported and eventually run by a Christian organisation, the London City Mission, it tried to find the ayahs work or a passage back to India. The Mission also hoped to convert the Hindu and Muslim ayahs to Christianity.

Source E

Around 1900, the ayahs' hostel moved to Hackney, London. This photograph shows the outside of the hostel, now called the Ayah's Home, and some of those who lived and worked there.

Source F

An illustration, published in 1889, of the inside of the Great Hall of the 'Strangers' Home for Asiatics, Africans and South Sea Islanders'. Opened in 1857 in Limehouse, London, the home was funded by the East India Company and the Peninsula and Oriental Steam Navigation Company.

Lascars

The East India Company (see pages 41 and 48) and other companies recruited Indians to work as crew (lascars) on their ships. Lascars were also recruited from Somalia and Yemen. British victory in a war against China (1839–42) opened up China to trade and led to a demand for Chinese lascars.

Shipping companies were responsible for their lascars while they were in Britain, and for their return passage home. Some companies used lascars to work on their ships during the return journey. Others simply abandoned them in the British ports. Some lascars chose to stay.

- Many found work in the ports. You can read on page 97 about the lascars in Liverpool.
- Some were destitute, roaming the streets, and begging or stealing. Many died from starvation or from the cold.
- In the 1880s, Yemeni lascars helped build the Manchester Ship Canal, settling in the Old Trafford area.
- Hostels were opened to help destitute lascars, providing them with food and clothing and helping them to find work. Christian missionaries worked in the hostels, hoping to convert the lascars to Christianity.

Activities ?

1 Ayahs and lascars were migrants. Were they treated in the same way when they arrived in Britain? Explain your answer.

2 Many lascars settled in the communities where they worked, but ayahs did not. Discuss with a partner why this was. What would have been acceptable to Victorian society at the time?

Europeans: Germans and Italians

Germans

Most Germans (see Figure 3.8 on page 77) migrated to Britain because they wanted the freedom to develop their skills, ideas and businesses. Because of this, the German population was spread across the towns and cities of Britain.

- Karl Marx and Fredrich Engels were two thinkers who published radical ideas. (See pages 89 and 90.)
- Engineers and scientists set up small companies that did well. For example:
  - Ludwig Mond was a research chemist who set up a company, Brunner-Mond, in Liverpool. It became the leading alkali manufacturer in the country.
  - John Merz was an electrical engineer who co-founded a company, Merz and McLellan, that supplied electricity to the north-east of England.
  - Paul Reuter set up a successful news bureau (see page 91).
- Hundreds of Germans set up smaller businesses in cities and towns throughout Britain. These were butchers, bakers and brewers; they ran restaurants and pubs, worked as shopkeepers and waiters – and introduced the sausage to Britain.

Italians

Most Italians were farmers so they had to find others ways of making a living. Many settled in Clerkenwell, London, where there were so many of them that the area was known as 'Little Italy'. Not everyone was happy with this, as Source G shows!

Source G

From *The Times* newspaper, 1856.

We endure them simply as idle people endure dirt and vermin – because we have not the moral energy to get rid of them. It is an evil that threatens to make London unbearable.

Key terms

Barrel organ*
A small pipe organ played by turning a handle.

Hurdy-gurdy machine*
A stringed instrument that is worked by turning a handle.

Source H

An engraving by Gustav Doré, a French Illustrator, for his book *London, a Pilgrimage*, published in 1872. He visited London and made sketches from what he saw.

Nevertheless, the Italians brought some fun to London and other cities, even though some people complained about the noise!

- Many Italians worked as street musicians. They played barrel organs* and hurdy-gurdy machines*, sometimes with a tame monkey dancing and playing tricks. By 1881 there were over a thousand street musicians in Britain. Many were young boys forced into labour for work gangmasters.
- Some Italians did hard, manual work many English people didn't want to do, such as laying asphalt on the new roads.
- Some Italians developed skills learned in Italy – making tiles, ceramics and plasterwork.
- The biggest and most important form of employment was making and selling ice cream. Italian entrepreneurs started small, but before long were running ice cream parlours in most major cities.

After a shaky start, Italian migrants flourished. They set up schools and hospitals, newspapers and shops.

Activities

1 How far does the evidence of Source H support Source G about the attitudes toward Italians? Use your own knowledge in your answer.
2 Most Italians and Germans settled successfully. What was the key to their success?

Exam-style question, Section B

Explain one way in which work opportunities for Huguenot migrants in the 17th century were different from those for Irish migrants in the 19th century.

Exam tip

You need first to identify just one difference. Be specific, not general. The question asks you to explain the difference, so don't just describe it. You need to use information from both periods.

3.2 Summary

- Thousands of migrants in British cities lived in overcrowded, unsanitary tenement buildings. Poor Irish migrants worked as navvies and labourers. Many Jewish migrants worked in sweatshops.
- Some black Africans who had fought for the British in the American Civil War were deported to Sierra Leone. The James Somerset case established no enslaved person could be taken from Britain and sold.
- Asian ayahs and lascars were often abandoned in Britain by those who brought them to the country.
- European Germans and Italians found different ways of making a living and generally settled well.

Checkpoint

Strengthen

S1 Which groups of migrants were the victims of forced migration?
S2 What was the Triangular Trade?
S3 What different ways did German and Italian migrants find to make a living?

Challenge

C1 When Irish people and Eastern European Jews arrived in Britain, they faced a range of problems. How far were the problems similar?

3.3 The impact of migrants on Britain

Learning outcomes

- Understand the impact of migrants on politics, political thought and culture.
- Understand the impact of migrants on trade, industry and the built environment.

Migrants settling in Britain brought a huge range of skills and abilities (see pages 72–77). Their impact was sometimes individual, such as Karl Marx, and sometimes collective. They all helped to begin to create a more diverse, multicultural Britain – although not every change was welcomed.

Politics and political thought

Any really big change had to have Parliament's agreement. For example, the building of the Leeds to Liverpool canal (largely built by Irish navvies) would not have happened without an Act of Parliament in 1770. It was the same with the abolition of the slave trade in 1807 and the abolition of slavery in the British Empire in 1833.

MPs had to pay attention to changing attitudes on a range of issues. Various action groups and individuals put pressure on MPs to take particular actions.

Abolition of the slave trade

A strong movement for the abolition of the slave trade emerged in the 18th century. In 1787 the Society for the Abolition of the Slave Trade was formed. It aimed to educate the public about the horrors of the slave trade. They held meetings, organised lecture tours and published books, pamphlets and posters. Black Africans were a very important part of this.

Around the middle of the 18th century, some black Africans living in England wrote about their experiences. What they had to say was essential to the success of the abolition movement. They opened people's eyes not only to the horrors of the slave trade, but also to what former enslaved people could achieve through writing and public speaking.

Olaudah Equiano (1745–97)
Equiano was kidnapped when he was 11 years old, living in what is now Nigeria. He was first sold to a Virginian planter, then a British naval officer and finally a Quaker merchant from whom he bought his freedom. He settled in Britain, where he published his autobiography. It was widely read and the account of his time in Africa and enslavement had a tremendous impact. Equiano travelled around Britain giving public talks about his experiences and condemning the slave trade.

Ottobah Cugoano (1757–91)
Born on the Gold Coast (modern-day Ghana) Cugoano was taken on a slave ship to Grenada. In 1772 he was bought by a British merchant, Alexander Campbell, taken to England and given his freedom. He worked as a servant for the artists Richard and Maria Cosway, becoming known to some leading politicians. He was part of an abolitionist group called the 'Sons of Africa.' With the help of Equiano he published *Thoughts and Sentiments on the Evil and Wicked Traffic of the Slavery and Commerce of the Human Species* in 1787. He called for the end of slavery.

Ignatius Sancho (1729–80)
Sancho was born on a slave ship crossing the Atlantic. When his parents died, his owner took the two-year-old Sancho to London. Sancho was given to three sisters, and was their slave until he was 18. Eventually Sancho started his own business as a shopkeeper. Because he was a property owner, he was able to vote in the general elections of 1774 and 1780, the first black African to do so. He quickly became involved with abolitionists. Published after his death, his book, *The Letters of Ignatius Sancho, an African*, was read widely.

Source A

From Olaudah Equiano's autobiography *The Interesting Narrative*, published in 1789. Here he writes about the horrors of the Middle Passage – the journey across the Atlantic from Africa to the West Indies and southern states of America.

I was soon put down under the decks and there I received such a stench in my nostrils as I had never experienced in my life. I became so sick and low that I was not able to eat, nor had I the least desire to taste anything. I now wished for death to relieve me… If I could have got over the nettings I would have jumped over the side, but I could not as the crew used to watch us very closely when we were not chained down to the decks… the heat of the climate – added to the number in the ship, which was so crowded that each had scarcely room to turn himself – almost suffocated us. This brought on a sickness amongst the slaves, of which many died… this wretched situation was made worse by the discomfort of the chains and the filth of the necessary tubs [toilets] into which the children often fell and were almost suffocated. The shrieks of the women and the groans of the dying, rendered the whole a scene of horror almost inconceivable.

Key term

Non-conformists*

People who were Christians but were not members of the Anglican church. They were, for example, Methodists, Presbyterians or Quakers.

Extend your knowledge

In 1833 Parliament passed an Act ending slavery in the British Empire. It was made illegal to own or sell a slave. Former enslaved people, however, had to stay on as employees for four more years while the plantation owners worked out how to run their estates without slave labour. Approximately £20 million (equivalent to £2.43 billion today) was paid out to the plantation owners to compensate them for their 'loss of property'. No enslaved person was paid any compensation whatsoever.

Black Africans played an important part in getting the slave trade abolished. But others were involved too.

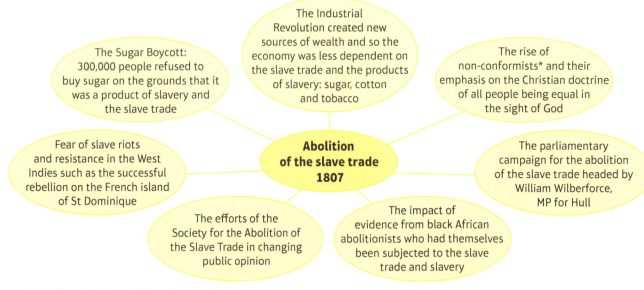

The Industrial Revolution created new sources of wealth and so the economy was less dependent on the slave trade and the products of slavery: sugar, cotton and tobacco

The Sugar Boycott: 300,000 people refused to buy sugar on the grounds that it was a product of slavery and the slave trade

The rise of non-conformists* and their emphasis on the Christian doctrine of all people being equal in the sight of God

Fear of slave riots and resistance in the West Indies such as the successful rebellion on the French island of St Dominique

Abolition of the slave trade 1807

The parliamentary campaign for the abolition of the slave trade headed by William Wilberforce, MP for Hull

The efforts of the Society for the Abolition of the Slave Trade in changing public opinion

The impact of evidence from black African abolitionists who had themselves been subjected to the slave trade and slavery

Figure 3.12 The abolition of the slave trade

Supporting the Chartists

Chartism was a mainly working-class mass protest movement. Its members were disappointed with the Reform Act of 1832 (see page 69). Working men had hoped the Act would give them the right to vote, and it didn't. They learned how to use posters and petitions from the impact of the anti-slave-trade movement. Two prominent Chartists came from immigrant families.

Feargus O'Connor (1794–1855)

O'Connor was a Protestant born in Ireland. He inherited an estate in County Cork and became its MP. A reforming landlord, he argued for the rights of tenants. He founded a radical newspaper, the *Northern Star*, and became a Chartist leader. His inspirational speeches drew huge crowds and his support of violent methods landed him in prison several times.

William Cuffay (1788–1870)

Cuffay was born in Kent, the son of a cook who had been a slave in the Caribbean. He worked as a tailor and then, in 1834, disgusted with being sacked after taking part in a strike, he joined the Chartists. Elected president of the London Chartists, he supported militant action. This got him into trouble, and he was transported to Tasmania. Once there, he again got involved in radical politics. He died a pauper* in a Tasmanian workhouse.

Activities ?

1. Design a poster that could have been used by the abolition movement to persuade people to oppose the slave trade.
2. Create a discussion between an MP who owns several sugar plantations in Jamaica, a female housekeeper buying foodstuffs, including sugar, for the household, and a black African who bought his freedom. What are their views on the slave trade? How will they try to persuade each other their views are right?
3. Are you surprised that migrants became involved in radical politics? Discuss this in your class.

Political thinkers

Some people migrated to Britain because of the freedom it gave them to develop their ideas, free from persecution by the state.

Karl Marx (1818–83)

Karl Marx's ideas were too radical* for his birthplace in Germany, and in 1850 he migrated to England. He lived in London for the rest of his life and spent most of his time working and writing in the British Museum.

Wrote *Das Kapital* stating that the capitalist system* only worked because workers were exploited. The bosses owned the means of production and this had to change.

Believed religion was a 'drug' used by the authorities to make the workers forget their misery.

With Friedrich Engels, wrote the *Manifesto of the Communist Party*. This argued society should be stateless and classless, with no private property.

'Workers of the world, unite. You have nothing to lose but your chains' is the last line from the *Communist Manifesto* and it terrified governments.

Figure 3.13 The impact of Karl Marx

Key terms

Pauper*

A very poor person, who often depended on the state to support them.

Radical*

A person who wants fundamental social or political change.

Capitalist system*

An economic system based on the private ownership of the means of production that are run for profit.

Friedrich Engels (1820–95)

Engels was born in Germany into a wealthy family who owned factories in Europe and Britain. He travelled to England to get experience of working in the family's Lancashire cotton mills.

Key terms

Communism*

An economic and social system where all property is owned by the community and each person contributes according to their ability and receives according to their needs.

Communication and trade

Canals and railways

Irish and Italian migrants worked as navvies (see pages 79–70 and 85) digging out canals, building locks and docks and, later, laying track for railways. The work was dirty and dangerous, but the impact it had on the British economy was huge. The economy couldn't have developed as it did without their work.

In Manchester studied the lives of the poor for his book *The Condition of the Working Class in England in 1844*. This had a huge impact on reformers and parliament.

Believed that England was a likely place for a communist revolution, where the oppressed workers would rise up and overthrow the privileged few.

Worked with Karl Marx to produce their *Manifesto of the Communist Party*, setting out the principles and policies of communism*.

Led a double life, working in the capitalist system by day and at night working with Marx to overthrow it. In 1869 he sold his share in the family business to support the Marx family and himself while he continued writing radical articles.

Figure 3.14 The impact of Friedrich Engels

Figure 3.15 The British canal network in 1830

Figure 3.16 The British rail network in 1852

The canal network and, later, the rail network meant raw materials and finished goods could move easily around the country. It also made it easier for migrants to settle in all parts of the country. This helped industrial towns grow more quickly.

Transport improvements also improved people's lives. Holidays became easier. Fresh fruit and fish could be moved quickly around the country, improving people's diets. Newspapers could also be circulated throughout the country.

News and newspapers

Paul Reuter (1816–99)

Born in Germany, Reuter created a telegraph system between Aachen and Brussels so that he could get news quickly and sell it on to newspapers. In 1851 he moved to London and set up Reuters News Agency.

Reuters News Agency was important because it was the first to report accurately on stories of international importance. Today, almost every major news outlet in the world subscribes to Reuters.

Shops and shopping

Many Eastern European Jews were involved in the clothing trade (see pages 80–81). In the 1850s, Moses Moss dealt in second-hand clothes. By the 20th century, the company Moses founded – Moss Bros – was a successful men's outfitters.

Montagu Burton fled to Britain in 1900 from Lithuania and founded Burton's Menswear, which, by the 20th century, was a successful chain of menswear shops.

Marks & Spencer

Michael Marks migrated to Britain in the 1880s, as did thousands of Russian Jews, escaping persecution (see page 74). In 1884 he set up a stall in Kirkgate Market in Leeds. His slogan was 'Don't ask the price – it's a penny'. And everything was. The business took off. Penny bazaars opened in Castleford and Wakefield, Warrington, Birkenhead, Bolton and Manchester.

Joined by Tom Spencer in 1894, Marks opened stores in Birmingham, Newcastle-upon-Tyne, Cardiff, Bath and London. Marks purchased goods directly from the manufacturer, cutting out the merchant middleman. Today Marks & Spencer is a successful international business.

Source B

Marks & Spencer's penny bazaar in Cardiff in 1901.

Activities ?

1 Draw a mind map showing how all the factors involved in communication and trade are linked. Remember, some factors are linked to more than one other factor. Now add another layer showing how migrants influenced and were affected by those factors and links.

2 Which factor do you think is the most important in your spidergram? Why?

Johann Jacob Schweppe: German-Swiss scientist who developed carbonated water. In 1792 he moved to London and started a company called Malvern Water. This later merged with Schweppes International.

Gustav Wilhelm Wolff: German Jew who moved to Liverpool in 1849 and went into partnership with Edward Harland. They founded the Harland-Wolff shipyard in Belfast. It built over 400 ships including RMS *Titanic*.

Contributing to British industrial success

Ludwig Mond: German chemist who set up the Brunner Mond company in Northwich, Cheshire. In 1926 Brunner Mond merged with three other British companies to form ICI; currently it is a subsidiary of Tata Chemicals, Europe.

Hugo Hurst: left Germany in 1881 for London. Opened a shop selling electric bells, coils and ignition systems. Partnered with Gustav Byng. Their company later merged with General Electric Company.

Figure 3.17 Contributing to British industrial success

Interpretation 1

From *Bloody Foreigners: the story of immigration to Britain* by Robert Winder, published in 2004.

They were extraordinary individuals and often progressive employers, but, like all entrepreneurs, they needed backers. They found them in the extraordinary network of German, or German-descended, bankers in the City of London: Barings, Grotes, Samuel Montagu and Rothschilds.

Source C

An ice cream seller in London 1878.

Industry and ice cream

Industry

Many migrants' companies became successes, helping the British economy grow. The four migrants featured in Figure 3.17 are examples of what migrants achieved. Their success, however, would not have been possible without financial backing, as Interpretation 1 explains.

Ice and ice cream

Until the 19th century, ice cream was difficult to make and only the rich could afford a cook with the time to make it. It was Italians in the 19th century who made ice cream a popular street food. By the 1900s, street sellers of ice cream were common and most towns and cities had a least one ice cream parlour. Glasgow had 300!

Case study

Carlo Gatti and ice cream

Carlo Gatti left Switzerland in 1847, settling in 'Little Italy', London (see page 85). His successful waffle and chestnut stall was followed by a cafe specialising in chocolate and ice cream. To get enough ice to make ice cream, Gatti made an agreement to cut ice from the Regent's Canal. He also sold ice cream from a stall in Hungerford Market, and it soon became a popular street food. In 1857 he built an 'ice well' off Regent's Canal that stored tons of ice (imported from Norway). Gatti went on to run many successful cafes, restaurants and music halls in London.

Extend your knowledge

Migrants bought many different foods to Britain, that have now become part of our everyday life. German sausages such as Bratwurst influenced British tastes. Queen Victoria's fondness for Indian culture helped make Indian curries more popular.

Activities   ?

1   Look back at the mind map you made showing how the factors involved in the section 'Communication and trade' were linked. Add to them using the information in this section 'Industry and ice cream'.

2   Marx and Engels did nothing practical to help build the British economy, like digging canals or setting up companies. Does this mean that their time in Britain was of no importance?

THINKING HISTORICALLY Change and continuity (2b)

Events or historical change?

The language that historians choose can help show whether they are talking about change or continuity. For instance, 'more' suggests a change from before.

Study the following events and changes.

Thousands of people migrate from Ireland.	Shipping companies run passenger services between India and Britain.	Italian migrants settle in Clerkenwell, London.	More and more people work in sweatshops sewing cheap clothes.	Increased pressure on Parliament to abolish the slave trade.
Barrel organs play a new kind of music in the streets.	Olaudah Equiano writes his autobiography.	Thousands of Russians settle in Spitalfields.	Navvies build miles of track for the new railways.	Homes for abandoned ayahs were set up for the first time.

1   Sort the points above into 'events' and 'changes'.

2   Match each change to an event.

3.3 Summary

- Black Africans played a large part in bringing about the abolition of the slave trade in 1807.
- Irish and Italian navvies dug roads and canals and built docks and railways.
- Jewish migrants established successful retail outlets such as Marks & Spencer.
- Germans helped set up successful industrial companies. Italians brought street music and street food to Britain.
- Individuals, such as Marx, Engels and Reuter, created new ideas and businesses.

Checkpoint

Strengthen

S1 How was the slave trade abolished?

S2 How did Irish and Italian migrants help the British economy?

S3 Describe how Jews contributed to the British economy.

Challenge

C1 What was the most important change brought about by migrants to Britain in the years 1700–1900? Explain your choice.

3.4 Case study: Liverpool in the 19th century

Learning outcomes

- Understand the growth of Liverpool as a port and the impact of this on migration.
- Know about Irish migration to Liverpool and the development of an Irish community in Liverpool.
- Know about other migrant groups in Liverpool, such as Indians, Chinese and West Africans, and their impact on the city.

The growth of Liverpool

Liverpool's port made huge profits from the slave trade (see page 71). When the trade ended in 1807, its merchants needed new markets.

Ships from Liverpool sailed straight into the Atlantic, meaning the city had a lot of trade with America. The city became very successful importing raw materials, especially cotton (from slave plantations in British colonies and America), for large factories in places such as Manchester. Liverpool merchants then exported the products made by the factories. The city's trading links and job opportunities in its port made it attractive to migrants.

Liverpool's growth as a trading port

- Liverpool's port grew dramatically; by 1900 Liverpool had over 7 miles of docks.
- During the 19th century, sailing ships were replaced by steamships. These were faster and could carry more goods. In 1850 the average ship carried 280 tons; by 1906 the average was 1,270 tons.
- From 1845 to 1895 Liverpool's docks went from handling 2.8 million tons of goods a year to 10.5 million tons.
- By 1905 Liverpool was the second most profitable port in the world, with goods worth £237 million a year moving through it (only London was larger).

Source A

A large number of goods moved through Liverpool docks every year. This photo from the late 19th century shows just one of the city's docks. You can see the warehouses where goods were stored and the ships waiting to be unloaded.

Extend your knowledge

Sailing ships needed people experienced in working with rigging, which took years to master. Steam ships needed skills that were quicker to learn. 'Stokers' shovelled coal into the furnaces that kept the ship moving; 'greasers' oiled the machinery; 'firemen' moved coal from storage to the engine room. These less-skilled jobs made it easier to recruit labourers to work on the ships.

The cotton trade

The cotton industry involved spinning and weaving cotton into fabric. In the 1860s almost 600,000 people were directly employed in the cotton industry, with another 4 million people depending on it either as family members of workers or in industries supporting it.

All raw cotton was imported from abroad. In the second half of the 19th century, England imported over 362,000 tons of cotton a year. Some 80% of this cotton came from the USA and arrived in Liverpool. From 1850 to 1900 cotton was the number one import to Britain.

Irish migrants to Liverpool

After the famines in Ireland (see page 73), hundreds of thousands of Irish migrants travelled to Liverpool.

- In 1846, between January and March 90,000 people arrived in Liverpool from Ireland.
- Between July 1847 and July 1848 another 300,000 arrived.
- In 1850 over 250,000 more migrants arrived in the city – nearly 78,000 of these were described as paupers by the city authorities.

Figure 3.18 Why did Irish migrants come to Liverpool?

Life in Liverpool was tough for the newly arrived immigrants. The *Liverpool Mercury* reported on the lives of these Irish migrants on 15 January 1847.

In the cold and gloom of a severe winter, thousands of hungry and half naked wretches are wandering about, not knowing how to obtain a sufficiency of the commonest food nor shelter from the piercing cold. The numbers of starving Irish men, women and children – daily landed on our quays is appalling; and the Parish of Liverpool has at present, the painful and most costly task to encounter, of keeping them alive, if possible.

Migrating to America

For many Irish migrants Liverpool was just their first stop. In 1851, 159,840 people sailed from Liverpool to America – five times more than from Le Havre (in France), the next most popular port for emigrants.

Ships to America would take migrants (for a fee). In the 1860s passenger shipping companies agreed to take Irish migrants. However, the price was high; in the 1880s the cost of a third-class ticket was £5 – about half the annual earnings of an Irish labourer.

Source C

This image from *The Illustrated London News* of 6 July 1850 shows Irish families boarding a ship in Liverpool to migrate to America.

Staying in Liverpool: the Irish community

Not all Irish migrants wanted to – or could – leave Liverpool. Some could not afford the passage to America or were cheated by people claiming to sell tickets. In 1841 there were 49,000 Irish people in Liverpool. But by 1851 there were 83,000 (over 20% of the city's population).

Working in Liverpool

Prejudice
Signs saying 'No Irish Need Apply' common. Trade unions were hostile to Irish workers.

Jobs for men
Mostly poorly paid manual labour jobs, often temporary, involding long hours, hard work and low pay. In 1881, 80% of Irish men were labourers.

Jobs for women
Few opportunities. By 1881, 84% of working women in Liverpool were maids.

Figure 3.19 The Irish experience of working in Liverpool

Irish migrants eventually dominated jobs at the docks.

- Many of the new docks were built by Irish navvies.
- Irish dock workers (called 'lumpers'), hired on a daily basis to load and unload goods from ships.
- By the 1870s almost 2,000 Irishmen employed as 'lumpers' and in warehouses.

Although life was hard, some Irish workers gained senior positions (such as foremen) or worked in skilled trades, such as repairing ships.

Source D

In a report to the Council of the Irish Federation in Dublin, written in January 1848, Liverpool businessman George Smythe discussed Irish labour in Liverpool:

The Irishmen in Liverpool perform nearly all the labour requiring great powers and endurance. Nine tenths of the ships that arrive in this great port are discharged and loaded by them... Out of the 1,900 shipwrights, 400 are Irish, or of Irish parents; and although Liverpool is a port rather for repairing than building vessels, there is one Irishman of the three of four master builders of the town, and many Irish foremen. In almost every branch of trade Irishmen, notwithstanding the many prejudices with which they have to contend, have risen to the highest promotion.

The Irish community in Liverpool

- Social areas for Irish people appeared. One of the first things Irish arrivals in the 1840s would have seen was a dockside pub run by retired Dublin-born boxer Jack Langan. This offered advice and support for new arrivals. Later other pubs, such as Shenanigans (1841), opened in the city.
- Other Irish-run businesses started to open, including butchers, bakers, tailors and greengrocers.
- The number of Catholic parishes grew from 18 in 1870 to 24 by 1916.
- Areas Irish people could afford to live in were poor and run-down. Many were paupers.

Extend your knowledge

The Irish community in Liverpool was so large, it was the only place in England to elect a member of an Irish independence party to Parliament. T. P. O'Connor (known as 'Tay Pay' because of the way he pronounced his name) was elected in 1885 and served as an MP for Liverpool for almost 45 years.

Local prejudice

Crime in the city was often blamed on Irish migrants – in February 1850 the *Liverpool Mercury* complained about a 'constant influx of Irish misery and crime'. In 1850 just over half of the nearly 6,000 people brought before magistrates for crimes were Irish.

Source E

An article from the *Liverpool Mail* in March 1851.

The Irish beggar is generally an idle and worthless wretch, always a disgusting object... Ireland they assure us is recovering; and yet these beggars still come in swarms of male shadows in indescribable rags, and horridly ugly barefooted nasty women carrying something like imps [little demons] in bags at their backs. This is pollution. Instead of exciting sympathy it produces nausea.

Illness and disease

Outbreaks of typhus* and other diseases were common. It was not helped by many of the Irish arrivals being weak and starving. In 1847, 60,000 people became ill with typhus.

The Liverpool Workhouse Infirmary supported the Irish community. An Irish Nurse, Agnes Jones, became its first Nursing Superintendent in 1865. She was one of the few superintendents training nurses in the country. She died of typhus aged only 35.

Key term

Typhus*

An infection spread by lice and poor hygiene that brings rash, fever, confusion and (if untreated) death.

Source F

This stained glass window in a Liverpool church shows Kitty Wilkinson, an Irish migrant. Known as 'the saint of the slums', Kitty opened one of the first washhouses in Liverpool in 1832 and became the superintendent of public baths in Liverpool in 1842. She was honoured by Queen Victoria and worked tirelessly to improve public health in Liverpool.

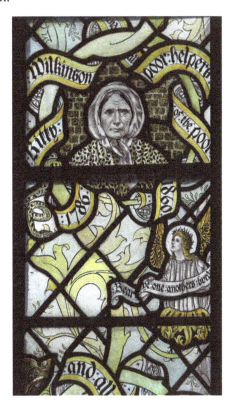

The legacy of Irish migrants

Today almost 75% of people in Liverpool have some Irish ancestry.

- The scouse accent largely comes from Irish speakers – Irish migrants changed the way the city sounded.
- Descendants of Irish migrants have been involved in the city's politics, businesses and culture – Paul McCartney and John Lennon of The Beatles both had Irish ancestors.
- Liverpool has several roads named after areas in Ireland, such as Ulster, Belfast and Donegal.
- The Anfield area, now home of Liverpool FC, was named after Annefield the family home of the Irish-born lord mayor of Liverpool in 1861, Samuel Robert Graves.

Migrant sailors in Liverpool

Liverpool's growth as a port meant migrants from all over the world found their way to the city. It became common to see Indian and Chinese sailors in Liverpool.

Indian sailors

Throughout the 19th century approximately 10,000 to 12,000 Indian sailors visited Britain each year, many arriving at Liverpool. Sailors were recruited from the West Coast of India (Gujarat and Malabar) and from modern-day Bangladesh.

The demand for Indian sailors increased with the introduction of steam ships. It was assumed that Indians were better suited than white sailors to the hot conditions in boiler rooms. They were also paid much less than white sailors.

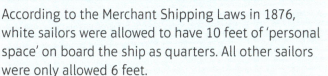

Extend your knowledge

According to the Merchant Shipping Laws in 1876, white sailors were allowed to have 10 feet of 'personal space' on board the ship as quarters. All other sailors were only allowed 6 feet.

Indian migrants in Liverpool

- Some continued to work as sailors. Others took up different jobs, becoming, for example, street sweepers or musicians; or they set up lodging houses for other sailors, like Meer Jan who ran a lodging house with his English wife.
- Many Indians who migrated to Liverpool married British women; this helped them to settle in Britain.
- An Indian community grew in Liverpool. In 1890 a mosque for Muslim Indian migrants opened in Liverpool.

Extend your knowledge

One of the first Indian-run trading companies in Britain, Cama and Company, was run by three Parsi businessmen. It had one of its two British branches in Liverpool in the 1850s.

Liverpool's Chinese community

Liverpool has the oldest 'Chinatown' in Europe. From the late 1850s, Chinese seamen arrived in large numbers as silk, cotton and tea were imported from Shanghai and Hong Kong.

Boarding houses in Liverpool housed Chinese sailors. From the 1890s, Chinese shops and cafes became common. Chinese sailors had a reputation for working hard, not drinking, and for looking after their families. Many of them married British women.

African sailors in Liverpool

As trade grew with Africa, African sailors also migrated to the city. Many came from modern-day Gambia, Ghana and Sierra Leone – some migrated from these countries to be hired as sailors.

Liverpool shipping companies, such as Elder Dempster, recruited African sailors to work in the ship's boiler rooms. These sailors were willing to work for lower wages and in harder conditions. Some stayed, often for a short time, living in hostels in areas like Toxteth.

Activities

1. What factors would an Irish migrant need to consider when deciding whether to stay in Liverpool or travel to America? Try to think of two reasons for and two reasons against for both decisions.

2. How do you think the arrival of Irish, Indian, African and Chinese migrants helped to make Liverpool a more important city? Write down a list of four factors and then share them with the rest of the group. How many factors can you come up with?

3.4 Summary

- Liverpool was one of the largest and most successful ports in the world, handling millions of tons of goods. The cotton industry, and trade with America, helped make it hugely profitable.
- After the Irish famines, hundreds of thousands of Irish migrants travelled to Liverpool – many of them looking to take ships to America. Others stayed in Liverpool.
- Life in Liverpool was hard, but Irish migrants built a strong community and have a huge legacy.
- Growing trade links with the world meant sailors from India, China and Africa became a common sight in the city. Migrant communities developed, bringing their own cultures to the city.

Checkpoint

Strengthen

S1 Why did Liverpool become such a successful trading city?

S2 Why do you think so many Irish people arrived in the city in the 1840s?

S3 How did the Irish migrant community change the city?

Challenge

C1 Why do you think that many people in Liverpool disliked the Irish migrants?

C2 What impact do you think migration had on the city of Liverpool?

Settling in Whitechapel and Spitalfields

Many of the 100,000 Jewish migrants in the 1880s/1890s landed at St Katherine's Dock, close to the Tower of London. This was a short distance from Whitechapel and Spitalfields, where there were established Jewish communities. Although less than 1% of Britain's population was Jewish, it is estimated by 1888 over 40% of the population in Whitechapel were recent Jewish migrants.

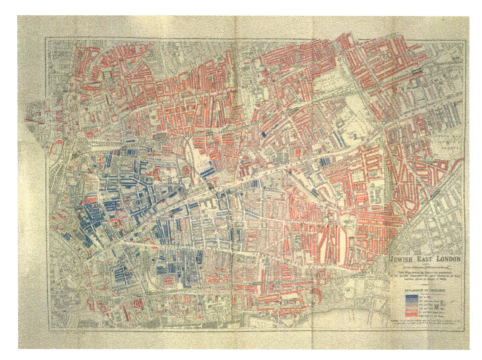

Figure 3.20 Jewish settlement (blue) in the East End of London (Spitalfields in Whitechapel), beginning of the 20th century

Whitechapel in the 1880s was a maze of tenement buildings with little or no sanitation, dark alleys and filthy courts. Many people lived in extreme poverty, lodging in cold, damp and overcrowded tenement buildings. Desperate people were forced into theft and prostitution. However, there were many in the Jewish community who worked hard to support the newly arrived immigrants (see page 74).

Source A

From *Life and Labour of the People in London*, a report written by Charles Booth in 1889.

The newcomers [Jews] have gradually replaced the English population in whole districts. They were formerly in Commercial Street. Now the Jews have flowed across the line; Hanbury Street, Fashion Street, Pelham Street, Booth Street, Old Montague Street, and they have taken over many streets and lanes and alleys. They fill whole blocks of model dwellings*; they have introduced new trades as well as new habits and they live and crowd together and work and go their own way independent of the great stream of London life surging around them.

Key term

Model dwellings*

Housing built to provide the basics of comfort and sanitation. Although they were intended for the poor, rents were generally higher than those charged for squalid lodgings.

Source B

From a report in the *Lancet*, a medical journal, describing the conditions its investigators found in Whitechapel. The report was published in 1884.

In Emily Place we found five persons living in one room, while in another house we came upon a Jewish potato dealer who kept his wife, five children and a large stock of potatoes all in one room, measuring five yards by six yards*. There was one bed in the room and probably some of the family slept on the floor.

In Hanbury Street we found… the first two floors of a house let out to lodgers who were Jews. Their rooms were clean but damp as water was coming through the rotting wall … the closet [toilet] was a source of trouble. A flushing apparatus had been provided, but the water came out under the seat and flowed across the yard to the wall opposite, which was eaten away at its base.

Source C

An engraving of Wentworth Street, Whitechapel, by Gustav Doré, dated 1876. This is one of a series of pictures he made while visiting London.

Key term

Yards*

This was a measurement of length before metrication in 1971, and so it appears in many documents before that date. 1 yard = 0.9144 metres.

Activities ?

1. How far does the map (Figure 3.20) and Source A help explain the pressures Jewish migration in the 1880s put on Spitalfields and Whitechapel?

2. Read Sources A and B. How far does Source A support the findings described in Source B?

3. Now look at Source C. Sources A, B and C were all made by people who had visited the East End of London. Which, in your opinion gives the best impression of what it must have been like to live there? Explain your answer.

Rising tensions and prejudice

There was unemployment in the East End before the rush of Jewish immigrants in the 1880s. Poverty, unemployment and the arrival of thousands of East European Jews, also looking for work, created a tense situation.

- The police were afraid to patrol the streets alone, especially in areas where the Irish and Jews lived.

- Many English people believed Jews were taking their jobs.

- Many Jews worked in sweatshops, for long hours in poor conditions for little pay.

- Trade unions had worked hard to establish basic working conditions. Sweatshop owners and workers ignored these and so were able to produce goods more cheaply than regulated factories.

- Sweatshops were illegal in Britain, but communicating this was difficult because some Jewish immigrants spoke only Yiddish, which the police did not speak.

- Parliament was concerned about the tense situation and prejudice in Spitalfields and Whitechapel and set up two committees of enquiry. Anti-Semitic hostility grew and attacks on Jews increased.

Source D

Evidence given to the House of Lords Committee on Sweated Trades in 1890 by Charles Freak, Secretary of the Shoemaker Society, a trade union representing workers in the industry.

There is no feeling against these foreigners as foreigners. These Jew foreigners work in our trade at this common labour for 16 or 18 hours a day, and the consequence is that they make a lot of cheap and nasty stuff that destroys the market and injures us [because it is sold at such a low price]. The Jewish labourers defeat the cause of the English workmen in their battle to attain higher wages. They do this by shameless blacklegging* during disputes and taking work out at any price.

Source E

From an article in the *Sunday Magazine* by a Mrs Brewer, published in 1892.

My first impression on going among them was that I must be in some far-off country whose people and language I knew not. The names over the shops were foreign, the wares were advertised in an unknown tongue of which I did not even know the letters, the people in the streets were not of our type, and when I addressed them in English the majority of them shook their heads.

Activities ?

1 Read Sources D and E. Explain why Charles Freak and Mrs Brewer found the East End Jews difficult.

2 How might a Jew have replied to Charles Freak and to Mrs Brewer? In pairs, work out what they could have said to explain their position.

Key terms

Blacklegging*
Working during a strike.

Hebrew population*
The Jewish community.

Shochetim*
A Jew who has been specially trained and licensed to slaughter birds and animals according to Jewish law.

The writing on the wall

Whitechapel was a place where murders and beatings were common. In 1888, between 31 August and 9 November, five women were brutally murdered. The Jewish community would have known some of them: Mary Ann Nicholls lived in Thrawl Street, Elizabeth Stride in lodgings in Flower and Dean Street, and Mary Kelly in Loleworth Street – all places where Jews lived. The police believed that the murders had all been carried out by one person, who was given the nickname 'Jack the Ripper'. Many people believed he was a Jew.

Reaction to the murders by the police and public give us an insight into the community's hostility towards Jews living in their midst.

Source F

From the *East London Observer*, September 1888.

On Saturday in several quarters of East London the crowds who assembled in the streets began to assume a very threatening attitude towards the Hebrew population* of the district. It was repeatedly asserted that no Englishman could have perpetuated such a horrible crime... and that it must have been done by a Jew – and forthwith the crowds began to threaten and abuse such of the unfortunate Hebrews as they found in the streets. Happily the presence of a large number of police prevented a riot actually taking place.

Knives

The injuries of the women were so awful that the police believed they could only have been done by a doctor or a butcher. Suspicion fell upon the shochetim*, the Jewish ritual slaughterers, and two of them were arrested. However, both had strong alibis. Furthermore, when the police surgeon examined the knives used by the shochetim, he found they were not pointed, whereas the women had been killed with a pointed-blade knife.

Graffiti

Part of the bloodstained apron belonging to Catherine Eddowes, one of the victims, was found under an archway a short distance from where her body was found. Above the archway was written the graffiti you can see in Figure 3.21.

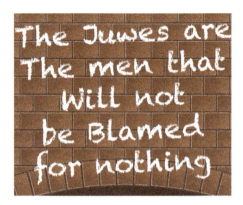

Figure 3.21 A copy of the graffiti seen above the archway where part of Catherine Eddowes' bloodstained apron was found

Key terms

Home Office*

The government department responsible for the police.

Inquest*

A legal enquiry into an incident – usually a death.

The graffiti was rubbed off before it could be photographed. The Chief Commissioner of the Metropolitan Police force, Charles Warren, explains why in Source G.

Source G

From a report written by Charles Warren, Chief Commissioner of the Metropolitan Police, sent to the Home Office* on 6 November 1888.

It was just getting light; the public would be in the streets in a few minutes, in a neighbourhood very much crowded with Jews and Christians and the writing would be visible to anybody in the street. After taking into consideration the strong feelings that existed in the area against the Jews, and fearing a riot, I ordered the writing to be wiped away. I took a copy of it and this I enclose.

Inquests

Inquests* were held into all the deaths. Statements were taken from people who had seen the victims talking to a man shortly before their bodies were found.

Source H

Part of a statement made by George Hutchinson, an unemployed labourer, at the inquest into the death of Mary Kelly. She was killed on Friday 9 November 1888.

He was aged 34–35 years old and about five feet six inches tall, with a pale complexion, dark eyes and hair and a little moustache that curled up at the ends. He wore a long, dark coat with a dark jacket underneath, with dark trousers and button boots. His shirt was white and his black tie was fastened with a horseshoe shaped pin. He had dark hair turned down in the middle. He was Jewish in appearance and respectable.

Source I

Part of a statement made by Elizabeth Long, who worked on a market stall, and saw Annie Chapman, another of the victims, talking to an unknown man.

He was dark and wearing a hat. I think he was wearing a dark coat but I cannot be sure. He looked shabby but respectable, He was a man over forty, as far as I could tell. He looked to me like a foreigner.

The hunt for the Ripper highlighted the hostility that existed against Jews in Whitechapel. Even so, there was something positive to come out of the unsuccessful hunt. It drew attention to a deprived area and spurred people to try to get rid of the worst slums and alleys in the East End of London.

Activities

1 Look carefully at the graffiti (Figure 3.21). People have argued for many years over what it means. What do you think it means? Discuss this in your class.

2 Now read Source G. Do you think Charles Warren was justified in having the graffiti rubbed out? Explain your answer.

3 Read Sources H and I. How far could they have added to the hostility against Jews in Whitechapel?

4 'Hostility against Jews in the East End of London has been very much exaggerated.' Write a paragraph explaining how far you agree with his statement.

3.5 Summary

- Thousands of Jews from Eastern Europe crowded into the East End of London, particularly Spitalfields and Whitechapel, in the years 1890–1900.
- Much of the area was a slum, with overcrowded houses, little sanitation and poor working conditions. Unions complained about sweatshop labour.
- Hostility towards Jews grew, especially during the hunt for Jack the Ripper.

Checkpoint

Strengthen

S1 Describe living conditions in Whitechapel and Spitalfields.

S2 Explain why there was so much hostility towards recent Jewish immigrants.

S3 Explain how the hunt for Jack the Ripper increased hostility towards Jews.

Challenge

C1 Describe the problems faced by Jewish people trying to live and work in the East End of London.

C2 Explain how the problems were linked.

Activity

What were the most important factors bringing about change in migration during this period? You have a bag of 100 weights. Copy the table to distribute them between the factors, according to which you think was the most important.

Remember that your total number of weights can't go above 100, and you need to explain your thinking in the final column.

Factor to balance	Number of weights	Reason why
Government		
Religion		
Economic influences		
Attitudes in society		

04 | c1900–present: Migration in modern Britain

In the years following 1900, Britain was involved in two world wars. People from all over the Empire fought for Britain. The world wars resulted in enormous movements of people, many of whom migrated to Britain.

The world wars disrupted British society. Cities, towns, ports and railways all needed rebuilding. The National Health Service (NHS) was created. Migrants were needed to help do all these things.

The British Empire was dismantled from 1946 onwards, causing more movement of peoples and migration to Britain. Britain formed new relationships with its former Empire through the creation of the Commonwealth and with Europe when it joined the European Union (EU).

Both of these led to a freer movement of people to Britain. This was limited, however, because in 2016 the British people voted to leave the EU. A major reason for this was resentment of migration and migrants.

Learning outcomes

By the end of this chapter, you will:

- understand how world events led to voluntary and forced migration
- understand how changes in British society led to increased migration
- know about the different experiences migrants had in Britain, and understand the reasons for these differences
- understand the impact migrants had on Britain
- complete a case study on the experiences of migrants in mid-20th-century Bristol
- complete a case study on the experience of Asian migrants in Leicester after 1945.

4.1 The reasons why people migrated

Learning outcomes

- Know about British society in the years 1900 to the present time.
- Understand the reasons why different groups of people migrated to, from and within Britain.

What was Britain like in the years 1900 to the present?

The period 1900 to the present was one where tremendous changes affected everyone in Britain, including migrants already in the country and those hoping to migrate.

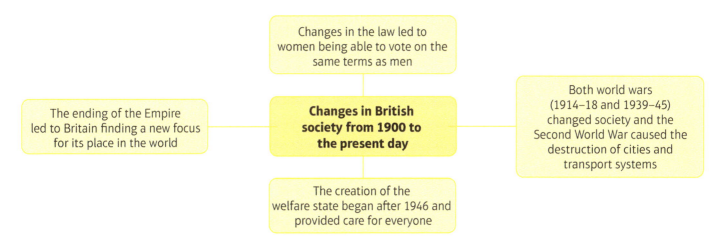

Figure 4.1 Changes in British society from 1900 to the present day

Changes in Parliament

In the years after 1900, laws were passed that not only made Parliament more representative of society, but which affected people's lives in many different ways. These changes all impacted migration.

Changes in Parliament	Impact on migration
Some women first given the vote in 1918, with all women having equal voting rights with men from 1928.	This helped give greater political representation to migrant communities.
In 1948 Parliament created the NHS. Paid for through taxation, people could use the service for free.	The NHS was in urgent need of staff, recruiting migrant nurses and doctors.
Legislation protecting workers' rights, e.g. Equal Pay Act 1970, National Minimum Wage Act 1998, Equality Act 2010.	Greater workers' rights made Britain a more attractive place to live and work.
Legislation passed regarding immigration and nationality, e.g. the Aliens Act (1905), Race Relations Act (1965).	Many migrant communities were given greater legal protection and rights.
In 1975, Britain joined the European Union. This affected legislation and the movement of people between Europe and Britain. In 2016 Britain voted to leave the EU.	Migration from Europe became easier, and Britain offered more support to asylum seekers. Leaving the EU was to change this.

Changes in industry and the economy

After 1900, the British economy had to adapt to changing world events.

Change in industry and the economy	Impact on migration
World wars demanded increases in production to supply the army. During the Second World War, factories and ports needed rebuilding after being bombed.	Britain's war effort relied on support from the people of its colonies. Britain encouraged migration after 1945 to help it rebuild.
Aeroplanes and large turbine-powered ships became more common, making the movement of people and goods around the world faster and easier.	With international travel easier, it made it easier for families of migrants to move longer distances, rather than just individuals. Communities of migrants became more common.
In the 1980s many businesses, e.g. shipbuilding, coal mining, iron foundries, etc., closed because of cheaper global competition.	Greater competition meant many companies were keen to recruit migrants, many of whom were often willing to work for lower wages.

Changes in the British Empire

The British Empire came to an end and Britain had to develop new relationships with the countries of the world.

Changes in the British Empire	Impact on migration
Soldiers from the Empire fought on the side of Britain in both world wars.	Many migrant groups felt stronger connections with Britain.
After the Second World War, the countries of the British Empire gained their independence.	Britain was keen to maintain links with its former colonies, encouraging migration post 1945.
British Commonwealth, set up in 1926, was renamed the Commonwealth of Nations in 1949. By 2010 it had 54 member states; many had been part of the British Empire.	The Commonwealth was seen by some as a 'family', encouraging greater migration links between members and Britain.

Attitudes in British society

The twentieth century was a period of huge change in British society. In 1900, Britain's population was largely white British. By 2000 Britain had become far more diverse. It was common for migrant communities – such as Leicester's Asian community – to be central to life in cities.

This often led to a hostile reaction from some who felt unsettled by the world changing quickly around them. Far-right, anti-immigrant parties, like the National Front, gained support. Anti-migrant feeling become more common, from complaints about jobs to landlords refusing to rent to black people.

It is important to note that many welcomed and supported migrants. But for many migrants, prejudice and racism was a part of everyday life.

The impact of the media

National newspapers and television became a part of everyday life during this period. They had a huge impact on shaping public opinion.

Many felt parts of the media encouraged feelings of hostility and suspicion against migrants. However, many in the media also campaigned against racism and prejudice.

Activity ?

In this chapter you will see how the media reported on different groups and events. What do you think their impact was? Take notes throughout this chapter on how the media reported on migrant communities. Use these to prepare a short argument for and against the media shaping public opinion on migrants.

Migration: where did people come from?

In the years from 1900, people migrated to Britain from many countries in the world.

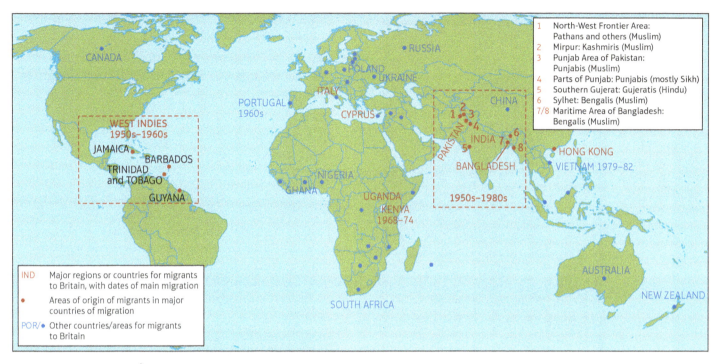

Figure 4.2 People migrated to Britain from many different parts of the world

Parliament passed several Acts affecting who could migrate to Britain and how they were treated once they arrived. You can read about these as you work through this chapter or look at page 123 if you want to find out more about it now.

Migration and the two world wars (1914–18 and 1939–45)

In 1914 the British government declared war against Germany. The British government turned to its Empire for support. The countries of the Empire contributed men, equipment, food and money.

- During the war, over 3 million soldiers from the Empire were moved, most usually to Europe, to fight Germany and its allies. Over 1 million of them came from India.
- Thousands of migrant merchant seamen served on the ships bringing food to Britain.
- In 1914, Germany invaded Belgium. Over 250,000 Belgians fled to Britain for safety.

1905 Aliens Act

Only people with money or jobs could migrate to Britain. This was the first time Britain put restrictions on who could enter the country. However, this Act was not applied to Belgian refugees fleeing to Britain after Germany invaded Belgium (see below).

Source A

A poster produced by the British government in 1915. It aimed to persuade men from the Empire to fight for Britain.

The lion standing on the rock symbolises Britain. The young lions gathered around the rock symbolise the countries of the Empire.

Source B

The British West Indies regiment in camp on the Albert-Amiens road in France, September 1916.

The peace that followed the war did not last. In 1933 the Nazi Party, led by Adolf Hitler, came to power in Germany. Before long it became clear that he was preparing for war, and in 1939 Britain was again at war with Germany and, again, needed the support of the Empire.

- About 8 million men from the British colonies and dominions volunteered, 2.5 million from India alone. Fewer soldiers went to Europe, but hundreds of thousands died all around the world fighting for Britain.

- Migrant merchant seamen again served on ships bringing food to Britain.

- Men and women from the Caribbean, Africa and other colonies migrated to Britain to work, supporting the war effort.

- Poland was occupied by Germany and Russia; approximately 160,000 Poles fled to Britain, around 14,000 joining the RAF.

Source C

A poster produced by the British government to encourage men in the British colonies* and dominions* to volunteer to fight in the Second World War. The men in the poster are (left to right) soldiers from India, East Africa, South Africa, New Zealand, a Canadian airman, an Australian soldier and a Royal Navy sailor.

Key terms

Colonies*

A colony is a country ruled by a larger one. Colonies in the British Empire, for example, were ruled by the British Parliament and monarch.

Dominions*

A dominion was a country with a high level of self-government while remaining within the British 'commonwealth' of nations.

Keeping children safe

Evacuees

When war began in 1939, the government made plans for evacuating children from cities likely to be bombed.

All children had a label tied to their coat or jacket. It just stated the child's name and age. The children didn't know where they were going, and neither did their parents. They were taken into the countryside to stay with strangers.

Children were allowed to take a change of clothing with them, but no toys or games. It looks as though this boy is with his younger brother and sister. Maybe he has all their clothes in that sack. There was no guarantee that brothers and sisters would be kept together.

Although the government authorised the evacuation of children, it was voluntary. No parent was forced to send their children away. The actual evacuation was managed by the National Federation of Women's Institutes. It was an enormous task as altogether 800,000 children were moved out of the cities and into the countryside.

This box contains a gas mask. Everyone in the country, including children, were issued one in case of a gas attack. One didn't happen, but the fear was there all the time.

Figure 4.3 Children being evacuated from their homes in Tyneside in north-east England; it was an area of heavy industry so was a target for German bombers

Kindertransport

Gradually, throughout the 1930s, it became clear that Nazi policies involved the persecution of Jews, and many fled Germany. The British government accepted about 60,000 Jewish refugees. However, it became more and more difficult for Jews to leave Germany, so attention turned to saving children.

- Jewish and Christian leaders persuaded the British government to drop visa and passport requirements and allow Jewish children to enter Britain immediately. This was called the Kindertransport ('kinder' means 'children' in German).

- The idea was that the children would return to Germany after the war, with the people looking after them paying the cost of their return. Families who couldn't afford this were helped by charities.

- The movement of thousands of children was organised by leaders of the German Jewish community.

- Between December 1938 and September 1939, 8,274 children travelled to Britain without their parents. War was declared in September 1939. The borders were closed and the Kindertransport stopped.

- No one knew then that the Nazis would go on to murder over 6 million Jews, among them the families of most of the Kindertransport children.

Interpretation 1

A statue at Liverpool Street station, London, commemorating the Kindertransport children.

Extend your knowledge

The Children's Overseas Reception Board (CORB) was a government-sponsored organisation for moving children from Britain so that they escaped the dangers of war. Some 2,644 children were moved to Canada, Australia, New Zealand and South Africa. They were called 'sea evacuees'. After two ships carrying children were torpedoed by German submarines, many drowned and the scheme stopped.

Activities ?

1   Look at Sources A and C. In both posters, the British government is trying to persuade people to migrate. What techniques is the government using? Are they the same in both posters?

2   Look at the photograph in Figure 4.3.

   a   Write down what you think, just from looking at the photo. For example, are they rich or poor? Happy or sad?

   b   Now choose one of the children. What is he or she thinking and feeling? Write a short paragraph, using what you noted down in (a) and what you know about their situation.

3   How far was the British government a factor in encouraging migration from 1914 to 1945?

4   Research Nicholas Winton. What did he do to save Jewish children?

Migration to rebuild Britain

After the Second World War, Britain desperately needed labour to recover.

- Houses and schools, factories, railway stations and churches needed rebuilding.
- The new National Health Service needed skilled workers.
- The whole transport system, particularly London Transport, needed rebuilding and staffing.

Workers from all over Europe migrated to help build up Britain. But there weren't enough of them.

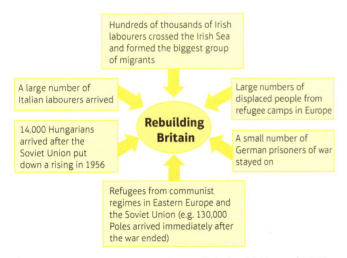

Figure 4.4 Europeans migrating to Britain, 1940s and 1950s

Parliament encouraged people from the colonies to migrate to Britain. Employers began looking beyond Europe in their recruitment drive, particularly to the Caribbean.

1948 British Nationality Act

British citizenship, and therefore British passports, were given to millions of people living in British colonies (e.g. Hong Kong) and in former British colonies (e.g. India). This gave them the right to enter Britain and to stay for as long as they wanted.

Migration from the Caribbean, 1947–60

Caribbean people arriving in Britain to help rebuild the country from 1948 to 1973 are often referred to as the 'Windrush generation'. The ship *SS Empire Windrush* brought over 800 Caribbean migrants, mainly from Jamaica and Trinidad, to London, docking at Tilbury, near London, in June 1948.

The migrants on board had many different skills. However, many were often forced to work in jobs they were overqualified for. This was usually due to prejudice and ignorance on the part of those employing them. You can read more about Caribbean migration in Chapter 5.

Extend your knowledge

Two ships brought migrants from the Caribbean before the *SS Empire Windrush*. In April 1947, 110 Caribbeans arrived in Liverpool aboard the *SS Ormonde*. In December 1947, 200 Caribbeans arrived in Southampton, having travelled from the Caribbean on the *SS Almanzora*.

The cost of sailing to Britain was too high for many people, and migration slowed down. It was easier and cheaper for Jamaicans to find work in the USA. Then two things happened to change this:

- In 1952 the USA put severe restrictions on immigration (from 65,000 to 800 per year), which reduced opportunities for workers from the Caribbean.
- In 1956 London Transport (which had been recruiting Caribbean people for some years) started paying migrants' fares and the workers paid it back over time from their wages.

Migration from the Caribbean rose steadily. In 1960, 58,000 Caribbean people settled in Britain.

Source D

Four Windrush migrants explain why they migrated to Britain.

1. Arthur Curling

I came to England in 1944 in the Air Force. I went back to Jamaica in 1946, but after spending two years there, it was too small for me. I had a reasonably good job in Jamaica… but it was just a matter of the island being too small. You don't realise how small until you've travelled. The *Windrush* came in 1948 and I returned to England and to more freedom.

2. Clinton Edwards

I first came to England during the war, in the RAF. When I went back home there was no work, so I decided to come back. There was a boat coming back, by the name of *Windrush*, and it was only £28, so I paid my fare and came back. The opportunity for jobs in England was better than back home in Jamaica.

3. Sam King

I was born in Jamaica in 1926. The 'mother country' was at war with Nazi Germany and I did believe in the British Empire and as a young man I volunteered to fight Nazi Germany. We as part of the former British Empire volunteered and contributed and I'm glad that we did. I came back to help build Britain.

4. Lucile Harris

I came here in 1948 because my husband sent for me. He and his brother came over a year before. They were at the dock waiting for me. I was very excited… because when he left we were just married. Jamaica in 1948 was all right. If my husband had not sent for me, I would not have come at that point. Maybe later.

Source E

A bus conductor on a London Transport bus.

Activities ?

1. What was the impact on migration of the 1948 British Nationality Act?

2. Read Source D. How similar were the migrants' hopes for the future?

3. Look at Source E. What 'message' is London Transport sending with this recruiting poster?

Asian migration to Britain from the Commonwealth after 1948

The 1948 British Nationality Act gave the right to live and work in Britain to millions of people. Many Asian people in India and Africa moved to Britain, which they often believed was a place of safety.

Migration from India and Pakistan, 1948–60

India gained independence from Britain in 1947 and the country was split into India and Pakistan. This partition led to extreme violence and many communities were badly affected. Thousands fled to Britain both at that time and in the years that followed.

- Although lumped together as 'Indians' by many white British people, these migrants came from a variety of backgrounds, each with different religions and customs. For example, Hindus from Gujarat, Sikhs from the Punjab and Muslims from Pakistan.

- Some were highly educated professionals, others rural labourers who had never been to a major city.

Migration from Kenya 1967

Asian people, mainly from India, had been migrating to Kenya since the 19th century. Many had become central to Kenya's prosperity, working as bankers, lawyers, teachers and doctors as well as in industry and business. When Kenya gained its independence from Britain, in 1963, over 100,000 Asians were living there.

Source F

Kenyan Asians arriving at Heathrow airport, 1967.

Source G

From the *Ugandan Resettlement Board, Bulletin 4*. This was a British agency appointed by the Home Secretary to help Ugandan Asians who were British passport holders.

Tons of treasured possessions were left behind – piled in heaps at Entebbe Airport to be wrecked by weather or pilferers. Of the baggage that did arrive in Britain, much had lost all identification

Activities ?

1. Make a list of all the similarities you can find between the migration to Britain of Asian people from Kenya in 1967 and Uganda in 1972. Now make a list of all the differences.

2. How similar was the experience of Asians migrating to Britain from Kenya and from Uganda?

> Following Kenyan independence in 1962, the prime minister, Jomo Kenyatta, told Kenyan Asians to choose between being Kenyan or British.

> Approximately 95,000 Kenyan Asians chose to remain British and so keep their British passports.

> In 1967 the Kenyan government ruled that all non-Kenyan Asians were foreigners and could only stay and work on a temporary basis.

> Fearing the worst, many of those with British passports fled to Britain.

Figure 4.5 Asian migration from Kenya to Britain

In 1967, 1,000 Kenyan Asians began to arrive in Britain every week. By 1968, 20,000 Kenyan Asians had migrated to Britain. The government put a limit on how many would be allowed in. This was a controversial decision with political consequences (see page 123).

Migration from Uganda, 1972

As in Kenya, the Asian community in Uganda played a large part in building up the country's economy. In 1962, when Uganda gained its independence from Britain, it was one of the most prosperous countries in Africa. Ten years later, almost 27,000 Ugandan Asians migrated to Britain. What had happened?

> In August 1972 President Idi Amin issued a decree expelling the entire Asian population.

> Idi Amin issued a second decree two days later stating that all professionals (e.g. doctors, teachers and lawyers) had to stay. If they left Uganda they would be commiting treason. All other Asians had to go.

> Britain tried to negotiate with the Ugandan government, and failed. So it offered the Ugandan Asians a choice of either an Indian or a British passport.

> Most chose a British passport, believing Britain would offer greater stability and security. They left Uganda with nothing more than they could carry.

Figure 4.6 Asian migration from Uganda to Britain

Exam-style question, Section B

Explain one reason why independence for Britain's colonies resulted in increased migration to Britain. **(4 marks)**

Exam tip

The question is asking you to explain **why** something happened. So don't just describe what happened, but look behind the migration to give an explanation as to why migration happened – and why the migrants should choose to go to Britain.

Migrants since the 1970s

For many years British governments encouraged people from the Commonwealth to migrate to Britain to work. These were economic migrants*. After 1973 another very large group of economic migrants were also able to work in Britain.

The European Union

In 1973 Britain joined the European Economic Community (EEC), which allowed people to move freely between member countries. In 1973 there were just nine members. By 2007, there were 28 and the EEC had become the European Union (EU). The idea was that free movement would help economies to prosper.

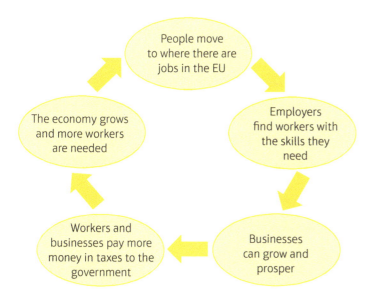

Figure 4.7 How the free movement of people can help economies to prosper

Many people were unhappy in Britain in 2004 when nine Eastern European states joined the EU. Why was this?

- Until 1990 these states had been communist; wages were low and their economies were weak.

- Thousands of migrants from these countries travelled to Britain, where they earned money to send back to their families. For example, by 2005 there were 300,000 people from Poland working in Britain.

- Migration rose steadily, leading to political and social issues (see pages 122–29). In 2016, Britain voted on EU membership: 52% voted to leave, some naming migration as their main reason for voting 'Brexit'*.

Asylum seekers and refugees

In 1951 Britain signed up to the United Nations* Convention on Refugees. What did this mean?

- Britain, along with the other countries who signed, promised to offer asylum* to foreign refugees who asked for it and who had evidence they were facing persecution in their own country.

- The numbers claiming asylum increased and the situation became more complicated. In 1987 there were 4,256 applications from refugees for asylum in Britain. By 2002 this had risen to 84,130.

- The system for checking asylum requests began to fail. There were simply too many requests and too few officials.

- Desperate refugees, often paying people smugglers*, tried to cross the English Channel in dangerous ways.

It is important to realise that there are accepted, legal ways of entering the country and claiming asylum. Crossing the Channel in inflatable boats or hiding on lorries are illegal methods of entry to Britain.

Key terms

Economic migrants*
People who move from one country to another, looking for higher wages and a better standard of living.

Brexit*
Short for 'Britain-exit' – leaving the EU.

United Nations*
An international organisation that aims to maintain world peace through various organisations.

Asylum*
The protection provided by a state to someone who has left their own country because of fear of persecution.

People smugglers*
People who illegally smuggle refugees across country boundaries for money.

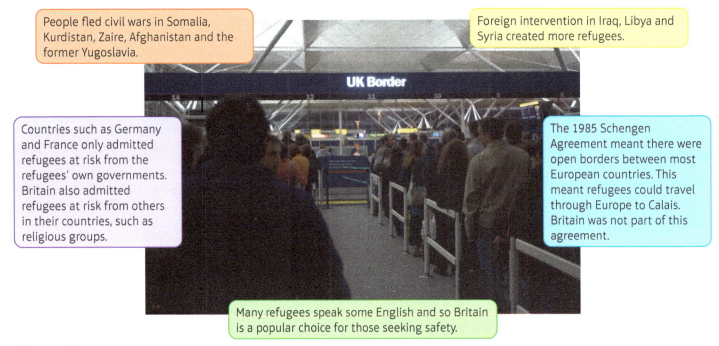

People fled civil wars in Somalia, Kurdistan, Zaire, Afghanistan and the former Yugoslavia.

Foreign intervention in Iraq, Libya and Syria created more refugees.

Countries such as Germany and France only admitted refugees at risk from the refugees' own governments. Britain also admitted refugees at risk from others in their countries, such as religious groups.

The 1985 Schengen Agreement meant there were open borders between most European countries. This meant refugees could travel through Europe to Calais. Britain was not part of this agreement.

Many refugees speak some English and so Britain is a popular choice for those seeking safety.

Figure 4.8 Asylum seekers

Activities ?

1   Why did migration to Britain increase as a result of its membership of the EU?
2   How far did signing up to the United Nations Convention on Refugees lead to changing attitudes to migrants in Britain?

4.1 Summary

- During both world wars the British government encouraged people from the Empire, and then the Commonwealth, to leave their countries and fight for Britain. Refugees from Belgium (First World War), Poland (Second World War) and Nazi Germany (60,000 Jewish children) also arrived in Britain.
- After the Second World War, Britain actively recruited workers, especially from the Caribbean, to help rebuild Britain. The 1948 Nationality Act gave British citizenship to members of the Commonwealth.
- Independence for Britain's colonies resulted in migration to Britain from India, Kenya and Uganda.
- Membership of the EU led to the migration to Britain of people from Europe.
- Refugees seeking asylum in Britain increased from 1951.

Checkpoint

Strengthen

S1 Which groups of people fled to Britain because of the world wars?

S2 Why did people migrate to Britain from the Caribbean in the period 1947–60?

S3 Why did migration from Europe to Britain increase after 1973?

Challenge

C1 Explain the role of the British government in encouraging migration during the years after 1900.

4.2 The experiences of migrants in Britain

Learning outcomes

- Understand the ways in which, and how successfully, migrants settled in Britain.
- Understand the differing relationships between migrants and the existing population.

The experiences of migrants in Britain in the years after 1900 were very different from one another. Some found local communities accepted them and settling in was relatively easy. Others struggled with racial prejudice. What life was like for immigrants depended on:

- when they arrived
- where they lived
- what their skills were
- what ethnic group they belonged to.

The First World War

The Belgians who fled the Germans were welcomed. Charities found homes for them and there was plenty of work available as so many men were away fighting. More than 60,000 Belgians worked in Britain during the war. Many set up their own businesses. The government made it clear that they were expected to stay only for the duration of the war.

In 1918 their jobs were ended, and all Belgians were provided with a free one-way ticket home. The Belgian government also needed them to help rebuild their country. About 90% went back.

Enemy aliens

It was different for the Germans. There were thousands living and working in Britain when war broke out. Hurriedly, in August 1914, Parliament passed the British Nationality and Status of Aliens Act that made it clear what was to happen. They were enemy aliens.

People living in Britain reacted in different ways to the German people who had been living and working amongst them. The media fuelled anti-German feelings, as you can see from the front page of the *Daily Sketch* on page 116.

Key term

Interned*

To hold someone prisoner, often for political reasons.

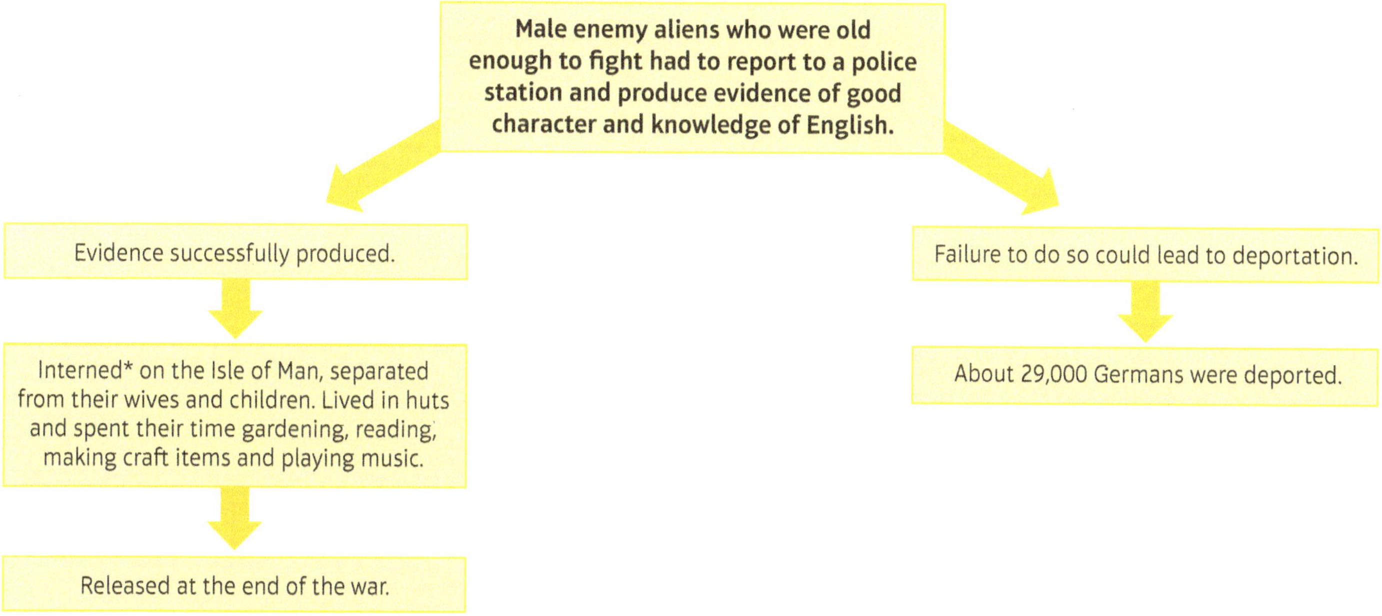

Male enemy aliens who were old enough to fight had to report to a police station and produce evidence of good character and knowledge of English.

Evidence successfully produced.

Interned* on the Isle of Man, separated from their wives and children. Lived in huts and spent their time gardening, reading, making craft items and playing music.

Released at the end of the war.

Failure to do so could lead to deportation.

About 29,000 Germans were deported.

Figure 4.9 What happened to the Germans living in Britain?

Mobs attacked and looted shops owned by Germans in Liverpool, Manchester, London and other cities. Violence increased after the Germans sank a British passenger ship, the *Lusitania*, off the west coast of Ireland.

The Royal Family changed its surname from the German 'Saxe-Coburg-Gotha' to the English 'Windsor'. Many ordinary families did the same.

German food was taken off menus and shopkeepers refused to stock German sausages.

Workers went on strike in factories employing Germans. There were demonstrations against German doctors and lawyers.

The government sent in the army to protect German properties and businesses in Britain.

Figure 4.10 Anti-German actions and attitudes

Trouble at the docks

When the war ended in 1918, returning servicemen wanted their old jobs back. Many were angry to find some jobs had been filled by migrant workers. The most serious resentments were at the docks.

- Merchant seamen had joined the Royal Navy, and lascars had filled their jobs on cargo ships.
- After the war, companies kept hiring lascars because they were willing to work for lower wages. The returning merchant seaman blamed them for making it harder to get their jobs back.
- Riots broke out in many ports, the worst being in Tiger Bay, Cardiff. The mayor of Cardiff blamed white seamen, but also said unemployed lascars should be sent back where they had come from.
- The National Union of Seamen, instead of inviting lascars to join the Union and fight for better wages for everyone, encouraged white seamen to believe the lascars were stealing their jobs.

This was to be a pattern throughout the century: fears over job losses were almost always blamed on immigrants 'taking our jobs'.

Source A

Police trying to remove a barricade built across Cable Street, Whitechapel, on 4 October 1936.

Key term

British Union of Fascists* (BUF)

A British political party formed in 1932 by Oswald Mosley. The party's Nazi-style anti-Semitism led to violent clashes with anti-fascists.

Case study

Battle of Cable Street

The 1930s were years of high unemployment. Some blamed Jewish migrants. The British Union of Fascists* (BUF) targeted the East End of London. The BUF planned to march through Whitechapel, the city's main Jewish neighbourhood, also home to Irish and Somali people.

On 4 October 1936 about 100,000 people – Jews, Irish, Somalis and other ethnic minorities, along with dockers, trade unionists and socialists, gathered in Cable Street, Whitechapel, to stop the march. They blocked the street with barricades, hoping to stop the march. However, 6,000 police, many on horseback, cleared the route, with running battles between anti-fascist demonstrators and the police. Eventually, after over 100 arrests and injuries, the BUF were turned back and escorted by the police into central London.

The Second World War

What happened to the Poles, Jewish children and evacuees after the war?

Polish servicemen

When the war ended in 1945, Poland was controlled by the Soviet Union, a communist dictatorship that soon became an enemy of Britain. Many Poles did not want to return home.

In 1947 Parliament passed the Polish Resettlement Act giving Polish servicemen the right to remain in Britain – something that 120,000 of them chose to do. The Act also allowed their families to join them.

The government wanted the Poles to work in British industries, particularly mining. At first, there was opposition from the unions, but gradually the Poles won acceptance, due largely to their war service and hard work. Before long, there were Polish communities in many large industrial towns.

Jewish children and British evacuees

There were both similarities and differences in the experiences of these children.

Figure 4.11 Looking after the children?

Enemy aliens

The British government set up tribunals to decide which Germans living in Britain posed a threat to national security. Many had lived and worked in Britain for a long time. Some were Jewish refugees from Nazism. People recognised that these migrants were no threat to Britain – or were also victims of Nazism. In the end, only 348 men out of 35,000 were interned.

This number increased in 1940 when Italy, an ally of Germany, joined the war. The British government began mass internment of Germans and Italians. This only lasted for about a year and then almost all internees were released. Public opinion had turned against internment. In July 1940 the *SS Arandora Star* carrying 1,150 German and Italian internees to Canada was sunk by a German U-boat. Over half the internees drowned. Events such as this made the public more sympathetic to the internees.

Activities   ?

1. Look at Figure 4.10. How is the newspaper, the *Daily Sketch*, stirring up anti-German feelings?

2. Why was there so much trouble in Britain's docks in 1918?

3. Explain why police and anti-fascist demonstrators fought in Cable Street on 4 October 1936. Use Source A in your answer.

4. Why were the Poles at the end of the Second World War treated differently from the Belgians at the end of the First World War?

1968: 'Rivers of Blood'

In the early 1950s migrants had been mainly single people. Over time it became more common for immigrants to be families looking to settle.

The arrival of the Kenyan Asians in 1967 (see pages 111–12) focused media and political attention on what some called the 'immigration problem'. That year a far-right political party, the National Front* (NF), was founded. It wanted to end immigration and expel immigrants from Britain.

Key terms

The National Front*

A small, far-right political party with fascist views that is opposed to immigration. It was founded in 1967.

Shadow cabinet*

Key members of the opposition party, chosen to 'shadow' cabinet members of the government.

Enoch Powell was the Conservative MP for Wolverhampton, one of the centres of Caribbean and Asian populations. He had been Health Secretary in 1960 and had recruited 18,000 Indian doctors for the NHS. On 20 April 1968 he made an explosive speech.

The speech became known as the 'rivers of blood' speech. It ended his political career. He was sacked from the shadow cabinet* and never returned. Powell's speech had a huge impact. London dock workers stopped work and marched through the city in support of him. A survey found 75% of people in Britain believed there were too many ethnic minority migrants living there.

Source B

Extract from the speech made by Enoch Powell on 20 April 1968. In the final sentence of this extract, Powell compared himself to an ancient Roman prophet ('the Roman') who predicted a Roman civil war and Rome's river Tiber being filled ('foaming') with blood. He was suggesting migration would lead to the same thing happening in Britain.

In 15 or 20 years, on present trends, there will be in this country three-and-a-half million Commonwealth immigrants and their descendants… How can its dimensions be reduced? By stopping, or virtually stopping, further inflow and by promoting the maximum outflow.

To the immigrant, entry to this country was admission to privileges and opportunities eagerly sought, the impact on the existing population was very different. For reasons they could not comprehend and on which they were never consulted, they found themselves strangers in their own country. They found their wives unable to obtain hospital beds in childbirth, their children unable to obtain school places, their homes and neighbourhoods changed beyond recognition.

As I look ahead, I am filled with foreboding; like the Roman, I seem to see the River Tiber foaming with much blood.

Race riots

The case studies on Bristol and Leicester (pages 131–34 and 135–38) and Chapter 5 on Notting Hill will tell you a great deal about the experiences of migrants in post-war Britain. Their experiences were mirrored in many towns and cities throughout Britain.

In some cities, tensions grew to breaking point. Immigrants, white English people, and the police fought running battles in the streets.

Brixton, April 1981

On 10 April 1981 rioting began in Brixton, south London, where about 25% of the residents were from an ethnic minority. Rioters fought the police for three days. The rioters were mainly second-generation young men, born to parents from the Windrush generation. More than 300 people were injured and about £7.5 million (the equivalent of £29 million in 2021) of damage was caused.

Source C

Rioting in Brixton, south London, April 1981.

The trigger was accusations of police brutality, but tensions had been building for years.

- Brixton was an area of poor housing, a higher-than-average crime rate and high unemployment, where about half of the young black men were unemployed.
- In early April 1981, the police started Operation Swamp 81 to target street crime, increasing the numbers of police officers in Brixton.
- The police used the SUS law (SUSpected Persons Law) to stop and search anyone they believed likely to commit a crime. In six days, over 1,000 people in Brixton were stopped and searched, most of them black.
- The black community argued that they were being persecuted – especially as the police were exempt from the Race Relations Act of 1976, which banned discrimination on the grounds of race.

Extend your knowledge

The Scarman Report

The government set up an enquiry into the Brixton riots, led by Lord Scarman. Scarman's report found there had been 'disproportionate and indiscriminate' use of the SUS powers by the police against black people; that 'racial disadvantage was a fact of current British life' but that 'institutional racism' did not exist in the Metropolitan Police. The SUS law was ended and a Police Complaints Authority created.

Burnley, June 2001

In 2001 tensions in Bradford, Oldham and then Burnley led to violence. These cities all had large, mostly Asian, migrant communities. All three riots had the same pattern of economic hardship and racism, made worse by the presence of the BNP*.

Outside a nightclub in Burnley, on Friday 22 June 2001, a fight broke out between rival drug dealers; some were white, some Asian. As the fight spread, an Asian taxi driver was attacked with a hammer by a group of white youths.

A rumour spread that the taxi driver had been killed. The next night a group of Asian men attacked the Duke of York pub in Colne Road, and its white customers fought back. Rioting continued over the weekend, with hundreds involved in firebombing and assaults. The riots turned into a racist conflict.

Key term

British National Party*

A far-right fascist political party that was founded in 1982.

Source D

Rioting in Burnley, Lancashire, in June 2001.

The trigger was a violent dispute between rival drug dealers, but again tensions had been building for years.

- Burnley had been a prosperous mill town, but in the 1980s cheap textile imports led to many mills closing.
- More than 25% of Burnley's houses were unfit to live in. At least 40% of households depended on state benefits.
- There was no multicultural community in the town. Whites worked with whites and Asians with Asians. Schools were almost all 'single race'.
- Asians felt the town council treated white communities better than them. White communities felt the opposite.

Prejudice or ignorance?

Not all the reactions to migrants were violent. Many were subtle, as you'll see from Sources E, F and G. Parliament passed legislation trying to improve relationships between different communities. But changing attitudes was far more difficult than passing laws.

Source E

Ivan Weekes, who arrived in Britain in 1955, remembers what it was like for black people.

I used to feel not only frightened but wondering what is going to happen next. I could get bumped off. And people would look at you, like spears, daggers. People would spit at you. If you went to sit down beside someone on a bus, they'd shuffle up. But then somebody would look at you, see that you are as frightened as hell and say 'Oh mate, take no notice of them. We're not all the same.' I think that's so important to say. That was my experience. Just those few words gave me two things: hope and comfort. People are not all the same.

Source F

Andrea Levy was born in London in 1956. Her parents were Jamaican. She became a famous novelist. Here she remembers what it was like to be a child in the 1950s and 1960s.

We were asked, 'When are you going back to your own country?', 'Why are you here?', 'Why is your food so funny?', 'Why does your hair stick up?', 'Why do you smell?' The clear message was that our family was foreign and had no right to be here. When a member of the far-right group the National Front waved one of their leaflets in my face and started laughing, I felt I owed them some sort of apology. I wanted them to like me. It would be years before I realised I could be angry with them.

The racism I encountered was rarely violent, or extreme, but it was insidious [subtle] and ever present and it had a profound effect on me. I hated myself. I was ashamed of my family, and embarrassed that they came from the Caribbean.

Source G

Comments made by a white, male delegate at the Trades Union Congress conference in 1958.

People talk about a colour problem arising in Britain. But how can there be a colour problem here? Even after all the immigration of the past few years there are only 190,000 coloured people in our population of over 50 million – that is only four out of every 1,000. The problem is not black skin but white prejudice.

Activities ?

1 List the reasons why riots broke out in Brixton in 1981 and in Burnley in 2001. How similar were the tensions that led to riots in Brixton and Burnley?

2 Both Ivan Weekes and Andrea Levy experienced racism. How far were their experiences the same? How do you think they might have replied to the TUC delegate (Source G)?

Exam-style question

Why did the experience of migrants in Britain change in the years after 1945?

You may use the following in your answer:

- the British Nationality Act of 1948
- the role of the police.

You **must** also use information of your own.

(12 marks)

Exam tip

The question tests an understanding of key features and causation. First, focus on those factors that enabled migrants to have a positive experience, and then those that made for a negative experience. Try to make links between the factors that will emphasise the reasons for the changes.

4.2 Summary

- During the First World War many British Germans were interned as 'enemy aliens'. In the Second World War there was much less enthusiasm for interning 'enemy aliens'. Polish veterans were welcomed.
- Tension over jobs was an issue. Lascars took on many shipping jobs during the First World War. Returning seamen wanted their jobs back. This led to violence in many ports.
- Groups like the BUF and BNP made racist campaigns against migrants. In April 1968 Enoch Powell's 'rivers of blood' speech called for sending immigrants back.
- Violence was a continual problem, from the Battle of Cable Street (1936) to riots in Brixton (1981), Burnley (2001) and other towns and cities.

Checkpoint

Strengthen

S1 What happened to Belgian refugees after the First World War and Polish airmen after the Second World War?

S2 Name two things that happened as a result of Enoch Powell's 'rivers of blood' speech.

S3 Give three reasons for the race riots of 1981 and 2001.

Challenge

C1 Explain why Germans living in Britain during the First World War were treated differently from Germans living in Britain during the Second World War.

4.3 The impact of migrants on Britain

Learning outcomes

- Understand the impact of migrants on politics and Parliament.
- Understand the impact of migrants on public services and the economy.
- Understand the impact of migrants on culture and the urban environment.

Migrants had a significant impact on Britain, politically, economically and culturally.

- Politically, racial tensions led to the rise in support for far-right political parties. This also led to organised opposition against them, and Parliament passing legislation to support diversity and equality.
- Economically, migrants worked in factories, mills, engineering works and in transport. They were essential to the functioning of the NHS.
- Culturally, migrants brought music, dance and food, changing the face of many cities.

Source A

A woman arrives from Barbados at Victoria Station on 4 January 1955.

Parliament and immigration

Immigration was a tricky issue for politicians of all parties. They had to balance the interests of:

- The economy – many employers depended on immigrant labour.
- The voters – many were against immigration and the National Front was gaining in popularity. MPs had to listen to their voters, otherwise they wouldn't get elected again.
- The immigrants – they needed the protection of the state, and many of them were voters too.
- Society – it needed to prevent racial tension, and the violence it could cause, in Britain's cities.

At different times, policy was driven by one or other of these demands, and sometimes by more than one.

What did Parliament do in the 1960s and 1970s?

You read about the legislation passed by Parliament in 1905 and 1948 (pages 105, 107 and 110). What did Parliament do after the immigration in the 1950s, when migrants arrived in Britain to help rebuild the country after the Second World War?

Date	Act	Comment
1962	**The Commonwealth Immigrants Act** introduced a voucher system. Only those with a valuable skill or who could take a job where there was a shortage of workers could get a voucher.	Ended the automatic right of Commonwealth passport holders to live and work in Britain. Aimed to restrict immigration from the Caribbean and Asia (migrants from there were thought to be unskilled workers). **But**, it also increased immigration as more than 130,000 people decided to migrate to Britain before it came into effect, more than the previous five years put together. This also happened with the 1968 Act.
1965	**The Race Relations Act** made it illegal to discriminate against any person because of their race. The Race Relations Board was set up in 1966 to handle complaints about discrimination.	The Board had no power to enforce its decisions.
1968	**The Commonwealth Immigrants Act** reduced the number of vouchers available. Applicants now had to have been born in Britain or have parents or grandparents born in Britain.	This favoured white immigrants from Canada, Australia and New Zealand. **But** there was outcry against using it to keep out Kenyan Asians, and the government let them in.
1968	**The Race Relations Act** made discrimination in housing and employment illegal.	Employers could still discriminate indirectly, e.g. claiming a white candidate had more experience.
1971	**The Immigration Act** replaced vouchers with work permits for specific time periods. This did not apply to people with British-born parents or grandparents.	This again favoured white immigrants from Canada, Australia and New Zealand. **But** there was outcry against using it to keep out Ugandan Asians, and the government let them in.

The Race Relations Act (1976) finally made it illegal to discriminate on the grounds of race, nationality or ethnic origin. It covered employment, education, training, housing, and the providing of any goods, facilities and services. It set up:

- tribunals to hear complaints from people believing they had suffered discrimination
- the Commission for Racial Equality to investigate and combat racism.

Source B

Notices like these were common in 1960s Britain.

Activities

1 Work with a partner. Do you think the legislation that followed dealt with that the issue of racial tension? Write a paragraph to explain your thinking.

2 The Immigration Acts of 1962, 1968 and 1971 have been described by some people as 'racist'. Explain whether you agree. [Hint: first define what you mean by racist, and then apply that definition to the Acts.]

Migrants take action

The aims of migrants were varied. Some urged decolonisation*, others the removal of the colour bar*. What united them all was the need to be treated equally with white people. Many of the initiatives started by migrants were supported by white British people.

1900 Pan-African Conference held in London. Organised by Trinidadian barrister Sylvester-Williams. Campaigned for full political rights for Africans worldwide. Met six times in the years to 1945.

Action before 1945

1931 Jamaican doctor Harold Moody founded the League of Coloured Peoples in London. Became an influential pressure group for black rights in Britain.

1925 Nigerian Ladipo Solanke, a student at London University, founded the West African Students' Union. campaigned against the British Empire and racism.

Figure 4.12 Migrants taking action before 1945

Doreen Lawrence: campaigner

On 22 April 1993 Stephen Lawrence, a black teenager aged 18, was stabbed to death while waiting for a bus in Eltham, south-east London. Five suspects were arrested but not charged. What happened next?

- Stephen's parents, Doreen and Neville, claimed the Metropolitan Police had not carried out a professional investigation into their son's murder. They said the police had been incompetent and racist.

- A massive publicity campaign began, led by Doreen Lawrence, with the support of many people in the community, media and politics. This led to a private prosecution* in 1994 that failed.

- In 1997 an inquest* was held into Stephen's death at which the five suspects refused to answer any questions. The *Daily Mail* publicly accused the suspects of murder.

- In 1999, the government set up a public enquiry into 'matters arising from the death of Stephen Lawrence'. The enquiry, led by the judge Sir William MacPherson, found the Metropolitan Police to be institutionally racist*. This, along with poor leadership, was the main reason for their failure to solve the case.

Case study

Harold Moody, 1882–1947

Harold Moody was born in Jamaica. In 1904 he travelled to London to study medicine at King's College Hospital. He struggled to find housing and was turned down for two jobs because he was black.

In 1931 Moody founded the League of Coloured Peoples and became its first president. For 30 years the League campaigned tirelessly for civil rights, helping thousands of British black people.

Moody died from influenza after a tour of the USA in the winter of 1946–47, raising funds for a colonial culture centre in London. The League continued, but a lack of funds caused it to close in 1951.

Key terms

Decolonisation*

The granting of independence to colonies.

Colour bar*

Denying ethnic minority people access to the same rights and opportunities as white people. This particularly applies to jobs, recreation, housing and promotion.

Private prosecution*

A criminal prosecution brought by a private individual or organisation, instead of a public prosecution brought by the Crown.

Inquest*

A legal enquiry to establish the facts surrounding a death.

Institutionally racist*

Racism embedded in an institution that influences the ways in which people work there.

Source C

There remained strong media interest in the Stephen Lawrence case, with the conviction of two of his murderers in January 2012 becoming front page news.

Doreen Lawrence had led the campaign to find justice for her murdered son. The campaign led to changes in attitudes to racism on the part of the public and the police.

It also led to a change in the law: the rule against double jeopardy (that prevented someone being tried twice for the same crime) was dropped. Two of Stephen's killers were found guilty of his murder in 2012. Doreen Lawrence didn't stop there.

Awarded honarary doctorates from the Open, Cambridge and West London universities. Became chancellor of de Montfort University 2016–2020.

Founded the Stephen Lawrence Charitable Trust to promote community relations and was awarded the OBE for her community work.

Doreen Lawrence's achievements

Became a life peer in 2013 as Baroness Lawrence of Clarendon in the Commonwealth Realm of Jamaica. She sits on the Labour benches.

Established the Stephen Lawrence prize, a bursary for young architects.

Figure 4.13 Doreen Lawrence's achievements

Pressure groups

Pressure groups usually come about in response to a particular event, and they often continue long after the event is over.

Fascist and anti-fascist groups, however, were founded in response to a general rise in the immigration of people of an ethnic minority.

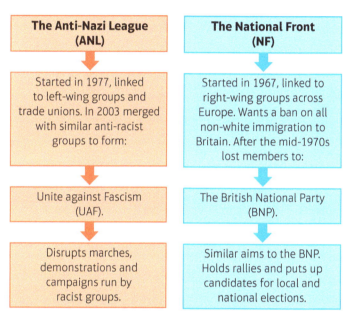

Figure 4.14 Fascist and anti-fascist organisations

Show Racism the Red Card (SRTRC)

A player shown a red card in football is sent off the pitch at once. SRTRC is a charity working with high-profile footballers as anti-racist role models. It began in North Tyneside in 1996 and spread throughout Britain and other countries. It works with schools and youth clubs as well as running workshops and training sessions.

Black Lives Matter (BLM)

The BLM movement began in the USA in 2013 protesting against police brutality and racially motivated violence against black people and demanding criminal justice reform.

It became an international protest movement in 2020 following the death in Minneapolis of George Floyd after police officer Derek Chauvin knelt on his neck. In 2021 Chauvin was found guilty of murder.

Source D

A Black Lives Matter march in Birmingham, June 2020, protesting the death of George Floyd.

However, it was in transport and the NHS where migrants were vital to meet the need for workers.

Transport

London Transport advertised in the Caribbean (see page 111) and set up a recruitment office in Bridgetown, the capital of Barbados. Not all recruits were employed via the official recruiting service; some were already in the UK and applied in the usual way.

Women were taken on as bus conductors, station staff and canteen workers. Later, they trained to be bus drivers. In 1968, London Transport had 73,000 employees, of whom around 9,000 were from an ethnic minority.

Activities ?

1 What, in your view, was the most important achievement of **(a)** Harold Moody and **(b)** Doreen Lawrence?

2 Harold Moody failed to raise enough money to keep the League of Coloured Peoples going; memorials to Stephen Lawrence have been defaced with racist graffiti. Does this mean Harold Moody and Doreen Lawrence failed?

3 What is the best way to combat racism? Discuss this in your class.

Case study

Ruel Moseley, bus conductor

Ruel Moseley worked as a bus conductor in Barbados before applying to work for London Transport in 1959. At first, he wanted to increase his skills, earn money and then return to Barbados for a better job.

Some passengers refused to touch tickets or change from a black man. Black migrants were promoted more slowly than their white colleagues. London Transport expected many migrants to fill only basic roles before returning home.

Housing was hard to find: Ruel was forced to share a room with five other men. He later said: 'However poor you were in Barbados you were not used to sharing a room. Here, you had to be in work by 6.30 am. You had to keep your dignity, you had to keep working. A lot of boys came here and had mental breakdowns because of that stress.'

Ruel never went back to Barbados. He married and had a family, working with London Transport until he retired in 1990. Like many Barbadians, he played cricket for transport company teams, including for Central Road Services cricket team, which went 26 years undefeated.

The economy: textiles, transport and the NHS

Britain desperately needed migrant workers to get the economy going after 1945 (see pages 110–11). Migrants played a vital role in rebuilding many parts of Britain's economy, for example, in 1971:

- Over 100,000 migrants were working in the textile industry. In Bradford's textile mills, immigrants, mainly from Pakistan, accepted lower wages than British workers. This helped the mills to survive.

- Nearly 300,000 migrants were working in manufacturing and engineering, mainly in the West Midlands.

The National Health Service

The National Health Service was launched in 1948 by the government. It provided medical care for the entire population 'from cradle to grave'. It needed a huge number of doctors and nurses as well as porters, cleaners and administration staff. Immigrants were vital to starting the NHS and continue to play a huge role in keeping it running today.

- In 1949 the NHS began recruiting nurses from the Caribbean. By 1955 there were recruitment campaigns in 16 British colonies and former colonies. By 1965 around 5,000 Jamaican nurses worked in the NHS.
- Between 1953 and 1955, 12% of NHS doctors were trained overseas – many were Jewish and European refugees from Nazi-occupied Europe. By 1977, 12% of student nurse and midwife recruits were migrants.
- By 1980, 18,000–20,000 NHS doctors were born outside the UK, with 50% from India and Pakistan.
- By 2003, 29.4% of NHS doctors and 43.5% of NHS nurses were born outside the UK.

> ### Extend your knowledge
>
> Jamaican Professor Jacqueline Dunkley-Bent and Trinidad-born Arona Ahmed were the midwives who delivered Prince George in July 2013 and Princess Charlotte in May 2015, the first two children of the Duke and Duchess of Cambridge.

Source E

Part of an interview given by Professor Donna Kinnair to the *Guardian* newspaper on 10 June 2020. Professor Kinnair was appointed Chief Executive and General Secretary of the Royal College of Nursing in August 2018.

After university, I signed up for Marks & Spencer's management trainee scheme. When I was pregnant with my first child, I went to see a nurse. I said to her: 'I've always wanted to be a nurse, you know.' She said: 'I don't see any reason why you can't be.'

I started my training in 1983 at the Royal London hospital when my son was six months old. My sister had applied to do nursing at that same hospital a year before me. When she went for her interview, they tried to persuade her to train as a state-enrolled nurse, which is a lower grade than a registered general nurse.

She told me: 'Watch out, they'll try to push you into a lower grade.' She was right... I said: 'No thank you, not with my qualifications, and if you don't want me, I've got an interview at [St Bartholomew's Hospital] down the road.' That was my first experience of racism in the NHS.

Sometimes patients would say: 'I don't want to have any black hands on me.' That was fairly common in the 1980s. It was obvious that some people didn't expect me to progress. They would be surprised that I had such a good education, as if black people couldn't go to university.

Changing cities and towns

Many migrants were forced to live in run-down and damaged areas of Britain's inner cities. Migrant communities regenerated those areas, introducing new businesses and cultural events.

- They rebuilt many houses, turning them into warm and comfortable homes.
- In the 1960s, many local stores closed because of competition from supermarkets. Asian entrepreneurs, in particular, revived these shops, providing local communities with a service and building successful businesses. Restaurants serving food from migrant communities – India, the Caribbean etc. – became common in towns and cities across the country.

> ### Activities ?
>
> 1 Immigrants were clearly needed to get the British economy going again. Why, then, did Ruel Moseley and Donna Kinnair face discrimination? Discuss this in your class.
>
> 2 Ruel Moseley and Donna Kinnair had very different careers, and they each faced two different kinds of prejudice. Describe what these were.

- Areas where migrant communities lived were often very close. Self-help organisations were formed to assist the community with problems. A community spirit helped provide a sense of security and familiarity for migrants and their descendants, especially when dealing with hostility from other groups.
- Many of these areas became lively places to visit, with food and music from other countries (such as India or the Caribbean) that, for British people, were exciting and different. Some migrant community areas, such as Chinatown in Manchester or 'the Golden Mile' in Leicester (see page 138) became tourist attractions.

(see page 138)

Source F

The entrance to Chinatown, Manchester.

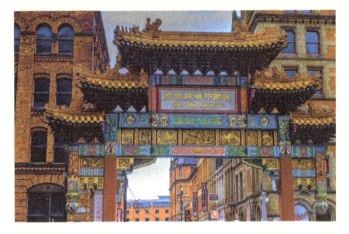

Religion

Migrants brought their religions to Britain. Particularly from the Caribbean, many migrants were Christian. Although there was some hostility, they helped to revitalise churches in Britain.

- Cities with large Muslim populations built splendid mosques. The festivals and celebrations of migrant communities became part of regular life.
- Immigrants from India and Pakistan brought Hindu and Muslim religions to the heart of British communities, with festivals like Diwali, the festival of lights, celebrated by Hindus, and the Muslim festival of Eid al-Fitr that ends the Ramadan fast.
- Pentecostal Christianity and gospel singing, brought to Britain by Caribbean immigrants, renewed Christianity in many inner cities and kept churches open that otherwise would have become disused.

Source G

The Shah Jahan mosque, Woking, Surrey.

Food and fun

Immigrants changed the British diet for ever!

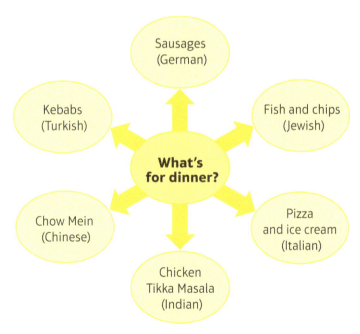

Figure 4.15 What's for dinner?

Sport, music and the media

Immigrants, first, second and third generation, have played a massive part in sport, politics, music and the media. Here are some of them.

Marcus Rashford plays football for Manchester United and campaigns for the homeless and ending child hunger. He has a West Indian grandmother.

Moira Stuart began working in TV and radio journalism in the 1970s. In 1981, she became the first African-Caribbean female newsreader to appear on British national television.

Lucian Freud was one of the most important portrait painters of the 20th century. He fled Germany with his Jewish family when Hitler and the Nazis came to power in 1933.

Jessica Ennis won a gold medal in the heptathlon at the London Olympic Games in 2012. She has a Jamaican father.

Mo Farah is a successful British track athlete, winning gold medals in the 2012 and 2016 Olympic Games. He was born in Somalia, migrating to England with his family when he was eight years old.

Ms Dynamite is a rapper, singer, songwriter and record producer. She has a Jamaican father and a Scottish mother.

Diane Abbott is an MP, and in 1987 was the first black woman to be elected to parliament. She has worked in the Labour Party's shadow cabinet. Her parents are Jamaican.

Rishi Sunak is a Conservative MP who became chancellor of the exchequer in February 2020. His father was born in Kenya and his mother in Tanzania and his grandparents are Punjabi Hindus who emigrated to Britain from East Africa in the 1960s.

Figure 4.16 Part of British culture

Exam-style question, Section B

The question is asking you about impact, so don't describe what migrants did, but think about the consequences of what they did. Then, when planning your answer, decide which was the most significant. Don't just say which you think was the most significant, but say why you think this.

Activities ?

1   Work in groups of two or three. Choose one area that particularly interests you: food, music, the media or sport, and research the impact of immigrants, using local examples where you can. Present your findings in any way you choose – a collage, a spidergram, a ferris wheel, for example.

2   In what ways did immigrants help make British culture more diverse?

The continuing story: Windrush scandal

The 'Windrush generation' played an important part in building up Britain's economy after the Second World War (see pages 110–11). So what was the scandal?

- In 2012 the government announced people had to prove they had a right to live in Britain.
- Many of the 'Windrush generation' arrived on their parents' passports. The Home Office had destroyed thousands of landing cards proving they arrived legally. People needed to show at least one official document from every year they had lived in Britain. For many this was impossible.
- Thousands of people, even though they had paid taxes and national insurance for years, were branded illegal immigrants. They lost their jobs and were denied healthcare. Some were deported.
- Newspapers reported the scandal in 2017. There was widespread shock and outrage.
- After an official enquiry, the government apologised and promised to compensate the victims. In December 2020 it promised an increase in payments and to speed up the process.

Exam-style question, Section B

'The impact on the economy was the most significant consequence of migration to Britain in the period 1700–2000.'
How far do you agree? Explain your answer. You may use the following in your answer:
- trade
- culture.
You **must** also use information of your own.

(16 marks)

THINKING HISTORICALLY **Change and continuity (3b)**

Significance to whom?

Historians are interested in in different aspects of the past – and ask different questions. The interest of the historian is a very important factor in their decision about what is significant and what is not.

Political historian	Economic historian	Religious historian	Social historian
How did the government try to control immigration and race relations?	How did migrants help the British economy in the years after 1945?	How did migrants turn Britain into a multi-faith society?	How well did migrants settle in Britain's towns and cities?

Look at the following events and changes:

The Immigration Acts of 1962, 1968 and 1971.	Government encourages soldiers from colonies to join the Allied forces in both world wars.	The building of mosques and the festivals of Diwali and Eid-el-Fitr.
Evacuee and *Kindertransport* children.	Migrants from the Caribbean working in the NHS and London Transport.	The Battle of Cable Street 1936.
The introduction of gospel singing and the development of Pentecostal churches.	Race riots in Brixton and Burnley.	The development of immigrant communities, such as Chinatown in Manchester.

1   Make a diagram linking each type of historian to the event or change that would interest them the most. Be warned – some events and changes might interest more than one sort of historian!

2   Which type of history do you find most interesting? Why?

4.3 Summary

- Immigration was restricted by Acts in 1962, 1968 and 1971. Equality for migrants was addressed in Acts in 1965, 1968 and 1976.
- Migrants worked in important industries, especially the NHS and transport, facing discrimination and racial abuse.
- The far-right National Front and, later, the BNP opposed immigration. They were opposed by pressure groups.
- Migrants helped to change the appearance of cities and towns and to enrich the culture with festivals, music, art, sports achievements and food.

Checkpoint

Strengthen

S1 How did Parliament try to restrict immigration?

S2 What is the significance of Doreen Lawrence?

S3 How did people experience racism in organisations such as the NHS and London Transport?

Challenge

C1 What was the most important impact migrants had on Britain in the years after 1945? Explain your choice.

Learning outcomes

- Understand the experiences of migrants in Bristol.
- Know about protests against discrimination, such as the bus boycott, and their impact.
- Know about the impact of migrant communities on the city.

Bristol's slave trade history

Bristol had been a major part of the slave trade. Ships from Bristol had taken almost 500,000 African slaves to work in British colonies in the Caribbean. Bristol businessmen grew rich from slavery and the sale of tobacco and sugar grown by slaves. They made large investments in the city, with buildings and streets named after them. In the 20th century, Caribbean migrants saw all around them reminders of how slavery had shaped Bristol. This is a difficult legacy, which Bristol is working hard to address today.

Extend your knowledge

Edward Colston statue

Bristol's legacy of slavery remains controversial today. In 2020, protestors pulled down and threw into the harbour a statue of Edward Colston, a 17th-century businessman. Part of Colston's fortune came from slavery. Many important buildings in Bristol are named after him and he gave millions to support charity in Bristol during his life. But, the protestors argued, that money had come from trading slaves.

Activity ?

The debate about slavery remains a very difficult subject. Think about what you have learned in this chapter. Read the speech bubbles in Figure 4.17 – who would you agree with in this debate and why?

Migration to Bristol

After the 1948 British Nationality Act (see page 110), Caribbean migrants started arriving in the city. They were looking for job opportunities and helping to rebuild a city badly damaged from the war.

By 1958 there were 1,500 Caribbean migrants in the city (less than 1% of the city's population). By 1962 this had doubled to 3,000.

Finding homes in St Paul's

- Similar to Notting Hill (see pages 159–60), the migrant community struggled to find homes. Many landlords refused to rent to black people.
- Migrants were forced to find homes in parts of the city where people were less keen to live, such as the war-damaged area of St Paul's. Landlords rented out bomb-damaged houses for high rents.
- Many houses in St Paul's were turned into HMOs – Houses of Multiple Occupation (see page 160). By the 1960s, half of Bristol's Caribbean population all lived within a few streets of each other.

Extend your knowledge

Princess Campbell was born in Jamaica and moved to Bristol in 1962. She faced discrimination daily, but was determined to help people. She trained as a nurse and, in the 1980s, became Bristol's first black ward sister. She set up the United Housing Association to help black people find affordable housing.

Colston's money came from crimes against Africans. We shouldn't celebrate him today.

We should remember that Colston helped the poor and built schools and hospitals. He made life for many people in the city better.

It was a long-time ago – does it matter today?

Colston's statue should be put in a museum with an explanation of what he did – good and bad.

Figure 4.17 Debates about slavery

Attitudes in society

- Some people were convinced migrants took jobs and housing from white residents. 'Colour bars' were common.
- Many migrants felt safer living closer together. In 1961 housewife Lisset Simpson told a local reporter 'There is still so much prejudice that we prefer to stay together.'
- Just as in Notting Hill (see page 172), people were worried about falling victim to racist violence.

Various groups developed to give the immigrant community a voice. In November 1962 Owen Henry and Roy Hackett helped found the West Indian Development Council (WIDC). The WIDC campaigned against racism and helped black people find better jobs, housing and education.

In 1975 it changed its name to the West Indian Parents and Friends Association and continues to fight racism and help the black community today.

The Bristol Bus Boycott

In many British cities black bus drivers and conductors were common. Bristol was different: in 1955 the Transport and General Workers Union (TGWU) banned 'coloured people' from being hired as bus drivers or conductors. The Bristol Omnibus Company, which ran the buses, agreed to this.

In October 1961 the manager of the company told the *Bristol Evening Post* his staff would not work with black people – and that Bristol's black population weren't good enough to work for the company.

> ### Source A
>
> From an October 1958 report to the Committee for the Welfare of Colonial Workers in Bristol, which was sponsored by the lord mayor and the bishop of Bristol.
>
> Fear of increasing unemployment has made many English people more conscious of the presence of coloured people. Many white people who had a 'live and let live' attitude to coloured people two years ago [in 1956] are now asking why coloured people should be allowed to come into this country and are showing hostility when speaking about coloured people, although not necessarily always when speaking to coloured people.

> ### Extend your knowledge
>
> **Barbara Dettering** was born in British Guyana and moved to Bristol in 1961. She was a social worker and teacher in St Paul's for 18 years and campaigned against racism. She worked with the WIDC and helped thousands of students to improve their lives.

> ### Source B
>
> From an interview with activist Owen Henry by historian Madge Dresser, 1986.
>
> It seemed illogical to me that in London where people were being recruited on the buses and indeed where London Transport were going recruiting in Barbados, that Bristol should have had a policy of no black people working on the buses… I didn't for a minute think I was going get much opposition [campaigning against that]. Oh no, I thought, once it's out people will say 'This is ridiculous'.

> ### Source C
>
> From an interview with Paul Stephenson by historian Madge Dresser, 1986.
>
> My line was simply this: this is an employment issue, if the unions don't like it they can go to Hell. What matters is the employer should say 'we're not accepting this kind of racism' and tell the workers if they don't like it they can lump it. The decision was for management. It was a moral obligation for the management!

Exposing racism

The WIDC decided to expose this racism. The WIDS partnered with Paul Stephenson, who was the first black man in Bristol to work as a youth officer. Stephenson suggested they find an applicant for the job who was so well qualified, that the only reason to turn him down would be racism.

Guy Bailey, a dedicated student, boy's brigade officer and amateur cricketer with excellent references applied. He was immediately given an interview. Stephenson then called the company to tell them Bailey was black. The interview was immediately cancelled. This was proof of racism.

The boycott

On 29 April 1963 the WIDC called for the black community to boycott Bristol's buses until the colour bar was lifted. This action cost the company a huge amount of money in lost ticket sales. Many white people, such as students and tutors at Bristol University, also supported the boycott.

On 6 May 1963 Stephenson, Hackett and Owen led the first black-led protest march in British history through Bristol. Almost 200 people joined the protest. Roy Hackett later led a protest to block buses from using one of the main roads into the town centre.

Victory?

The campaign received national attention. Local MP Tony Benn and Labour Prime Minister Harold Wilson spoke in support of the boycott. Sir Learie Constantine, a famous ex-cricketer and Trinidadian High Commissioner* wrote to the company to condemn the bar.

The TGWU attacked the protesters in the press, in particular Paul Stephenson. Stephenson later sued a union official for libel, and won – the first libel victory by a black man in British history.

Eventually, public pressure forced the company to scrap the colour bar on 28 August 1963. A month later, the company hired a Sikh graduate, Raghbir Singh, as a conductor.

In 1965, the government passed the Race Relations Act. This made it illegal for anyone to discriminate against a person because of their race (see page 123).

However, progress was slow. By 1966 there were only four ethnic minority drivers and 39 ethnic minority bus conductors in Bristol – less than 2.5% of the total number of drivers and conductors. Official colour bars were illegal – but many thought unspoken colour bars remained.

Interpretation 1

A mural in St Pauls, Bristol, celebrating Roy Hackett – one of seven murals in the area celebrating 'The Seven Saints of St Pauls', including Hackett, Owen Henry and Barbara Dettering.

Key term

High Commissioner*

The senior ambassador from a Commonwealth country to the United Kingdom.

The cultural impact on Bristol

The Bristol Bus Boycott played a large part in helping Bristol start to combat racism. Bristol became one of the first cities in the country to have its own Race Equality Council, which Roy Hackett served on from 1965 to 2005. The council worked to improve housing and education for the migrant community, particularly after a brief riot after a police raid on a cafe in St Paul's in April 1980.

The migrant community continued to face discrimination, but also helped make Bristol more diverse. In 2015 a series of murals celebrating black history in the city were revealed. The murals celebrated 'seven saints of St Pauls', including Roy Hackett, Owen Henry and Barbara Dettering.

Extend your knowledge

During the 1990s c5,000 Somali refugees moved to the city to escape persecution after a coup in Somalia. There are over 20,000 people of Somali descent in Bristol today and the city hosts a popular Somali festival every year.

St Paul's Festival

In 1968 Roy Hackett bought together local residents and activists for the first St Paul's Festival. People opened up their homes and gardens, playing music and selling home-cooked food. What started as a street festival grew into an event that by the 2010s was attracting thousands of people a year.

In July 1979 the festival became a platform for African and Caribbean artists. Some festivals had themes, e.g. 'Survival' (1979), 'Resistance' (1980) and 'Not Guilty' (1981), which responded to events happening to the black community across the country. From 1991 it became known as the St Paul's Carnival.

Activities

1 Why do you think the bus boycott was so effective at getting national attention and support? Write down a list of the reasons and then try to put them in order of importance. Compare your list with those of the rest of the group.

2 The bus boycott wanted to end the colour bar and racism in job applications. How far do you think it succeeded in achieving these two goals?

4.4 Summary

- Bristol has a complex slave-trading legacy, which it is still addressing today.
- West Indian migrants faced discrimination and lived in low-quality housing, paying high rents.
- The Bristol Omnibus Company had a racist policy to not appoint people from an ethnic minority as bus drivers or conductors. The black community proved this was racist and successfully campaigned to have the ban brought to an end by encouraging people to boycott the buses.
- The migrant community helped make Bristol a more culturally diverse city.

Checkpoint

Strengthen

S1 Why did so many Caribbean migrants end up living in the St Paul's area of Bristol?

S2 Why was the Bristol Bus Boycott successful?

Challenge

C1 Why did so many people across Britain find the Bristol Omnibus Company's policies so shocking?

C2 The Race Relations Act (1965) made open racism illegal – but did it manage to stop unspoken racism?

Learning outcomes

- Understand the reasons for migration to Leicester in the 1950s and 1960s.
- Understand the 'Africanisation' policy in Uganda and its impact on migration to Leicester.
- Know how Asian migrants influenced the economy and culture of Leicester.
- Understand the local and government reaction to Asian migration to Leicester.

Migration to Leicester, 1948–72

Since the end of the Second World War, Leicester has been an attractive destination for migrants. The city had a very strong textiles and shoe industry – it was famous as the city that 'clothes the world'. In 1950 two-thirds of its 283,000 population worked in these industries – and there were always more job vacancies than there were people to take up jobs.

Source A

In his book *Postwar Leicester* (2006), Ben Beazley describes job opportunities in Leicester in the 1950s.

A situation existed where anyone could apply for three jobs: attend an interview for the first, decline it, accept the second and not bother to go to the interview for the third. So dire were the employers' needs for labour that it was more likely the prospective third employer would later contact the applicant asking whether, despite the missed interview, they were still interested.

The job opportunities and available housing encouraged migrants, many of them Punjabi Sikhs, as well as families from Pakistan and Bangladesh, to travel to Leicester. In the 1960s many Gujarati and Punjabi families from former British colonies in East Africa also migrated there.

Table 1 The growth of the Asian population in Leicester

Census year	Asian population of Leicester
1951	624
1961	3,566
1971	20,190
1981	59,709

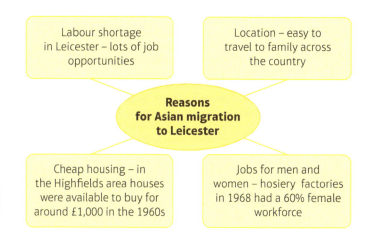

Figure 4.18 Reasons for Asian migration to Leicester

The early Asian community in Leicester

Many of the first Asian migrants to Leicester settled in the Belgrave and Highfields estate, where houses were affordable and available. Asian communities started to grow in the city.

- By 1972 there were three Hindu temples, three Sikh Gurdwajas, two mosques and an Islamic foundation.
- By 1972 there were 40 Asian social and welfare clubs in Leicester.
- In 1968, a spokesman for the Indian Workers Association described Leicester as being a place where 'not only can men and women earn a decent wage [but] there is less discrimination than elsewhere'.

Reaction in Leicester

As in Bristol, there was hostility from some and colour bars were common. In 1964 The Belgrave and District Working Men's club announced it would not allow more than 10% of its members to be from an ethnic minority. In 1967 the council's education committee stated schools were being 'flooded' by Indian children, many of whom 'do not speak English'.

However, some sympathised with the Asian community – students demonstrated against the colour bar and there was widespread outrage at KKK (see page 180) action in the city.

Source B

This letter from 'Some Leicester residents' was published in the *Leicester Chronicle*, 24 May 1964. *(Note: This source contains offensive racist language, reflecting the writer's attitudes.)*

Where are the white people who used to live in the Highfields area? It is only common sense to say that they have had to leave because of the deterioration of the district, with its overcrowded houses, smells and noise. At the rate coloured people are coming into the country, given preference in everything such as unemployment pay... without paying a penny into these schemes, we think England has quite enough to do to look after the interests of the English.

Activities   ?

1   What do you think was the most important factor attracting migrants to Leicester?

2   Read Source B. What does this source, and your own knowledge, tell you about the attitudes Indian communities faced in Leicester?

Ugandan Asians and Leicester

In August 1972 President Idi Amin threw the entire Asian population of Uganda out of the country. He claimed this 'Africanisation' policy was to 'give Uganda back to Ugandans'. Many fled to Britain (see page 112).

'Full up'

Many Ugandan Asians hoped to move to Leicester, some to join family, others because they felt the city's Asian community would offer safety and support. Leicester City Council were worried – in August 1972 they complained to the Home Office that the city was 'full up'. In September 1972 they ran an infamous advertisement in the Ugandan press (see Source C) to discourage immigrants.

Source C

This is the text of an advert Leicester City Council published in the *Ugandan Argus* in September 1972. The advertisement failed to discourage migrants from travelling to Leicester.

The City Council of Leicester, England, believe that many families in Uganda are considering moving to Leicester. If <u>you</u> are thinking of doing so it is very important you should know that <u>present conditions in the city are very different from those met by earlier settlers</u>. They are—

<u>Housing</u> — several thousands of families are already on the Council's waiting list

<u>Education</u> — hundreds of children are awaiting places in schools

<u>Social and Health Services</u> — already stretched to the limit

In your own interests and those of your family you should accept the advice of the Uganda Resettlement Board and not come to Leicester.

Despite this, over a fifth – nearly 6,000 – of the Ugandan refugees arrived in Leicester to make new lives. The British Asian Welfare Society and other volunteers helped the new arrivals find homes and jobs. Over the next ten years the Asian population of the city more than doubled to nearly 60,000.

Suspicion and hostility

The National Front targeted Leicester. There were NF marches in 1974 and 1979; and in 1976 the party won 19% of the local council vote. However, its support fell in the 1980s as many voters were shocked by its racism and violence.

Unions were worried jobs would be 'lost' to immigrants and that they would not 'fit in'. Many early Asian migrants had to take on work they were overqualified for and yet they were still paid less than white workers.

The impact of the Asian community on Leicester

Leicester City Council had at first been hostile to the idea of an Asian community in the city. Today the council celebrates Leicester as a multicultural city. How did this change?

Economic impact

Many migrants had been successful businessmen in Uganda. They were 'twice migrants' (who had migrated first to Uganda then Britain) and had experience of building a business in a new city.

At first Asian migrants found work in existing industries – often for low pay. They worked hard and saved money.

↓

In the 1970s, traditional industries in Leicester started to close. This left many shops and factory spaces empty.

↓

British Asian businessmen invested in this empty space – corner shops, greengrocers, clothing, jewellery and food shops became common.

↓

This helped the city economy recover. In the 1980s Leicester Chamber of Commerce worked with the Asian community to support more businesses and to help them grow.

↓

Many of the new business owners had contacts in Africa and Asia, opening new trading opportunities for the city.

Figure 4.19 How Asian businesses started to grow in Leicester

A study found many of these business owners (20%) were educated to degree level, compared to 3% of similar white business owners. In 1986 the Leicester Asian Business Association (LABA) was founded to help British Asians 'take an active part in the economic prosperity of their communities'.

By 1994 there were 1,446 Asian-owned businesses in Leicester. By 2004 there were over 10,000. Businesses owned by British-Asians employ thousands of people and contribute millions of pounds to the country's economy.

Asian entrepreneurs

Many of Leicester's Asian businesses flourished – these are only a few of the success stories:

- Aziz and Rashid Tyub started running a corner shop in 1976. They later formed a company called Crown Crest which owns Poundstretcher and had a turnover of £442 million in 2019.
- HKS Retail was formed by the Thakrar brothers in 1984. It started as a single garage forecourt and grew to control 70 sites with a turnover of £225 million a year when it was sold in 2017.

Extend your knowledge

Imperial Typewriter strike

Asian manual workers in Leicester experienced prejudice at work. At the Imperial Typewriter plant 1,100 of the 1,600 workers were Asian migrants. In 1974 almost 500 of them went on strike after not being offered the same bonuses given to white workers. The union refused to support them. The factory closed in 1975, but public pressure forced the union to support similar strikes elsewhere in Britain.

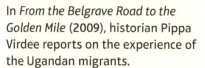

Interpretation 1

In *From the Belgrave Road to the Golden Mile* (2009), historian Pippa Virdee reports on the experience of the Ugandan migrants.

Jaffer Kappasi spoke about his experiences of coming to Leicester from Uganda in 1972. He reflected on the fact that the majority of Ugandan Asians were self-employed and had never worked for anyone. For him the Ugandan Asians were pivotal in reviving the economy of Leicester at a time when businesses were closing; the refugees were enterprising and took over flagging shops and manufacturing.

Cultural impact

The British-Asian community in Leicester has had a huge impact on the city's culture. By the 2000s the city was celebrating the diversity of its communities.

An annual fete that began in 1982 grew to become Belgrave Mela Festival, attracting over 120,000 people from around the world by 2004. Today it celebrates all communities in Leicester.

Belgrave Road: The Golden Mile

One of the most famous streets in Leicester is Belgrave Road. It is called 'the Golden Mile' because of the number of jewellers on it. The road had been a shopping street, but in the 1970s many of these shops were empty. Asian migrants took over these abandoned shops and many became successful, selling clothing and food at first for the Asian community and then for a wider market.

Today the road is a major tourist attraction – 'the closest Britain comes to an Indian bazaar'. The street hosts the largest Diwali festival outside India.

Source D

The Golden Mile today, where Asian businesses have turned a street of empty shops into a thriving tourist attraction.

4.5 Summary

- Leicester was attractive to migrants in the 1950s to 1960s as there were many housing and job opportunities. This led to a strong Asian community developing in the city.
- This helped make the city a popular destination for Ugandan Asians expelled from their homes.
- Although the immigrants were met with some hostility, they settled and rebuilt their lives.
- Many Asian businessmen became very successful. Asian businesses improved the city's economy.

Checkpoint

Strengthen

S1 Why did the growing Asian community make Leicester more attractive for other migrants?

S2 Why do you think the local council was eager to work with Asian businessmen?

Challenge

C1 What similarities are there between Idi Amin's 'Africanisation' ideas and the views of organisations like the National Front?

C2 Why do you think so many of the Asian businessmen were able to become successful?

Summary: Migration from 800 to the present

You have been considering migrants to Britain in four periods: 800–1500, 1500–1700, 1700–1900 and 1900 to the present. Of course, people didn't live neatly in those periods. Someone migrating to Britain in 1480 could have lived well into the 1500s; a migrant arriving in 1890 might have easily lived until the middle of the 20th century.

Factors that brought about change in 1680 could still exist in 1720, and attitudes to migrants in 1100 might still be the same in 1900.

You are now going to look at the whole time span, identifying different threads and patterns that worked together to bring about change.

Activities ?

The impact of institutions: government, the Church and the media in bringing about change

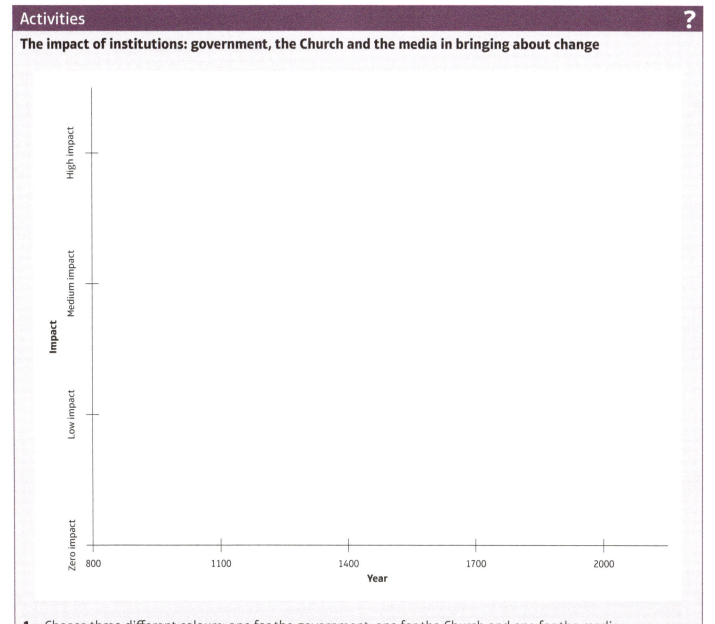

1 Choose three different colours: one for the government, one for the Church and one for the media.
2 Work through each section of the book, identifying the impact each of the three institutions had on the process of change.
3 Complete the graph, plotting the impact of each institution with the colours you have chosen. You might find, for example, that the Church had a higher impact in the early years but far less later on. For the media, it will probably be the other way round.

Activities ?

Did Britain's response to migrants change over time?

1   Copy the table below, selecting as many examples as you can from each section of the book. You should choose at least two groups from each chapter.

Date	Evidence of welcome	Evidence of rejection

2   Now answer this question. How far do you agree with the statement 'Britain always welcomed migrants'?

Activities ?

Did people's reasons for migrating to Britain change over time?

1   Copy the diagram on the right, enlarging it as much as possible.

2   For each of the reasons in the six boxes, complete the two empty boxes with examples from anywhere in the book, but they must be at least 200 years apart.

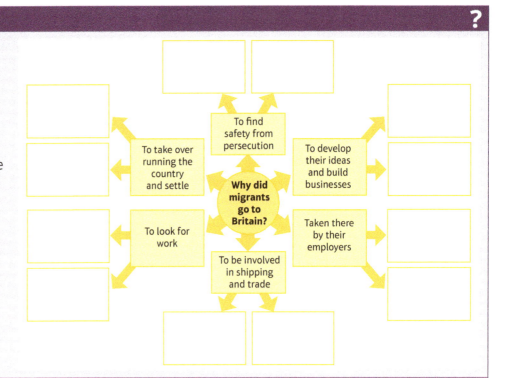

Why did migrants go to Britain?

- To find safety from persecution
- To take over running the country and settle
- To develop their ideas and build businesses
- To look for work
- Taken there by their employers
- To be involved in shipping and trade

Activities ?

The influence of the media from the 20th century

1   From the early 1900s the media (newspapers, television and later the internet) increasingly affected people's opinions on migration and migrants.

2   Look at every source from the media in this chapter, whether written or visual. Then draw up a new grid based on the example below. Add in as many rows as you think you will need, and complete the grid.

Source	Attitude to migrants	How is this shown?

3   Write a paragraph to explain whether, in your view, the media was racist or anti-racist. Remember to give examples to support your view.

Preparing for your GCSE Paper 1 exam

Paper 1 overview

Your Paper 1 is in two sections, which examine the Historic Environment and the Thematic Depth Study. Together they count for 30% of your History assessment. The questions on the Thematic Study: Migrants in Britain, c800–present, are in Section B and are worth 20% of your History assessment. Allow two-thirds of the examination time for Section B. There are an extra four marks for Spelling, Punctuation and Grammar (SpaG) in the last question.

History Paper 1	Historic Environment and Thematic Depth Study			Time 1 hour 15 minutes
Section A	Historic Environment	Answer 3 questions	16 marks	25 mins
Section B	Thematic Depth Study	Answer 3 questions	32 marks + 4 SPaG marks	50 mins

Section B: Migrants in Britain c800–present

You will answer Questions 3 and Question 4, and then **either** Question 5 or Question 6.

Q3 Explain one way... (4 marks)

You are given about half a page of lines to write about a **similarity** or a **difference**. Allow five minutes to write your answer.

This question is worth just four marks so keep the answer brief. Only one comparison is needed. You should **compare** by referring to both periods named in the question – for example, 'xxx was similar because in the Middle Ages… and also in the 16th century…'

Q4 Explain why... (12 marks)

This question asks you to explain the reasons **why something happened**. Allow about 15 minutes to write your answer.

You are given two information points as prompts to help you. You do not have to use the prompts and you will not lose marks by leaving them out. Higher marks are gained by adding in a point not covered in the prompts.

You will be given at least two pages of lines for your answer in the booklet. This does not mean you should try to fill all the space. Aim to write an answer giving at least three well explained reasons.

Q5 OR Q6 How far do you agree...? (16 marks + 4 marks for SPaG)

This question, including SPaG, is worth 20 marks – more than half the marks for the whole of the Thematic Study. Be sure to keep 30 minutes of the exam time to answer it and to check your spelling, punctuation and grammar.

You can **choose** between Questions 5 and 6. You will have prompts to help you, as for Question 4.

The statement can be about the concepts of: significance, cause, consequence, change, continuity, similarity or difference. Try to think about which concept to use to answer the question.

You should think about **both** sides of the argument. Plan your answer before you begin to write, putting your points under two headings: 'For' and 'Against'. Make a point and then support it with details from your own knowledge.

In this question, four extra marks are given for good spelling, punctuation and grammar. Use full sentences, paragraphs, capital letters, commas, full stops, etc. Also try to use the specialist terms you have learned, e.g. 'migration'.

Analyse
- Useful information
- What does it suggest?

+

Evaluate
- Contextual knowledge
- Its strengths and limitations

Paper 1, Questions 3 & 4

Explain **one** way in which the invasion of England by the Vikings in the 9th century was similar to the invasion by the Normans in the 11th century.

(4 marks)

Average answer

The Vikings landed in East Anglia with a Great Army and fought the Anglo-Saxons. Then in the eleventh century, the Normans also landed in England with an army and defeated the Anglo-Saxons too.

The answer identifies similarities between the Viking and Norman migrations, but the examples are vague. The words 'also' and 'too' show some recognition of similarities but the detail of the similarity is not spelled out.

Verdict

This is an average answer because:

- the candidate has provided very general comments about the similarities between the two invasions
- the candidate has not provided enough specific detail about the similarities, only that both groups landed with armies and fought the Anglo-Saxons.
- Use the feedback to rewrite this answer, making as many improvements as you can.

Explain why migration to Britain increased in the years c1900 to the present day.

You may use the following information in your answer:

- the World Wars
- the British Empire

You **must** also use information of your own.

(12 marks)

Average answer

From 1900 to the present day, thousands of people migrated to Britain. People came from the Empire to fight with British troops but also to escape from the problems of war in Europe. Belgians came over in the First World War, but most went back afterwards. Poles came over in the Second World War when the Nazis invaded Poland and most stayed on here afterwards. Kindertransport helped Jewish children escape. The ending of the British Empire meant that people from the colonies, like the Ugandan Asians, came to Britain. Migrants came from the Caribbean at the end of the Second World War to help build up Britain and in this century people have come from the EU to work.

There is an attempt to structure the answer, but it lacks organisation and structure. For example, paragraph one mentions the Empire but gives no examples. Paragraph two mentions workers from the EU, but the main thrust of the paragraph is about the ending of Empire.

The information provided is accurate but too generalised.

There is little attempt to focus on the question, which asks for an explanation, not a description.

Verdict

This is an average answer because:

- there is some focus on the concepts of the question, but it needs to be more explicit
- there is accurate and relevant information, but it is not precisely selected – some of it is not useful in explaining the reasons for change

- the answer does not fully develop a third aspect. For example, the EU migration is only very briefly mentioned and could be developed further.

Use the feedback to rewrite this answer, making as many improvements as you can.

Paper 1, Questions 3 & 4

Explain **one** way in which the invasion of England by the Vikings in the 9th century was similar to the invasion by the Normans in the 11th century. **(4 marks)**

Strong answer

Both invasions captured a city to use as a base for conquest and settling. In 865 the Vikings landed in East Anglia with a Great Army that was really made up of three separate armies, each with its own commander. The Vikings captured the city of York in 866. They used the city as a base for conquering most of eastern England where they finally settled.

In 1066 the Normans landed on the south coast of England. The Normans captured the city of London, where Duke William was crowned king. They used the city as a base for conquering the rest of England where they settled.

This answer describes the similarities between both invasions. It gives specific examples and focuses on the similarities between the two invasions.

Verdict

This is a good answer because it uses specific information about the topic to demonstrate similarities in the invasions that happened two hundred years apart.

Explain why migration to Britain increased in the years c1900 to the present day. You may use information on the world wars, the British Empire and **must** use information of your own. **(12 marks)**

Strong answer

A range of events led to migration increasing over the last one hundred and twenty years: the Second World War, the ending of the British Empire and Britain's membership of the EU have all been important.

The two world wars had a great impact on increasing migration. For example, Belgians fled to Britain at the start of the First World War and Poles at the start of the Second. The greatest impact, however, came at the end of the Second World War when thousands of people from the Caribbean migrated to Britain to help build up industry and transport after the devastation caused by German bombing.

The ending of the British Empire also played a significant part. The violence that accompanied Indian independence in 1947 led to many Indians fleeing to Britain. Kenyan independence in 1967 led to 20,000 Kenyan Asians arriving in Britain because of restrictions put on them by the new regime. There was a similar situation in Uganda in 1972.

The ending of the British Empire led to Britain looking for new commercial links with the EU and this led to more migration. Britain's membership of the EU (1973-2016) meant Europeans could work and live in Britain. When Britain joined there were only 9 member states. By 2007, there were 28, and many more Europeans could migrate to Britain. For example, Poland joined the EU in 2004 and many Polish people went to Britain to work in the care industry. Bulgaria joined in 2007 and many Bulgarians do seasonal work in agriculture, picking soft fruit in East Anglia and daffodils in Cornwall.

This answer begins with a clear focus on the question.

The reasons for change are clearly shown. The answer focuses on the two given factors and adds a new one.

A new aspect, not mentioned in the stimulus points, is clearly explained.

Verdict

This is a strong answer:

- it has included only relevant information and used it to support valid points

- the explanation is analytical, relating to the factors causing migration.

- the line of reasoning is consistently developed in each paragraph of the answer.

143

Paper 1, Questions 5 & 6

'The impact on the economy was the most significant consequence of migration to Britain in the years c1300–c1700.'

How far do you agree? Explain your answer. You may use the following information in your answer:

- trade
- culture

You must also use information of your own.

(16 marks + 4 for SPaG)

Average answer

During the period c1300 to c1700 migrants played an important part in the British economy.

Weavers arriving from the Low Countries in the 1330s boosted cloth production. They were encouraged to come by the king who wanted high quality cloth to be produced in England not on the continent. Hansa merchants had a base, the Steelyard, by the Thames. They dealt in cloth, as well as other goods, and their links with the Hanseatic League meant that trade increased and the economy prospered. Lascars helped ship British cloth to countries overseas and so they also played an important part in the economy.

The Flemish migrants in Canterbury and Sandwich had their own churches and wealthy people had houses built in the Flemish style. Their language and customs became part of British culture. Huguenot silks were in demand from rich women to make fashionable dresses. Huguenot words like 'brocade' and street names like 'Threadneedle Street' became part of the English language. Migrants like Hans Holbein and Anthony van Dyck were important artists who painted portraits of royalty.

Other factors, like finance, were also important. Therefore, impact on the economy was important but there were other factors too.

> Accurate information is given. Although there is some analysis of the impact of migrants on the economy, the treatment is mainly descriptive.
>
> Some of the information is too general.
>
> The impact of migrants on other aspects, apart from trade and culture are missing.
>
> 'Most significant' in the question is not directly addressed, but asserted.
>
> Spelling, punctuation and grammar are all correct.

Verdict

This is an average answer because:

- it includes valid information but does not analyse consequences enough to be a strong answer
- the answer does not go beyond the prompts given, except for a brief reference to finance.
- there is some analysis of the question but this is not consistent throughout and the answer lacks a clear, supported, overall judgement.

Use the feedback to rewrite this answer, making as many improvements as you can.

Paper 1, Questions 5 & 6

'The impact on the economy was the most significant consequence of migration to Britain in the years c1300–c1700.'
How far do you agree? Explain your answer.

(16 marks + 4 for SPaG)

Strong answer

Migration to Britain in the years c1300–c1700 had many consequences, the most significant of which was the impact migrants had on the economy. Trade, particularly in wool and woollen cloth, was a huge source of income for merchants and the treasury. Financial services, for example, the lending of money and investment in industry, contributed greatly to the economy and migrants were involved in both aspects of the economy. Other consequences of migration at this time were in culture such as language and art.

The impact migrants had on the cloth trade was huge. Flemish weavers, migrating in the late 14th and early 15th century, brought skills to England that transformed the cloth trade. Hansa merchants, working from the Steelyard beside the river Thames, controlled most of the highly profitable English cloth industry by the mid-1400s, using their links with the Hanseatic League. Later, between 1650 and 1700, the Huguenots' silk-making skills expanded the cloth trade, making Britain the world centre of cloth production. Gradually, migrants had changed the British economy from one based on raw materials to one based on manufacture.

Closely linked to this changing economy was banking. Money was needed to finance the changes. Bankers from Lombardy, invited to England by Henry III, not only supported the monarchs but merchants and entrepreneurs too. Jews, after their return to England towards the end of the 17th century, used their financial skills developed before they were expelled in 1290. Thus migrants began the process whereby London became an international financial centre.

Agriculture was an important part of the British economy. Towards the end of the 17th century, Dutch migrants completely transformed the Fens by draining them and turning hundreds of acres of marsh into productive arable land. Although this was important, it mainly benefitted the wealthy landowners.

In a similar way, migrants' impact on culture mainly benefitted the rich. Lightweight silks were used by clothes' designers to create new fashions for wealthy men and women. While words like 'taffeta' and 'brocade' were used by those weaving the new fabrics they were only really used by those buying and using the new material. Portraits of royalty and nobility, painted by artists like Holbein and van Dyck, could only be commissioned by the rich.

Thus, it can be seen that during the years c1300–c1700, the most significant impact made by migrants was on the economy. This was because the economic impact of trade, agriculture and finance affected the prosperity of thousands of people, whereas the cultural impact of migrants affected mainly the rich.

The answer begins with a clear focus on the question. There is good use of precise information to support each clearly developed point.

The answer goes beyond the bullet point prompts and makes several clear, relevant points.

Individual paragraphs and the overall answer follow a clear structure.

The evidence selected to support the analysis shows a strong grasp of the wider context and the inter-relationships between consequences.

Verdict

This is a good answer because:

- there is a clear focus on the question throughout
- there is a consistently analytical focus, backed by a range of precise knowledge
- there is a clear line of reasoning running through a well-organised answer
- there is a clear basis for the judgement made.

05 | Notting Hill c1948–c1970

Notting Hill was a centre for Caribbean migration from the 1940s to 1970s. Black people, some of whom had fought for Britain in the Second World War, arrived on the transatlantic boat services (such as the *SS Empire Windrush*), docking at Tilbury, Southampton, Liverpool or Portsmouth. They then took trains to central London.

The Notting Hill area is a short walking distance from Paddington train station. It became a hub for recent arrivals looking for a place to stay. At the time, London was still suffering from bomb damage from the war. Many firms needed workers and there were lots of jobs available as Britain started to rebuild its economy.

People from Caribbean islands were subjects of the British Empire. The British Nationality Act in 1948 made them all British citizens with the right to live and work in Britain. Their schooling and upbringing had taught them to see Britain as 'the Mother Country'. This idea was promoted by the British during the Second World War, to encourage people to contribute to the war effort.

They were, therefore, very surprised when they moved to Britain and to Notting Hill to find they were hostility and discrimination.

Note: The language used to discuss race has changed a great deal over time. Throughout this period words many people consider offensive today, such as 'coloured', were often used – including by members of the black community. Similarly, during this time some people used racist and offensive language to refer to people in the black community.

While we condemn racism today, we think it is important to report these attitudes. However, we have used asterisks (*) to strike out some unacceptable racist language that may cause particular distress.

Learning outcomes

By the end of this chapter, you will:

- know about the national and regional context for migration to Notting Hill
- understand the local context and housing problems in Notting Hill
- know about the influence of Caribbean culture in Notting Hill
- understand the impact of racism on the black community in Notting Hill and the impact of institutional racism in the police
- know about the impact of anti-immigrant groups and political movements
- understand the growth of black activism in Notting Hill, and the impact of the Notting Hill Carnival and the Mangrove Nine.

Sources, information and evidence

In the examination you will be given two sources. You are asked to do two things with these sources:

- comment on the **usefulness of both sources** for an enquiry
- write about **a detail in one source** that you would **follow up**. You will need to:
  - consider the question you would ask about that detail
  - consider what type of source might provide an answer to that
  - explain why that type of source helps to answer the question.

Because most of the marks in this section of the examination are for your work with sources, there are more sources in this chapter than in the rest of the book. Sources A and B in this section are examples to help you understand how the examination works.

Source A: Notting Hill riots

Source A is about the situation in Notting Hill in 1958. It is a news report from the BBC during the riots. It was referenced in a book by Colin Grant published in 2019, called *Homecoming: voices of the Windrush generation*. Grant attempts to capture the experiences of the men and women who came to Britain from the Caribbean in the late 1940s and early 1960s. The source reveals the racial tensions that existed in Notting Hill.

Source B: Teddy Boys*

Source B is a photograph that shows a man who may have been one of the 'Teddy Boys' being arrested by police officers. This photograph was comes from a book by Clair Wills published in 2017 called *Lovers and Strangers: an immigration history of post-war Britain*. Interestingly, this book challenges the idea that Britain was open to migration. The reasons behind the Notting Hill riots are complex, but they involved race, racism in policing, poor housing and xenophobia* from anti-immigration groups such as the White Defence League (WDL).

Usefulness (utility)

No source is useful (or useless) until you have an enquiry. Our enquiry is: How useful are Sources A and B for an enquiry into the reasons for the Notting Hill riots of 1958?

To answer this question, you will need to explain the criteria* for your judgement, based on your analysis of the content, provenance* and context* of the source. You should also consider asking how useful each of these makes the source.

Key terms

Criteria* (singular: criterion)

Benchmarks by which you judge something. It is vital that you know your criteria before judging a historical source.

Provenance*

Where a source comes from – who made it, when and why.

Context*

The wider setting. Historical context means the other information available on the same topic.

Criteria	Questions you might ask about a source
Content	What does the source tell you?
Provenance	What was the original purpose of the source?
Context	How does the source fit in with what you already know about the tensions in Notting Hill?

How does this work in practice?

Content

Source A tells us that racial violence from white youths towards black men and women became a major problem in Notting Hill. This suggests to us that racism from anti-immigration groups contributed to the Notting Hill riots as the Caribbean community responded to protect itself.

Provenance

Source A was written by BBC News and is attempting to inform the public of the reasons behind the social uprising in the Notting Hill area. Since it is being produced by a credible news outlet, it might suggest to us that the information is reasonably accurate. This source does seem to be condemning the violence. However, it is only a partial extract and we may not be able to trust it fully, because many organisations in Britain at the time were either biased against the black community or institutionally racist. It praises the police response to the violence, but it doesn't talk about the reasons for the violence. We need to be careful and think about what the source says and also what it does not say – how far does it help us understand the experience of migrants in Notting Hill?

Context

Always try to use your knowledge to evaluate the source. This is known as 'context'. When you have studied this topic a bit more, you could show how this source fits into your knowledge by pointing out that there were racist anti-immigrant groups such as the White Defence League and Teddy Boys who racially harassed black people. Or you could link the problem of racist practices within the Metropolitan Police that targeted the black community with stop-and-search tactics or through the use of violence towards these individuals. Our own knowledge can help us understand if a source is reflecting the typical situation at the time.

Following up on a source

Where possible, historians try to use as many different types of source as they can. There is a good reason for this. Each different type of source has different strengths and weaknesses.

The second question about sources asks you to pick a detail from one of the sources and then explain how you would follow up that detail with a different type of source. Figure 5.1 shows the range of different types of sources a historian can use.

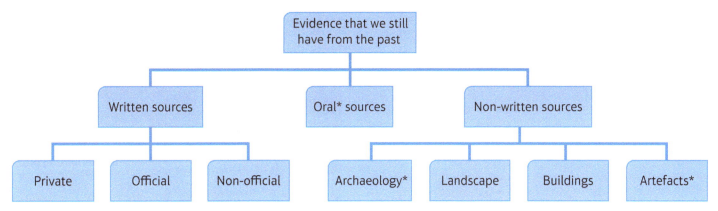

Figure 5.1 Types of sources used by historians

Key terms

Oral*
Spoken.

Archaeology*
The study of objects found buried in the ground.

Artefact*
A historical object.

Activities

1 Make a list of questions you could ask of Source B to judge its usefulness.

2 Using the categories from Figure 5.1, make a list of sources that could be used to study your life.

   a Give at least one example source in each category.

   b Explain why each example would be useful.

Source C

From an interview with retired Police Commissioner Sir Peter Imbert in 2002, published in an article on the police's relationship with the Caribbean community 1950–1970. Imbert ran the Metropolitan Police from 1987 to 1993.

When we saw black youth hanging around street corners we couldn't understand why. We automatically thought, quite wrongly of course, on every occasion, that they were up to no good. But that was because of a lack of understanding of their culture and way of life.

Provenance

Historians think very carefully about their sources. They test them to check whether they are really appropriate for the way they want to use them. The tests are as follows.

What is its purpose?

When, where and why was the source created, and who by? When we read something about living in Notting Hill during the 1950s by someone who was there, it helps to know if they wrote this at the time or 50 years later.

But just because it was written at the time doesn't mean it is true. A policeman from Notting Hill in the 1950s might have purposely underplayed information that was written to prevent himself or his team from getting into trouble.

The purpose of the source might be to ensure the wrongful arrest of someone from the Caribbean community, rather than to tell the whole truth – that race and racism were a major issue in Britain during the 1950s.

What is the opinion of the author or artist?

Does the person have a particular point of view? For example, if you are reading a criticism of the British Black Panthers (BBP), it might be useful to know whether it was written by an opponent or a supporter of this black activist group, which fought for the civil rights of the black community. Sometimes the BBP were looked upon as freedom fighters – but for other people they were seen as troublemakers.

Is the source trying to change people's views?

Propaganda* is deliberately created to change people's views. It might be exaggerated, it might leave things out, or it might be simply not true. This doesn't mean historians don't read propaganda – it provides a lot of useful evidence – but the use might be revealing what the government wanted people to believe, rather than what really happened.

Key term

Propaganda*
Deliberate mass persuasion.

Is it part of the action or reflecting on the action?

What is the difference between a live radio commentary on a football match, and an account of that same game written years later in a player's autobiography? Both have their strengths – but they are very different accounts.

Turning a source into evidence

A source is only useful, and it can only be turned into evidence, when you have a question or enquiry. For example, to find out more about racism and policing in the Notting Hill area. If we consider Source B in isolation, it is neither useful nor not useful. If we have an enquiry into the problems of racism and policing in Notting Hill (for example, attitudes of the police towards black people either a) in the 1950s or b) during the 1959 Caribbean Carnival), then we can think about whether Source B is useful or not. In the case of enquiry a) it is useful, and in the case of enquiry b) it is not.

Source D

A police report from PC Dennis Clifford made on 3 September 1958.

On Tuesday 2 September, 1958, at 10:35 pm, in St Luke's Road, Notting Hill, I saw Miguel Defreitas of 10 Kensal Road W10 with other coloured men surrounded by a large hostile crowd. I said to the accused, 'Get out of the area quickly'. He replied, 'I don't need you to f****** protect me.' He walked slowly up the road, and stopped to talk to a white woman. I asked him to keep moving, and he said, 'I'll go when I am ready.' The crowd became menacing, so I arrested him, taken to Notting Hill Police Station, where he was charged. When cautioned he said, 'I suppose I'm to blame.'

Source E

Police stopping and searching a black man, published in the *Daily Express* on 3 September 1958.

Judging sources

Start with the **provenance** (the nature, origin and purpose of the source). Does this suggest strengths or weaknesses when using this source? For example, we don't know if Source E was taken as propaganda to suggest that the police needed to stop and search black men.

Move on to **content**. What can you learn from the source that is relevant? What can you work out from it?

It is easier to use photographs as sources if we know **why** the photo was taken. The same is true of sketches drawn. Often, we don't know why – so the best you can do is think carefully about the context and content of the drawing or photograph.

Evidence (1b & c)

The message and the messenger

There are many sources of information about the past. Historians use these sources to help them draw conclusions.

Study Sources B, C, D and E about policing in Notting Hill during the 1950s.

Read Source C. In this source former Police Commissioner Paul Imbert says a number of things. He is speaking retrospectively after the major event. Time had passed, which meant that he could be open, honest and candid about the incidents. He did know, however, that what he said would be:

a read by historians and academics

b could be discussed by people in the country

c would be available to his bosses at the Home Office (the government department in charge of the Metropolitan Police).

What information does the source contain? What was Paul Imbert saying? Answer the following questions to find out:

1 Which group does he say was unfairly targeted by the police?

2 What does he say about the treatment of black people at the hands of the police?

3 What reasons does he give for their poor treatment by the police?

Historians are not usually interested in information for its own sake. Historians are interested in using information to work out answers to questions about the past. Use the information you have just taken from the source, and the information about its context provided above the source, to try to work out answers to the following questions:

4 What can we tell about Paul Imbert's intentions in making this statement for a public audience after the riots of 1958?

As a historian investigating racism and policing in Notting Hill from the 1950s to the 1970s:

5 What can we tell about Paul Imbert's intentions in discussing this after the riots of 1958?

6 What evidence might you look for in responses to Paul Imbert's statements?

7 What other types of sources might you want to look at to gather evidence?

Activities ?

In groups, consider the enquiry: 'Was the treatment of Caribbean people by the police a reflection of Britain's anti-immigration stance?' Study Source D.

1 Think about the provenance of Source D. What do you learn about policing towards Caribbean people? How might this change how you view the source?

2 What do you learn from the source about police methods?

3 How can Source D help with our understanding of the police reaction to the Caribbean community during the riots of 1958?

4 Using your answers to these questions, is Source D useful for the enquiry above? Give reasons.

THINKING HISTORICALLY — Evidence (2a)

Information and evidence

Information only becomes evidence when we use it **to work something out** about an issue in the past.

Information needs to be questioned before we can use it as evidence to draw conclusions. Without a question, information doesn't tell us very much.

Study the following questions about the Notting Hill Riots:

1 How did the riots start?	2 What sort of problems existed in Notting Hill before the riots?	3 Why did the black community respond in the way that it did?
4 Who led the protest?	5 How did the police force react?	6 What did people think about the actions of the black community?

Study Sources A to E.

1 Which of the six questions would the sources **not** help us answer?

2 Which question is Source C most useful in providing evidence for?

Look at Source D. Draw up a table with three columns labelled 'Question', 'Inference' and 'Evidence'.

3 Write out 'What were the causes of the Notting Hill riots?' in the first column. Use Source D to fill in the other two columns with ideas that answer the question, and evidence for this question from Source D.

4 Write out the sixth question in a new row. Add ideas and evidence from Source D to this new row.

5 Look at the ideas you've added from Source D. Are they the same for the two questions?

6 In your own words, explain how the question you ask affects what evidence you use in a source.

Britain after the Second World War

After the Second World War, Britain was exhausted from years of fighting. Rationing* was still in effect and many cities – particularly London – were badly damaged from bombing. Hundreds of thousands of people had been killed or disabled in the war. Britain was almost £21 billion in debt and had lost nearly 30% of its pre-war wealth, which was directly linked to its Empire.

The colonies in Britain's Empire had played an active role in fighting for the Allies in the war. Millions of people from Britain's colonies, including the Caribbean, had served in the armed forces, such as the army and the RAF. All of Britain's colonies sent money to support Britain during the war. Germany had also attacked the Caribbean with submarines, causing goods and food shortages.

Key term

Rationing*
A government policy that says that people can only buy a fixed amount of things, e.g. food or household goods, every week, to make sure there is enough for everyone.

War damage to Britain

Across the UK, 43,000 people were killed in German bombing raids. Nearly every major city in Britain had been attacked. In London, the damage was huge:

- 70,000 buildings had been destroyed and 1.7 million damaged
- one in six Londoners had been left homeless at some point during the Blitz.

With soldiers returning from the war, there was a huge growth in demand for houses. Rebuilding would take decades and need thousands of workers.

Extend your knowledge

John Henry Smythe
from Sierra Leone flew 26 RAF bombing missions before being captured and spending 18 months as a POW. Smythe then served as the senior official on the *SS Empire Windrush*, helping to support Caribbean migrants on their journey to Britain.

Source A

Some of the damage to an area in London, April 1945.

Emigration from Britain

With Britain heavily in debt and badly damaged, there were shortages in everything from houses to food supplies.

Many people decided to migrate to colonies such as Australia and Canada where they could live a better life with less hardship. Between 1945 and 1960 almost 1.5 million people left Britain.

Extend your knowledge

The 'White Australia' policy

At this time Australia only accepted European migrants. The 'White Australia' policy continued until the 1970s. British people who moved to Australia had their tickets subsidised and often paid only £10. However, Caribbean people who wanted to come to Britain paid the full price of £65–£75.

Exam-style question, Section A

Describe **two** features of Britain after the Second World War. **(4 marks)**

Exam tip

For each feature identified, develop it with some supporting information.

Reconstruction and the demand for labour

Rebuilding the country would be a lot of work. But between 1945 and 1946 the working population fell by 1.38 million. As well as emigration, many married women either left the workplace or were forced to do so because some jobs (e.g. teaching) did not allow women to continue working after marriage. Many older people had delayed their retirement during the war, so they also left their jobs.

Interpretation 1

The historian, Professor David Olusoga, talked about the challenges facing post-war Britain in a lecture he gave in 2019.

Post-war Britain was battered, it was war-torn, its industries and its infrastructure were in need of a vast programme of improvements, modernisation and repairs. One in seven homes, according to one estimate, had suffered some degree of war damage … [Factories] and whole industries that had been brilliantly retooled for wartime production now had to be returned to their pre-war functions or found a new economic niche. There was a colossal, unprecedented task of rebuilding facing the nation and not enough workers to do it.

On top of this the new post-war Labour government had created many new organisations, such as the NHS and British Railways. These organisations also needed to recruit workers. To help recruit more workers, the British government passed the British Nationality Act in 1948 (see page 110). This gave everyone in the Commonwealth the right to live and work in the UK.

The British Empire and Commonwealth

The British Empire was run to benefit Britain.

- Much of the wealth from the oil fields, sugar plantations, gold mines, copper mines or diamond mines in the African and Caribbean colonies did not stay in those countries but was invested in Britain.
- This meant there was a lack of jobs in the Caribbean and elsewhere – and many of the best jobs didn't go to local black people but to white migrants from Britain. Low wages and limited jobs were a legacy of Empire.

Despite this, many people in the Caribbean felt very loyal to Britain. Many thought of Britain as 'the Mother Country'. In countries such as Jamaica, Trinidad, British Guyana and Dominica, children didn't learn about their own African history – for example, Nanny of the Maroons, the ancient universities of Timbuktu or the Great Temple of Zimbabwe – but about British history.

The 1948 Act was a wonderful opportunity. Wages in Britain were about three or four times higher than wages in the Caribbean.

Many Caribbean people were used to migrating to other countries for a short time to find work. Many thought they would work in Britain for a few years, earning money to send back home. Others liked the idea of making a new home in 'the Mother Country'.

Exam-style question, Section A

Study Source B and Source C. How useful are these two sources for an enquiry into the reasons for Caribbean migration to the United Kingdom after the Second World War? **(8 marks)**

Source B

An interview with 82-year old George Warner from December 2020, remembering schools in St Lucia.

At secondary school, in the subjects Geography and History, 'Great Britain' was a topic. We learnt about its economy, industry and education system, the make-up and functioning of its society. We also learnt about Great Britain's position in the world, its conquests and its Empire. When we went to the cinema the British national anthem would play and we had to stand up for it.

Exam tip

Go through these steps when preparing your answer.

- Always concentrate on the enquiry in this question (the reasons for Caribbean migration to the United Kingdom after the Second World War) and then identify points from the content.
- Think about the provenance (nature, origin, purpose) of both items of information.
- Think about what you know about the context – wartime Britain had been destroyed through bombing and the country needed workers to help rebuild.
- Link together the content, provenance and context in your answer and include how the provenance and context affect the usefulness of the content.

Caribbean settlers travelled over 6,000 miles looking to find jobs and start new lives in Britain. They included engineers, nurses and musicians. Thousands of people were to follow to fill the 1.38 million job vacancies. Although some in the British government tried to discourage them, Caribbean newspapers displayed job advertisements for British firms, encouraging people to migrate.

Source C

From Sam King's book *Climbing Up the Rough Side of the Mountain*, published in 1998. King was a Second World War RAF veteran from Jamaica, who arrived on the *SS Empire Windrush* and became the first black mayor of Southwark.

Coming to England was the chance of a lifetime... As soon as immigrants settled and found employment and lodgings, families and friends would be sponsored. There was a recruitment drive in Barbados, Trinidad and Jamaica to fill vacancies in various areas such as London Transport... [There was an] acute shortage of skilled and unskilled labour. This situation offered new hope and was attractive to people who had been constantly threatened with floodings, hurricanes, earthquakes and the consequences of these disasters. Immigrants would go anywhere at any time and take any job, whereas the [British] natives would pick and choose.

Source D

Passengers on the *SS Empire Windrush* waiting to disembark at Tilbury, near London, 21 June 1948, published in the *Daily Herald*.

Employment opportunities in Great Britain

With the rebuilding after the war, there were many job opportunities in Britain for migrants. Two of the largest employers were London Transport and the NHS (see also page 126).

- London Transport hired many migrants as drivers and conductors. During the 1950s it lent the fares for travel to Britain to over 3,500 people from Barbados so that they could work for the company. In 1956 black underground workers were paid £7 10 shillings a week – less than the national average wage of £11 10 shillings. Many black people worked long hours in shifts others didn't want, such as early morning and late night.
- The newly created NHS ran recruitment programmes in 16 Commonwealth countries during the 1950s. By 1965 there were around 5,000 Jamaican nurses working in British hospitals.

However things were far from perfect. In the workplace, there were no laws against discrimination. Many employers paid black people less than white people for the same jobs. Over half the people arriving from the Caribbean took jobs for which they were overqualified: for example, trained engineers worked as cleaners.

Black people found promotion difficult due to colour bars*. Trade unions were worried migrants were taking jobs from their members, despite the massive job vacancies – and many trade unions supported limits on immigration.

Source E

From an interview with Georgiana, an NHS nurse from the Caribbean, in *Working Lives: gender, migration and employment in Britain, 1945–2007*, by Linda McDowell, published in 2013.

We were told to clean lockers and the beds, we were made to go and clean the wheelchairs and the commodes… we did a lot of menial jobs… the older patient was not used to black people so they were very nasty. They will take their things and throw at you or call you black and whatever and things like that, but you look beyond that because you know what you want out of your life eventually… Black people, we were treated differently… but we didn't worry because we know what we wanted to achieve and what we had to do and we did it, and we did it by making jokes with each other and laughing and doing our work properly.

Key term

Colour bar*

Denying ethnic minority people access to the same rights and opportunities as white people. This particularly applied to jobs, recreation, housing and promotion.

Source F

From an interview with Charlie Phillips, a famous photographer, in 2020. Here he talks about his parents' experience of migrating to Great Britain from Jamaica in 1956.

My parents got caught up with 'Come to England, Come to England! You must come to the mother country' fever. Up to now I can't understand why. It was one of the biggest mistakes because a lot of us didn't have to come here and my parents were entrepreneurial, it took a lot of our skilled people to come out to England and do menial jobs. In those days you could only get jobs in London Transport, Post Office or the hospital. You weren't supposed to have any aspirations above that… I still say this now, they took the best of our talent.

Poverty in London

Many Caribbean migrants were shocked by the bomb damage to London and how grey and dirty everything was. Many areas had changed very little since the Victorian age. Rationing and housing shortages had a huge impact on the lives millions of people. A freezing cold winter in 1947 had ruined food crops and killed thousands of farm animals. Nearly everything from electricity to bread was rationed. Fabric shortages meant most clothes were extremely old and recycled.

The 'Swinging Sixties'

During the 1950s, the British economy improved dramatically. In the 1950s only 3% of the population were unemployed. Rationing slowly came to an end. Young people had more time and money for leisure. In the 1960s, this greater sense of freedom that some felt became known as the 'Swinging Sixties'.

London became known as one of the most exciting cities in the world, with British music and fashion (like the mini-skirt) becoming internationally popular.

The new generation was more radical and wanted to change the world. Young people took part in marches, rallies and protests supporting anti-war and civil rights causes.

Many in the black community had been politically active for decades, but black activism increased during the 1960s.

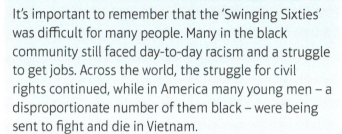

Extend your knowledge

It's important to remember that the 'Swinging Sixties' was difficult for many people. Many in the black community still faced day-to-day racism and a struggle to get jobs. Across the world, the struggle for civil rights continued, while in America many young men – a disproportionate number of them black – were being sent to fight and die in Vietnam.

Activities

1   What can you learn from Source B about the upbringing of people living within the colonies?

2   What problems might this lead to when making a decision on migrating to Britain?

3   What other types of sources might help you understand problems with views of the 'Mother Country' held by people from the colonies?

5.1 Summary

- Britain after the Second World War had been damaged very badly. Britain had relied heavily on its Empire, with many citizens of the Commonwealth providing soldiers and money.
- Britain needed help to rebuild the country and it encouraged people from the Empire to come to Britain. This resulted in the 1948 Nationality Act.
- There were job opportunities in Britain, but black employees were often discriminated against.
- The 1960s saw a number of changes within Britain including the growth of black activism.

Checkpoint

Strengthen

S1   Explain all the different problems Britain faced after the Second World War and the reasons why it wanted to encourage migration from the Empire.

S2   What key changes took place in Britain during the 'Swinging Sixties'?

Challenge

C1   How might changes during the 'Swinging Sixties' have affected the Caribbean community in Britain?

5.2 The local context of Notting Hill

Source A

From an interview with George Warner in December 2020. He remembers why he left St Lucia in 1957 to live in Notting Hill.

I left with the intention of bettering myself and helping others by becoming a doctor. The thought of returning to St Lucia was strong but life in England was more appealing.

I left on the 10th May 1957. I had bought the ticket from the agents of the Italian liner Franca 'C', which travelled through the Caribbean Islands picking up passengers from the other small islands. The ticket cost $350 for a through trip to London. That was a lot of money in those days. Three to six months' salary depending on your job. My mum saved up to pay for the ticket.

Extend your knowledge

In the novel *The Lonely Londoners* (1956), by Samuel Selvon (a Trinidadian-born migrant, who based the novel on his own experiences), the central character is a volunteer welfare officer who helps guide new arrivals 'around by houses he knew it would be all right to go to'.

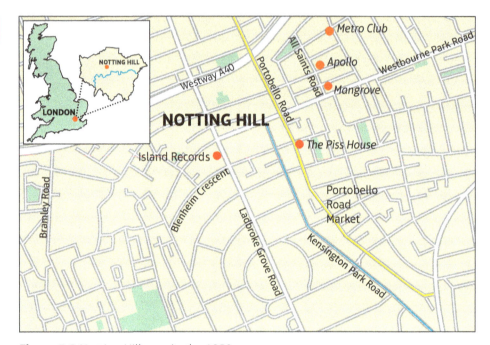

Figure 5.2 Notting Hill area in the 1950s

Caribbean migration to Notting Hill

In 1950, it was estimated that there were no more than 20,000 people from ethnic minorities living in Great Britain, although black people had lived in Britain since the time of the Romans. But, during the 1950s, the country saw mass migration of people from the Caribbean.

Why did people move to Notting Hill?

Migrants who arrived by ship would catch the boat train to London. One train route stopped at Paddington, very close to Notting Hill. There, officials from the High Commissions of several Caribbean countries, such as Jamaica and Barbados, and volunteers like Baron Baker (see page 174) would try to welcome new arrivals and help them find a place to stay.

There were not enough officials and volunteers to support everyone. People also relied on the advice and help of friends and family already living in London – and this often meant they moved into areas where those contacts were already living.

Lack of available housing

The biggest problem on arriving in London was finding somewhere to live.

- Many landlords were not willing to let to black people. Racist signs (e.g. 'No Blacks') in the windows of houses were common. Today this would be illegal, but in the 1950s there was nothing to stop this.

- This prejudice meant black people had very few choices where to live. They could only choose landlords who would let houses to them, which were often run-down properties with mould and draughts.

Notting Hill was one of the few places where landlords were willing to rent to black people – even if they often overcharged them. Many black servicemen during the war had stayed in the area.

Source B

A young Caribbean man looking for accommodation in London in 1958.

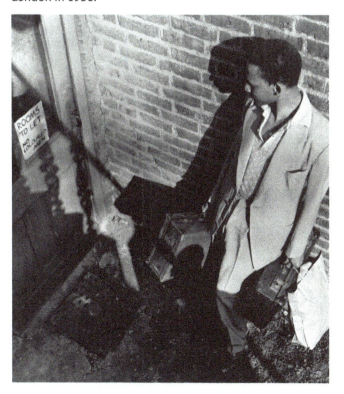

The growth of a community in Notting Hill

There were several reasons for the growth of the black community in Notting Hill.

- Many migrants had been surprised at the hostile reaction they had received on arrival. They felt safer and more secure living in an area where there was an existing black community.

- Lodgings were hard to find in London, so Notting Hill was attractive as black people could get homes there.

- Word spread among newly arrived migrants, making Notting Hill one of the first areas where people looked for housing.

- As the Caribbean community in the area grew, Notting Hill began to adapt to support them. Market stalls started selling Caribbean food and ingredients (such as on Portobello Road Market). Restaurants and cafes that either served, or were run by, black people appeared (particularly on All Saints Road).

- This made the area even more attractive to migrants, making it more likely that people would move there.

Activities ?

1 Why did Caribbean people move to Notting Hill in particular?

2 Make a list of all the different reasons for settling in Notting Hill. Read through the reasons you have written down. Can you put them into what you think is the order of importance?

Housing problems

If you had walked around the streets of Notting Hill in the early 1950s you would have seen dirty houses, boarded-up windows and rubbish on the streets. Nearly all the houses needed repairs, and some had fallen down and not been rebuilt.

Notting Hill was seen as an unattractive area to live. Landlords in Notting Hill struggled to rent out their properties. They solved this problem by renting to Caribbean migrants, who were often refused accommodation in other parts of London.

- Many landlords took advantage of the lack of choice migrants had by charging very high rents, sometimes two or three times what they charged white tenants. Four or five strangers or whole families could end up sharing rooms. Overcrowding in rented properties was very common.
- Landlords also avoided spending too much money on improving their houses. Any improvements they paid for in the buildings would affect their profits from renting the houses to Caribbean migrants.

Source C

Claude Ramsay, a Barbadian Second World War army veteran, talked about his experience of first living in England.

My first home in England was a house in Notting Hill Gate shared with about 30 other people, with only one bath and toilet between us. The conditions were appalling and it cost me £3 a week in rent. [£3 a week in 1950 is the equivalent of £105 a week today.]

Source D

Data from the UK census 1951–71. It shows the number of people living in Kensington and Chelsea (the London borough containing Notting Hill), its population density (the number of people living per square mile) and the average population density for London. Kensington and Chelsea is 4.7 square miles and was the most densely populated borough in London during this period.

Year	1951	1961	1971
Population	219,117	218,528	177,091
Population density (per square mile)	47,634	47,506	38,498
London average population density (per square mile)	13,185	12,856	11,852

Houses of Multiple Occupation (HMOs)

Many landlords applied to change their properties into Houses of Multiple Occupation (HMOs). This meant a house could be rented to many tenants, rather than just one tenant or a single family. Landlords made fortunes from doing this.

- These houses often contained private bedrooms, but even these could be shared by 2 or 3 people – sometimes even sharing a bed, one person sleeping while the other was out working and vice versa.
- Areas like the kitchen and the bathroom were shared by the whole house. They were often poor quality.
- Each person paid their own rent. There were no laws controlling how much a landlord could charge for the rent in these houses. Many landlords charged as much as they felt they could get away with.

Source E

Housing in Notting Hill, 1953.

Activities

1. Look at Source D. What can this data tell us about living conditions in Notting Hill at the time? Think about how it compares with the rest of London.
2. If this many people were living per square mile in this borough, how could this have affected the number of people living in each house?

Slums with no legal protection

One of the biggest problems Caribbean migrants faced was lack of rights. White tenants who had statutory tenancy* were encouraged to move out. Landlords often took advantage of people's prejudices by moving Caribbean migrants nearby – this led to many white people leaving. The Caribbean migrants could be overcharged or thrown out at any time. These houses became known as slums and some of the landlords became infamous.

Peter Rachman: a landlord's story

One of the very few landlords in Notting Hill who rented to black people was Peter Rachman. By 1959 Rachman owned 80 properties in Notting Hill and was making £80,000 a year from renting to Caribbean migrants (over £1.5 million today).

- Rachman may have believed he was helping the Caribbean community, giving them homes when no one else would. Many were grateful that he was willing to rent them homes. Charlie Phillips remembered in 2020 that he '… came in because he saw the gap, bless him he would rent to us, he did put a lot of people up but we never had no health and safety'.

- However he also rented out crowded homes. Every part of each of his buildings was turned into rooms to be rented out, from the basements to the attics. Some of these were in poor condition, with high rents.

- Many said the real problem was not Rachman but the lack of action taken against other landlords who refused to take black tenants. Rachman, himself a migrant, could be seen as a scapegoat in a city where signs like "no coloured people" were common.

Rachman died in 1962. The Rent Act was passed in 1965. It introduced a system to ensure people were charged fair rents for accommodation.

Source G

From *The People*, 14 July 1963, which published an exposé on Rachman after his death. Some felt the newspaper coverage of Rachman was anti-Semitic.

The flood of West Indian immigrants to Britain was at its height. Rachman soon found that he could make fantastic money if he could force out white families and pack each room with seven or eight immigrants. And even greater profits could be made by putting prostitutes into the rooms... Rachman would pack every room in the house with coloured people – often two, three or four to one room, and each individual paying rent... The houses were controlled for him by a gang of strong-arm thugs and a team of rent collectors who turned Alsatian dogs on anyone who refused to pay the rents demanded.

Key term

Statutory tenancy*

A lease on a rented property given to a tenant, which a landlord cannot cancel unless certain legal requirements (such as non-payment of rent) are met. It also controls how much the landlord can charge in rent.

Source F

From an article in *The Kensington Post* published 24 November 1967. The article was written as part of a series by Pat Philo, a Trinidadian journalist. Here she talks about tenants' struggles to get fair rents.

[The law] permits a landlord to give notice at will to tenants in furnished accommodation. The upshot of this is that tenants now fear taking over-charging landlords before the rent tribunal. The choice is: suffer a high rent, or take the landlord to the tribunal and start looking for somewhere else to live. Says a Jamaican housewife: 'When anybody ask what rent I pay for this room. I don't answer. What the use of taking the landlord to court? When the court changes the rent from £5 to £2 I may not be allowed to stay to enjoy it because the landlord will give me notice. Then I will be on the street. I have two children and with children it is harder.'

Activities

1 What can you learn from Source F about some of the difficulties faced by Caribbean people in Britain?

2 How might the attitudes of some people in Britain have led to tensions between the two communities going forward?

3 Read Sources F and G. What do you think these newspapers can tell us about the decisions Caribbean migrants needed to make about finding a place to live?

Bruce Kenrick and Notting Hill Housing (NHH)

Bruce Kenrick was a minister in the United Reformed Church. He moved to Notting Hill in 1963 and was shocked at the housing conditions. Kenrick believed improving people's housing would help solve many other problems. He was determined to do something to help.

Kenrick wanted to raise money to buy a house that he could improve and rent out to poor families, both white and black. Many of the people who took up this opportunity were black families. He recruited high-profile supporters – such as the Church and *The Guardian* – and his first campaign raised £20,000.

Kenrick founded Notting Hill Housing in 1963. The charity raised money to provide good quality, affordable housing to people.

- In its first year, NHH bought five houses and housed 57 people.
- By 1970 it was housing nearly 1,000 people in West London.

Associations like this helped to start to change housing conditions in Notting Hill, and improve the lives of ordinary people.

Pardner schemes led by people like Sam King (see page 168) also had a huge impact on helping people find housing.

Source H

From a parliamentary speech by Arthur Jones, 15 May 1969. Jones (a conservative MP representing Northampton) was keen to bring attention to housing problems in the UK.

Notting Hill is a crisis area in which the long history of bad housing is taking its toll… This, as will be well known, is the area of multi-occupation and exploitation…

In North Kensington the largest group born outside the United Kingdom are West Indians – 16.1%. Of this group 63.5% live in unfurnished lodgings in multiple-occupation accommodation. On average they pay more much more than United Kingdom residents by way of rent. About one-third of West Indians pay £6 to £7 a week for grossly overcrowded conditions… little is being achieved in improving housing standards throughout the country, and indeed nothing in such places as Notting Hill.

Source I

From *Come out of the Wilderness*, a memoir written by Bruce Kenrick in 1964.

What struck me painfully was the extent to which people's problems stemmed from damnable housing conditions. Marriages broke up because one or other partner could no longer stand the strain of living in one room with a stove and sink squeezed into one corner.

Portobello Road Market

Portobello Road runs through the centre of Notting Hill. There has been a market on Portobello Road since the 19th century. At first the market had mostly sold fruit and vegetables. However, after the Second World War a lot of antiques started to be sold at the market. This was because people living in bombed-out houses had started selling many of their possessions in order to survive.

In the 1950s, black people had to travel to Brixton to get the food and vegetables they were used to eating in the Caribbean. Breadfruit, yams, dasheens and sweet potatoes were not familiar to British traders. When the market traders realised there was demand for goods among the black community, the market on Portobello Road started to stock these items.

Some black people also managed to start businesses at Portobello Market. Charlie Phillips' parents opened a cafe, *Las Palmas*, which served Caribbean food – although this business, and others run by black people, faced racism and police persecution.

Extend your knowledge

Portobello Road has a direct link to the Caribbean. It was named after a Royal Navy victory against the Spanish near Porto Bello in Panama, Central America. The British captured a great deal of treasure and several areas in Britain were renamed 'Portobello' to celebrate the victory.

In the late 1960s there was also a strong music scene in Portobello Road. In 1969 Island Records, a music company founded in Jamaica, moved its base near to Portobello Road. It had started with jazz music from Jamaica and later also managed ska and calypso artists as well as rock and folk musicians. Their artists included Bob Marley. Their arrival helped to encourage music shops and live music venues to appear in the area around the market, helping to build an exciting black music scene locally.

Exam-style question, Section A

Describe two features of the development of Portobello Road Market. **(4 marks)**

Exam tip

For each feature identified, develop it with some supporting information.

5.2 Summary

- Many Caribbean people arriving in Britain faced discrimination and struggled to find housing. Most of the housing in the Notting Hill area that they found was very poor in quality.
- Some landlords preyed on the vulnerable and exploited their situation.
- Bruce Kenrick and others worked to improve the bad housing conditions in the Notting Hill area.
- Portobello Road Market started to sell food for the black community in response to the demand from the Caribbean people in the local area.

Checkpoint

Strengthen

S1 In your opinion, what was the most important reason for Caribbean migration to Britain?

S2 Give examples of some of the discrimination and prejudice faced by Caribbean people in Notting Hill.

Challenge

C1 Explain which of the different reasons for Caribbean migration to Britain you think was the most important. Give reasons for your answer.

C2 Why do you think that many of the housing problems in Notting Hill during this period saw so little improvement?

5.3 The influence of Caribbean culture

Learning outcomes

- To describe the way the black community developed its own identity in Britain.
- To explain the importance of the development of All Saints Road.
- To describe the different mutual self-help organisations created by the black community.

When a group of people move halfway around the world, they want to maintain their customs and culture. Socialising is a major part of human behaviour. When Caribbean people found time for leisure, they wanted to do things like attend church, go to the cinema, walk in the park, visit the library or go to concerts and nightclubs.

However, there was no space free from racial discrimination and the black community had to develop ways to cope. Some of those practices had a lasting influence.

Extend your knowledge

Black churches

Going to church was a major social obligation in the Caribbean. Many British churches though were hostile to black people who tried to join congregations. Black Christians started to form their own churches. In 2020 the Church of England apologised for the racism experienced by black people from the 1950s onwards, admitting many people had stopped going to church because of it.

All Saints Road

One of the main roads in the Notting Hill area is All Saints Road. As the black community in Notting Hill grew, this road become one of the centres of the community. Black-owned shops and restaurants opened on the road from the 1950s – although they had to fight against racism and police harassment (see pages 170–73).

In the late 1960s, All Saints Road became one of the hearts of black activism in London. In 1968 the British Black Panthers held meetings on All Saints Road.

Frank Crichlow opened the *Mangrove* restaurant at 8 All Saints Road, which supported activists and the organisers of the Notting Hill Carnival. The road was the starting point for the march that led to the arrest of the Mangrove Nine. You can read more about this in Section 5.5.

Shops and markets

Many people especially missed the foods they grew up with in the Caribbean. They were used to well-seasoned food flavoured with spices. Scotch bonnet, thyme, fresh ginger, pimento, cloves, hot pepper/tabasco sauce and other herbs and spices normal in the Caribbean were totally missing from the British diet.

This created an opportunity for traders to supply the food and ingredients people wanted. Black people began to rent premises and stalls not just on All Saints Road but also Portobello Road and other local streets. These businesses found an eager market of hungry Caribbean people.

Pubs, cafes and restaurants

Black people were not welcome in many pubs, cafes and restaurants. Racist owners often stopped black people from entering. Racial abuse and signs saying 'No blacks' were common.

But with fewer places for black people to go, there were opportunities for business owners willing to be different. *The Apollo* on All Saints Road was one of the first pubs to serve black people in London – a decision that helped make the owner a lot money as black people from across London came there to drink. Other pubs, such as *The Piss House* on Portobello Road, tried to attract working-class white and black customers (see Source D).

Source A

Front page of *The West Indian Gazette*, April 1961. It reports the story of Archie Spencer, who was told in a pub in Ladbroke Grove in Notting Hill, 'We don't serve coloured people here.'

Source B

In a 1964 article for *Flamingo* magazine (run by Dominican journalist Edward Scobie), Valerie Wilmer reported on the atmosphere in a pub called *The Coleherne*. Black people travelled across the city to the pub, as it was one of few that would serve them.

At 12 noon *The Coleherne* opens its doors and five minutes later you're lucky to find a seat in the place. Half an hour later, if you can force your way through the jostling crowd of beer-swigging West Indians and Europeans, brother, you've got wider shoulders than I have!

Just as with shops, black business people also started to set up their own cafes and restaurants.

- In 1959 Frank Crichlow opened the *El Rio* cafe. The cafe was popular with newly arrived migrants. It served good Caribbean food and became a gathering place for the local community.
- Crichlow later opened the *Mangrove* (see page 184), which served Caribbean food. It was the first black restaurant in the area, but became a victim of police harassment.
- Other businesses also suffered from police harassment, for example the *Las Palmas* restaurant set up by Charlie Phillips' parents (see page 162).

Source C

From an interview with Charlie Phillips in December 2020. Phillips remembers what it was like for black people setting up their own businesses in Notting Hill in the 1960s.

There were a lot of black businesses in All Saints Road but they all closed down due to pressure from the police. Frank was the only one who stood up to them. Many of the rest closed down and some went to the USA or Canada. My family did that too. If you tried to open a grocery shop or a bakery you could expect problems.

Source D

Customers in *The Piss House* on Portobello Road, a Caribbean and Irish pub, 1969. Photo by Charlie Phillips.

Activities

1. In pairs, make a list of the things the Caribbean migrants would have missed from their lives in the Caribbean. What opportunities could this present to businesses?

2. Study Sources A to D. What can these tell you about the reaction to the black community from local businesses? How representative are these sources of the black experience in Notting Hill? Draw up a list of points in all four sources that you would need to explore further.

Key term

Pirate station*

A radio station that broadcasts without a licence.

Extend your knowledge

Black-inspired music

Many famous bands were heavily inspired by black musicians. One of the Beatles' first promoters was the calypso singer Harold Phillips ('Lord Woodbine'). Blues musician Muddy Waters was one of the main inspirations for the Rolling Stones.

Extend your knowledge

Rent parties

Many people threw 'rent parties' to help pay their rent. Friends paid a small entrance fee and paid for drinks. These were a good way of meeting people, sharing experiences and coping with the stress of dealing with racism. It was also one of the few ways you could listen to and dance to black music.

Source E

From a letter to the editor from a 'regular reader' in *The Kensington Post*, 7 July 1950.

I have often wondered if there are other people who live in North Kensington, like myself, who are persistently annoyed by neighbour's noisy parties or 'ding dongs' as they prefer to call them... These parties are allowed, apparently, to go on until 3 or 4 o'clock in the morning, they usually start at 11 pm. I have not known a policeman to take any notice to attempt to lessen this nuisance.

Music and entertainment

Calypso singer Aldwyn Roberts, 'Lord Kitchener', arrived on the *SS Empire Windrush*, and many of his records became bestsellers. He often sang about life in London, helping to create a community identity.

Despite this popularity, in the 1950 to 1960s most radio stations and nightclubs did not play black music. Motown became popular in the 1960s but reggae, calypso, R&B (rhythm and blues) were only played on foreign stations or pirate stations*. Many houses had a radio that could pick up overseas stations, so they could listen to this music.

Like radio stations, mainstream record shops didn't stock black music. Ska, Rock Steady, Dub, Lovers Rock, Roots, Soca, Blues and Soul were unknown to white-owned record shops. This again created opportunities for new businesses.

Basing Street Studios opened in 1969 just off All Saints Road. The studio was used by famous performers such as Bob Marley and the Rolling Stones. Musicians – for example, Marvin Gaye, Diana Ross and Sarah Vaughan – would hang out at the *Mangrove*.

Nightclubs

Many nightclubs also refused to let black people enter. They would be told the place was full or that they were not welcome, so the black community had to set up their own nightclubs.

The *Metro Club* opened on St Luke's Road, one road on from All Saints Road in 1968. This was a youth club, community centre and nightclub, one of the only clubs in London for black people. Young black people from all over London came – sometimes there would be queues of 400 people waiting to get in. Reggae legends such as Alton Ellis and Aswad performed there. The police regularly raided the premises.

Shebeens

Many people found it was easier to host clubs at their houses or in abandoned buildings. These unofficial clubs were known as *shebeens*. People could smoke, drink, gamble and listen to music there, until early in the morning. Some people ran these parties full time. *Shebeens* helped to give black people entertainment and share music like blues, reggae and ska.

The police would often raid these events and violently break them up. They argued that these parties were nightclubs, and were selling alcohol without a licence (this was, and is, illegal). Partygoers at *shebeens* often had to be careful with the noise levels so their neighbours wouldn't call the police.

Source F

From *Black Scandal* (a memoir of life in Notting Hill) by John (Johnny) Edgecombe, published in 2012. Edgecombe wrote about how his *shebeen* worked:

When it was full, we had about twenty to thirty people inside the flat. There was a front room where you could listen to the latest sounds… we served every type of drink you wanted. Next door in the bedroom was the casino. The only furniture… was a table and chairs, where people sat and played poker… The shebeen had no fixed hours and just stayed open each day until the last people left… on a good week, my shebeen could earn up to £400.

Sound systems

Sound systems transformed how music was recorded and listened to in Britain and the world. They came from Jamaica, where they were used to play rhythm and blues music to large audiences in the streets. People set up their own speaker systems for house parties. These speaker systems – many of them homemade – were a real novelty in Britain in the 1950s.

Parties sometimes featured 'sound clashes' between two different systems to see who had the best speakers or DJs. They also became a major part of the Notting Hill carnival.

Source G

From *Changing Britannia: life experience with Britain* edited by Roxy Harris and Sarah White, published in 1999. Michael La Rose, an activist and later a successful businessman, remembers the influence of music and sound systems on house parties in the 1960s.

You made your own boxes (speakers) and amplifiers … The actual sound was very important… [Records] were imported from Jamaica… Like a lot of young people at that time, we used to go to what they called blues [shebeens], that's a party where they sold drinks. A sound system would be played and all the youths would come and go all through the night… We had to have our parties and and our blues in condemned houses because that's all that was available. You couldn't hire a hall, you couldn't hire a hotel, that's how it was at the time.

Extend your knowledge

Duke Vin

Duke Vin was the original sound system pioneer in the UK after he arrived as a stowaway in 1954. He performed as a DJ in the Ladbroke Grove area. He used a speaker and an amp to set up his system and played Jamaican reggae at house parties. He had a huge influence on making reggae and ska popular in Britain and performed at several clubs in London as well as being a regular at the Notting Hill Carnival.

Source H

From the Noise Abatement Act 1960, which the police stated they were enforcing when breaking up loud parties.

```
... a complaint of the existence of a
statutory nuisance may be made by any...
three or more persons each of whom is the
occupier of land or premises and is in that
capacity aggrieved [are annoyed] by the
nuisance.
```

Activities ?

1 How do you think the racism of pub and nightclub owners affected the development of the house party culture in the black community?

2 Until the 1950s sound systems – and the music played on them – were unknown in Britain. How do you think this might have affected the reaction to them outside the black community?

3 Look at Sources E to H. Why did *shebeens* develop and why did the police think they were a nuisance? Debate this as a group, with one side taking the view of the police, and the other side taking the view of the hosts of the *shebeens*.

Mutual self-help organisations

One of the ways the black community in Notting Hill helped to grow its own identity was through working together. This could involve anything from housing to childcare to activism. Organisations were set up by members of the community to support each other. They included:

- **The London Free School** was a community action project set up in 1966. It arranged dances, workshops for children, childcare and, later, street carnivals. Many childminders refused to take black children. Having an organisation that offered this for black families was a huge help.
- **The Unity Association** helped house homeless young black people in two properties in Notting Hill, donated by Notting Hill Housing (see page 162). Among its founders was Rhodan Gordon (one of the Mangrove Nine). It also helped young people with professional training.
- **The Black People's Information Centre** was founded in 1970. It provided legal advice, welfare support and education on black history and political causes. Its headquarters was in Portobello Road.

Exam-style question, Section A

Describe two features of the mutual self-help organisations for the black community in Notting Hill during the 1950s. **(4 marks)**

Exam tip

Make sure you develop each feature you identify with some supporting information.

Pardner schemes

Pardner schemes helped black people buy their own homes. It was especially hard for black people to get a mortgage: some banks would not let black people open an account let alone give them a mortgage. Without a mortgage it was nearly impossible for people to save the money they needed to buy a home.

Sam King, a Second World War RAF veteran who arrived in Britain on the *SS Empire Windrush*, set up saving systems all across London called 'pardner schemes'. Pardner schemes were based on a tradition dating back to pre-colonial West Africa. They helped people save to buy houses. Many of these houses still belong to black families to this day.

Source I

From his book *Now You Know*, published in 2015, Allan Wilmott, a Jamaican Second World War ex-RAF serviceman, explains how pardner schemes worked.

The partners contribute a regular sum weekly, fortnightly or on a monthly basis. Every week, fortnight or month, one member of the group is given the total amount contributed by the partners over that period. The 'banker' determines the order in which members can make their 'draw' and will normally give the priority to the more established and trusted members, leaving those who are least reliable until last. In those days it was difficult for black people to obtain accommodation because of overt racism… So the only solution was to buy our own houses with the use of a 'pardna'.

Source J

In his biography *Climbing up the Rough Side of the Mountain*, published in 1998, Sam King remembers the advantages of pardner schemes.

The system allowed members to take it in turns to draw the entire amount each week with no interest and repay the loan within fifteen weeks. This method of saving was the quickest and most successful way of accumulating enough in a short time to deposit on a house or make other purchases. A house was the main aim, as the average immigrant was finding lodging hard to get. Ex-servicemen were the avant-garde of a method of saving which was to be adopted by early immigrants whose main intention was to buy a house and which they more often than not achieved within three years of arrival.

Activities

1 Using the information from this section draw a table with three columns headed: Problems faced by Caribbean migrants, The community response, Impact of developments.

2 Read through this section of the text and add notes to the different columns in your table.

3 Which developments from the 1960s still exist in the black community today? Why do you think this is the case?

5.3 Summary

- When Caribbean people came to Britain they were denied access to leisure activities due to discrimination. In response, to help cope with the challenges they faced, the black community developed their own identity and leisure activities.

- This led to the emergence of a distinct culture that featured Caribbean shops, pubs, food, restaurants, music and entertainment.

- Mutual self-help organisations supported the community with finance, childcare, housing and legal advice.

Checkpoint

Strengthen

S1 Explain how the following were important developments in the creation of an identity for the Caribbean community: All Saints Road, Caribbean music, pardner schemes.

S2 Identify some of the problems that the Caribbean people faced in their leisure time.

Challenge

C1 From your list of problems, which ones do you think would be particularly challenging for Caribbean people trying to settle in Britain? Discuss your answers as a group.

C2 The impact of culture on people's lives and society can be difficult to measure. Think about why this is and how it might affect the questions you ask when reviewing sources.

5.4 Racism and policing

Learning outcomes

- To describe the problems of racism and policing in Notting Hill.
- To explain the reasons for the Notting Hill riots in 1958.
- To analyse the effects of the murder of Kelso Cochrane on race relations in Notting Hill.
- To evaluate the impact of anti-immigration groups on Caribbean people in Notting Hill.

The Metropolitan Police

In the 1950s the Metropolitan Police was mostly white, overwhelmingly male and often ex-military.

- In 1952 there were approximately 16,400 officers in the Metropolitan Police.
- Over 97% of these police officers were white and male.
- The police made little effort to build relationships with the black community or to understand the people they were policing.

Black people who attempted to join the police force were refused entry because of the colour of their skin. Many police officers displayed racist attitudes and the force was not respected or trusted by the black community.

Extend your knowledge

Norwell Roberts

Norwell Roberts, from Anguilla in the Caribbean, was the first black officer to join the Metropolitan Police after the Second World War (and only the second in its history). He joined in 1967. He had tried to join in 1965 but had been refused with no reason given. He experienced racism, isolation, bullying and blocked promotion. He served for 30 years in the force and was an inspiration to many future black officers.

Racism in the police

In the 1950s there were no laws against racial harassment or attacks. The police had the power to stop, search and arrest people they suspected of intent to carry out a crime – this was most often used against black people. Beatings of black people were common, as was the planting of evidence. 'N****r hunting' was the name the police gave to deliberately searching for black people to arrest.

Extend your knowledge

Race Relations Act (2000)

At this time the police kept no records of racially motivated crimes, describing them as hooliganism or thuggery despite evidence from the victims. This means it is very hard to identify how many black people were victims of racist attacks. Things only changed with the introduction of the Race Relations Act in 2000 after a campaign led by the parents of the black teenager Stephen Lawrence, who was murdered in 1993.

The term institutional racism* was not widely accepted in British society until the early 2000s. When black people complained about racism, they were ignored or accused of exaggerating and having an 'attitude problem'. Some police officers accused the black community of being full of troublemakers.

The black community argued that the police were not interested in looking after them. Black people were angry at:

- being denied entry to pubs, shops and other places simply because they were black
- police officers supporting the business owners in these situations
- racist attacks, where the police let the white attackers go, and tell the victim to 'go back home'.

Key term

Institutional racism*

When an organisation deliberately treats a group unfairly, because of its race. Typically, this behaviour is encouraged by the organisation or, at the very least, goes unchallenged.

Source A

From an interview with Charlie Phillips, conducted by Tony Warner in 2020. Here Charlie remembers his childhood in Notting Hill and facing racism from the police.

If you got arrested by police they would flush your head down the toilet or beat you with a wet towel so the marks wouldn't show. They would arrest you for no reason and then give you a choice of a wallet or some drugs. If you chose wallet they charge you with theft if you chose drugs they charge you with supply, sometimes they'd choose for you or say you were carrying a weapon and produce the weapon themselves. A lot of people got sentences and went to prison like that. The other thing they would do is come up real close to you, in your face, step on your toes with their boot and when you naturally pushed them away they'd arrest you for assaulting a police officer in the pursuit of his duty. That was the trick.

Lack of training and top-down racism

Many police officers made the same racist assumptions as many other people in Britain. The problem was, unlike the general public, the police were responsible for law and order and protecting the black community. The racist views of some police officers were not challenged by their superior officers. The West Indian Federation (WIF) suggested to Police Commissioner Sir Joseph Simpson that he could improve the situation if he worked with the WIF to train police officers about Caribbean culture. Sir Joseph was not interested.

Source B

Sir Joseph Simpson's minutes of the meeting between himself and the West Indian Federation (WIF), July 1959, from the Metropolitan Police records.

I explained that this was very difficult and that it would have to be for me to decide how best to carry out any agreed improvement in understanding of the problem by police. For the moment I do not propose to do more than to let them tell me... the sort of thing they want to get over. I can then decide how best, if at all, to get [it] over.

Police training on racial and cultural issues was very poor. Most officers received only a half-hour talk on race during their training. Very rarely – if ever – was this talk given by a specialist.

Unlike today, the police were not interested in community links or understanding the people they policed. Many officers found things about the Caribbean community – from the clothes people wore to the music people listened to, and even their food – threatening and un-British.

Source C

From N****r Hunting in England, a report looking at the police's treatment of the black community, written by Joseph A. Hunte, a black civil rights activist born in St Vincent, published in 1966. *The report deliberately used a racist word that has been blanked out.*

It has been confirmed from reliable sources that sergeants and constables do leave stations [to go] 'n*****r hunting', that is to say, they do not get orders from superiors to act in this way, but among themselves they decide to bring in a coloured person at all cost.

The general attitude of police officers to the coloured community is strained and the sooner the authorities can realise this distasteful situation and … get through to those who now serve as police officers that… human relations are essential when dealing with people, the call to the populace to assist policemen will [fall] by the wayside.

Activities ?

1 Study Source A. What does it tell you about racism and policing in Notting Hill towards Caribbean people?

2 Study Sources B and C. What weight would you give these sources as evidence of institutional racism within the Metropolitan Police in the 1950s and 1960s?

3 Institutional racism can be very hard to measure, as it is often not stated or obvious. As a historian, what sort of evidence would you look to collect if you were making an enquiry into racism in the police?

Source D

From a memorandum in the archive of the Trades Union Congress (TUC), 5 September 1958, which refers to a visit to a TUC representative by a group of Jamaican migrants, including a restaurant owner. The TUC representative was shocked by the dangers they faced and their lack of trust in the police.

The most disturbing feature of the conversation was that [they] did not believe that if they stayed at home they would be left in peace, since a bomb had been thrown through the window of the Calypso Club in Notting Hill last Tuesday... nor did they believe that the police could or would give them adequate protection. They said that police had used foul language to them particularly in the Harrow Road Police Station. The restaurant owner said that... after the police had dispersed a threatening crowd they had come in to search for weapons and kicked the door down so that it would not now shut.

Exam-style question, Section A

How could you follow up Source D to find out more about the experiences of the black community with the Metropolitan Police? **(4 marks)**

Exam tip

Tackle the question in four stages. The example shows you what to do at each stage.

1 *Pick a detail*: e.g. The general attitude of police officers to the coloured community is strained.

2 *Choose a question*: e.g. What were the consequences of the police attitudes on the black community?

3 *Suggest the type of source to use*: e.g. Oral accounts from Caribbean people who lived in Notting Hill in 1958.

4 *Explain how this would help answer the question*: e.g. Oral accounts will give a first-hand insight into the attitudes of the police force towards the Caribbean people in the community.

The impact of anti-immigrant groups

There were several racist and anti-immigrant groups in Notting Hill in the 1950s. These groups were violent and helped build an atmosphere of fear in the black community. Many black people felt the police did not do enough to protect them from these groups.

- Teddy Boys roamed the streets, some of them threatening black people. Many of these gangs of young people drove into Notting Hill from local areas, deliberately looking for black people to attack.
- The White Defence League (WDL), a neo-Nazi group, campaigned violently against black migrants, demanding that Britain should be 'kept white'. It published a monthly magazine with a circulation of 800. Members of the WDL come into black areas to take part in what they called 'n****r hunts'. Its office was in Princedale Road, in Notting Hill. It later united with other groups to form the British National Party.
- The Union Movement was a far-right political party, led by the fascist Oswald Mosley. Mosley made violent speeches against immigrants and the party encouraged attacks on black communities. Mosley's rallying cry was 'Keep Britain White'. Its offices were in Kensington Park Road, which is in Notting Hill.

These organisations, and others, had promoted racial tensions in Notting Hill. Racist violence became more common. This increased the black communities' distrust of the police, as they felt less and less protected.

Source E

From an interview with Colin Jordan, founder of the White Defence League, *Panorama*, BBC, 13 April 1959. Jordan spoke about the aims of his organisation.

The [aims] of the White Defence League are to keep Britain the white man's country that it has always been, to preserve the white civilisation, which is the product of our race, to preserve our northern European blood, which in our opinion is our greatest national treasure... if mass immigration continues as it is doing now, it will inevitably lead to a coffee coloured, half breed, Britain of the future, and we are going to fight to stop that.

Source F

From an interview conducted in December 2020 by Tony Warner with his uncle, 82-year-old George Warner, who lived in London in the 1950s.

The public would stare with disapproval if I was with a white girl. We were walking in Waterloo in 1965. This white guy, who was on the opposite side of the street shouted 'Leave our white women alone and **** off back to Africa!' It was embarrassing but I ignored him. Then he crossed the street, walked up to me and shouted more vile abuse. He was waving his hand in my face. I would normally avoid confrontation, but I was very angry and I decided not to wait for him to touch me. I gave him a solid right hook and watched two of his teeth explode from his mouth.

Source G

Teddy Boys, Portland Road, North Kensington, 1956. Photograph by Roger Mayne.

The Notting Hill riots, August 1958

The Notting Hill riots were triggered by a fight that broke out when a mixed-race couple were confronted outside a pub. However, it is important to remember that the 'riots' were not because of just one incident. Racist groups and violence had been building tension in the area for years.

Racism was rising across Britain. In Nottingham, riots against the migrant community had started a few days earlier and were still going on. In Notting Hill, a week before the riots, a gang of white youths had been arrested for committing serious assaults on six Caribbean men.

The riots

On the night of 30 August a mob of almost 400 white people attacked the homes of Caribbean people on Bramley Road. It was the start of six nights of violent attacks. Petrol bombs were thrown at the homes of black people and many of the mob were armed with iron bars, scissors, cricket bats, knuckle dusters and knives.

Some members of the black community counter-attacked to defend their homes and neighbourhoods. They were also accused of rioting, even though they were defending their homes. The violence became worse and worse. However, the police denied race had anything to do with the violence.

Source H

Police clashing with rioters in Notting Hill, published in *The Mirror*, 31 August 1958.

Source I

From *Black Britannia: a history of blacks in Britain* by Edward Scobie, published in 1972. Scobie, a Dominican-born ex-RAF bomber pilot and reporter, writes about witnessing the riots.

From that Sunday there was an uninterrupted, chaotic, senseless, repetitive sequence of rioting and arson, day and night… Marauding whites came from all over London looking for a 'punch up' ready to do grievous bodily harm to blacks… more and more sightseers watched greedy-eyed for the sight of bashed-in black heads…

Although most of the more realistic black people remained indoors… the more militant and indignant, primarily Jamaicans, came out of doors to defend themselves. [They] collected empty milk bottles, rocks and some hand-made bombs… [shelling] the baying, jeering white mobs in the streets from vantage points on the rooftops. These houses were bombarded with petrol bombs and bricks. There were attacks and counter-attacks. The Notting Hill Riots were race riots, and cannot properly be described otherwise.

Source J

From an interview with Hubert 'Baron' Baker in a BBC 4 documentary, *Timeshift*, 1 July 2003. Baker founded a black self-defence group based at 9 Blenheim Crescent. In the interview he remembers the resistance to white mobs that he organised during the riots. *Baker quotes racist and offensive language, which has been blanked out.*

I saw from Kensington Park Road to Portobello Road a massive lot of people out there and I distinctly hear when they say 'Lets burn the n*****s! Lets lynch the n*****s!' and from those spoken words, I said, 'Start bombing them!' and then we started to see the Molotov cocktails coming out from number 9 Blenheim Crescent and then they said 'Oh they are bombing us too!'

I said open the gates and throw them back where they're coming from… when the police saw the amount of people that was in number 9 they [rammed] the gates and said 'Not another one of you black b*****ds coming out!' I was arrested immediately but from then on the rest of my colleagues took over.

Exam-style question, Section A

How useful are Sources I and J for an enquiry into the reaction of the black community to the Notting Hill riots? **(8 marks)**

Exam tip

Make sure you consider the content of both sources. Highlight or underline any information to help you.

- Consider the importance of the provenance from each source. What is the nature of the source? How does this affect how much you can trust it? Use your own knowledge of the historical context to evaluate the source.
- How comprehensive is it?
- How accurate is it? Does your own knowledge support or challenge what it says?
- How typical is the source? Does it capture the common feelings at the time or is it out of place?

The aftermath of the riots

The public were shocked by the violence. The Notting Hill race riots were some of the worst race riots ever seen in British history. *The Times* wrote about 'groups of men in a public house singing… punctuating the songs with vicious [racist] slogans. The men said that their motto was Keep Britain White.' The *Daily Mail* blamed the black community, publishing an article called 'Should We Let Them Keep Coming In?', demanding greater controls on black immigration.

After the riots, 108 people were arrested. Amazingly, although there were several very serious injuries, nobody had been killed.

- According to the police, of the 108 arrests, 72 were white and 36 black. Charges included grievous bodily harm, affray, possessing offensive weapons and riot.
- In September 1958 over 170 cases connected to the riots were heard at courts across London, with sentences from prison time to fines. Although race wasn't always recorded, the majority (almost 75%) of these people were white.

Source K

From the Institute of Race Relations report of a trial at the Old Bailey of 13 men (3 of them black) in September 1958. *This report quotes attitudes and uses words which are rightly unacceptable today.*

> A police sergeant giving evidence was asked how long there had been disturbed feelings between white and coloured, and what was the cause. He replied that the feeling had been 'boiling up' for about 12 months in the Notting Hill area. He believed the cause to be 'the housing situation plus the white women associating with coloured men'. One of the acquitted men, a former Jamaican policeman, stated that he was going home: 'I came to the Mother Country because I believed there was no colour bar. Now I know there is.'

The Notting Hill riots helped the continued growth of black activism (see pages 179–87). The black community objected to the events being described as a 'riot' – they argued they were the victims of an attack and had no choice but to defend themselves.

The police refused to accept there was any racist motive behind the riots. Instead, they blamed the violence on white thugs and the black community. However, as Source M shows, the police were very aware of the racism behind the riots.

Source L

Statement from London-based Afro-West Indian Union, a civil rights movement, 4 September 1958.

> The Afro-West Indian Union considers that the attacks made upon the black population in Britain by a section of British white citizens have created a dangerous and deplorable situation which could have far reaching consequences... the union holds the British Government responsible for the conditions which have given rise to this racial violence.

Source M

From *The Guardian*, 24 August 2002. Two police officers remember the Notting Hill riots. *This source contains offensive racist language that has been blanked out.*

PC Richard Bedford said he had seen a mob of 300 to 400 white people in Bramley Road shouting: 'We will kill all black b******s. Why don't you send them home?' PC Ian McQueen on the same night said he was told: 'Mind your own business, coppers. Keep out of it. We will settle these n*****s our way. We'll murder the b******s.'

The murder of Kelso Cochrane

In 1959 another violent incident again made the black community feel abandoned by the police.

Kelso Cochrane was a 32-year-old man, working as a carpenter to raise money to study law. He had moved to Notting Hill in 1954. While walking home on 17 May 1959 he was stabbed by a gang of white youths, dying an hour later in hospital. In the aftermath of the riots, the murder received national attention.

Activities

1. Study Source K. What does it tell you about the reasons for the Notting Hill riots?

2. Study Sources K and L. In what ways do these two sources disagree about the causes of the Notting Hill riots?

3. Now look again at Sources K, L and M. Suggest two reasons why these might be useful as evidence about how the police and government responded to the issue of race in Notting Hill.

4. Which source do you think is most useful for an inquiry into the Notting Hill riots and why?

Source N

Illustration of the murder of Kelso Cochrane by cartoonist Ken Sprague, published in *Searchlight*, a socialist magazine, in June 1959. It shows a swastika-wearing Nazi urging on the killer.

Source O

Frank Crichlow, owner of the *Mangrove* restaurant, speaking in 1990. Here Crichlow gives his opinion on the police investigation into Kelso Cochrane's murder.

Neighbours said they saw the killer and up to now that killer has not been found and I don't think it's because the killer himself was very clever, it was because the police wasn't making no effort at all.

Source P

From the *Daily Mirror* article of 19 May 1959. In the article, some key words were written in capitals to make them stand out.

A senior Scotland Yard officer told me yesterday: 'You will be doing the community a service by refraining from any suggestion that this is a racist murder.' He went on 'We are satisfied that it was the work of a group of about six anti-law white teenagers who only had ONE MOTIVE in view – ROBBERY... the fact that he happened to be coloured does not, in our view, come into question.'

The police investigation

- Although arrests were quickly made the suspects were released in hours. The murderers were never caught. Years later a Union Movement member claimed his group were responsible for the crime.
- The investigation angered many in the black community as they believed the police were more interested in claiming there was no racial motive to the attack than capturing the killers.
- It's possible the government and the police were worried that if they acknowledged that race was the motive, it could lead to more riots.

Media coverage

- Most newspapers reported that the killing was not motivated by race, angering many black people. On 19 May 1959 the *Daily Mirror* placed the case on the front page with the headline 'It was not a racial killing'.

The black community response

The response to Kelso Cochrane's murder was immediate. Norman Manley, the prime minister of Jamaica, visited Notting Hill to meet local people and find out what was going on. Once, when he was standing on a street corner in Notting Hill, the police told him to 'move along'.

One of the main impacts was the growth of more black organisations to promote civil rights. The West Indian Standing Conference (WISC) was formed just after the riots; it fought for racial equality over the next 50 years. WISC also campaigned for greater understanding between races and worked to provide leadership in the Caribbean community.

Kelso Cochrane's funeral

- On 6 June 1959, hundreds of people – white and black – attended Kelso Cochrane's funeral. Over 1,200 more people lined the streets outside. Among those helping to organise the funeral was Claudia Jones (see page 179). Jones helped form the Inter-Racial Friendship Coordinating Council.

- The Council wrote to the prime minister, asking him to make racially motivated violence a crime and stating that 'coloured citizens of the UK have lost confidence in the ability of the law enforcing agencies to protect them'. The government didn't do this – but it did give permission to the White Defence League to hold a rally in Trafalgar Square on 24 May 1959.

Kelso Cochrane's murder became an important moment in the growth of civil rights and opposition to racism. For many black people it was a sign that if they wanted their rights and lives to be protected, it was up to them, not the police or the government, to do it.

Source Q

Members of the Coloured People's Progressive Association protesting the racist murder of Kelso Cochrane, near Downing Street, May 1959.

Activity ?

Look at Sources N to Q. What can these sources tell you about how the reaction to Kelso Cochrane's murder helped lead to a growth in black activism and a greater awareness of civil rights?

Oswald Mosley's Union Movement

In the 1930s Oswald Mosley had founded the British Union of Fascists. During the Second World War Mosley had been imprisoned. Many people believed he was a traitor. In 1948 he formed the Union Movement, a racist anti-immigrant party.

Extend your knowledge

Mosley's British Union of Fascists at its height had 50,000 members. He supported Hitler and led his 'Blackshirts' in marches and violence against many groups, especially Jews, most famously at the Battle of Cable Street (see page 116).

Mosley believed encouraging racist tensions and anger about immigration would help him win support. From 1958 he was active in Notting Hill, where his stirring of tensions helped lead to the Notting hill riots:

- Mosley held mass meetings, attended by hundreds of people. He attacked the black population and other minorities, with the message 'Keep Britain White'. Some of these meetings were held at the centre of the Caribbean community, for example, outside 9 Blenheim Crescent (see Source J).

- The Union Movement played on the fears and prejudices of white people in Notting Hill. A pamphlet released after the murder of Kelso Cochrane tried to promote racial tension (Source R).

- Black war veterans – for example 'Baron' Baker – were furious. They had fought for, and settled in, Britain only to have a Nazi-supporter like Mosley argue that black people should 'go back to where they came from'.

Source R

Union Movement pamphlet from May 1959. Note that the text of the pamphlet does not directly call for violence, but urges people to 'take action'.

```
Take action now. Protect your jobs. Stop
coloured immigration. Houses for white people
- not coloured immigrants.
```

Key term

Election deposit*

Any candidate standing in a British Parliamentary election must pay a fee to do so. This fee is repaid to the candidate after the election, unless they have received less than a set percentage of the votes (in 1959 this was 12.5% (6,433) of the 51,469 registered voters)

Source S

Results for Kensington North constituency, 1959 election.

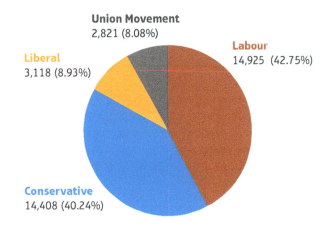

Union Movement
2,821 (8.08%)

Liberal
3,118 (8.93%)

Labour
14,925 (42.75%)

Conservative
14,408 (40.24%)

Mosley's 1959 election campaign

In 1959 Mosley ran for Parliament, trying to win the seat of Kensington North, which included Notting Hill. His campaign was based on racism. He claimed black migrants were criminals and rapists.

Mosley was humiliated in the election. He came fourth and received such a small share of the votes that he lost his election deposit*. He and the Union Movement never recovered from this embarrassment. However, racism – and political parties that support and encourage racism – continued to receive support, and still do today.

Activities

1. How do you think Mosley's campaign in Notting Hill impacted tensions in the area?

2. As a group debate Mosley's election defeat. How far was this a rejection of racism by the voters and how far was it due to the unpopularity of Mosley?

5.4 Summary

- In the 1950s racism in the police was a major barrier that prevented them from protecting the black community. Many officers believed racist stereotypes, leading to harassment and unfair treatment.
- Anti-immigration groups and figures like Mosley created an atmosphere of fear for the black community with acts of violence and intimidation. These issues were not addressed by the police.
- Institutional racism from the police force and violence from anti-immigration groups helped build tensions in the Notting Hill area – tensions that erupted into the 1958 riots.
- The riots and Kelso Cochrane's murder became a catalyst for the growth in civil rights groups.

Checkpoint

Strengthen

S1 In what ways did the black community suffer at the hands of racism within the police force?

S2 When did the Notting Hill riots begin?

S3 What impact did anti-immigration groups have on the black community?

Challenge

C1 Why might some historians argue that the police response to the Kelso Cochrane murder led to the murder of Stephen Lawrence?

5.5 Black British activism in Notting Hill

Learning outcomes

- To describe how the Notting Hill Carnival developed and the reasons for its success.
- To explain the growth of activism in the black community through the work of people like Claudia Jones.
- To evaluate the importance of the *Mangrove* restaurant and the trial of the Mangrove Nine.

Since before the Second World War, black people in Britain have organised groups to help their community and to fight discrimination and institutional racism in society. The riots of 1958 motivated even more people to join existing equality groups as well as to establish new organisations to fight for human rights.

Many of these groups were self-funded and began by meeting in cafes, churches or someone's front room (due to discrimination it was hard for these groups to rent meeting rooms). These groups demanded the right to be treated as human beings in a racist society.

Extend your knowledge

Black self-help groups before 1958

In the 1780s The Sons of Africa, led by the Nigerian Olaudah Equiano, lobbied for equal treatment of black and white people. In 1925 Ladipo Solanke established the West African Students Union to campaign against racism. In 1931 Jamaican Dr Harold Moody founded The League of Coloured Peoples. All these groups demanded the right to be treated as equal human beings in a racist society.

Claudia Jones and the *West Indian Gazette*

Claudia Jones was a Trinidadian woman who spent her life fighting for equality. She was active in the US civil rights movement, organising rent strikes against racist landlords overcharging black people.

Source A

Claudia Jones at the offices of the *West Indian Gazette* in 1962.

In 1955, because she was an active and successful anti-racism leader and communist, the US government imprisoned and then deported* her. Claudia moved to Britain and, in 1958, set up a newspaper called the *West Indian Gazette*, which became Britain's first major black newspaper (see Source A, page 165).

Key term

Deported*

Forced by the government to leave a country you are visiting or living in where you are not a citizen. (Note: this is different from the Windrush deportation scandal where black people who had been living and paying tax in Britain for decades were suddenly deported due to changes in government policy.)

The *West Indian Gazette* gave a voice to the black community in London and it soon gained a circulation* of over 15,000 people.

- In the 1950s, without the internet or social media, newspapers were how you found out about jobs, accommodation and events as well as the news.
- At the time major newspapers only rarely featured stories about the black community and, if they did, they tended to be negative or sensational.
- The black community had nowhere to get information on issues that were important to them and there was no platform for their voices to be heard.
- Newspapers were also a vital way to help arrange or publicise campaigns for equal treatment.
- The office in Brixton, South London, received huge numbers of racially abusive letters and was attacked by the Ku Klux Klan (KKK). Letters sent on KKK-headed notepaper boasted that 'Communism Enslaved, Jewish Usurers Invented It. England Awake, Keep Britain Pure and White. Put the Traitors to the Stake'.

Source B

West Indian Gazette, 18 August 1958, letter from the London Branch of the Ku Klux Klan, a racist organisation. It was addressed to 'Mr B. Ape' and sent from 'A. Whiteman'. *This source contains offensive racist language that has been blanked out.*

```
Possibly you are wondering
why we have so-far failed
to pay attention to your
audacity in setting up
this filthy hack-trash of
a paper? Pray good Sir,
We, The Aryan Knights miss
nothing, close attention
has been paid to every
issue of this rag, and so
I sincerely assure you,
the information gleamed has
proven of great value to
the Klan. May we take this
opportunity to wish your
n****r paper every success
whilst you are able to
continue printing it.
```

Source C

Interview with Billy Strachan, former Second World War RAF bomber pilot and a member of the Caribbean Labour Congress, in BBC documentary *Eye to Eye*, 1989. Strachan spoke about his work with Claudia Jones.

```
We were just getting people to get jobs. I remember,
we were going to Barclays Bank and trying to get a
black girl a job there, and there was no chance, [they]
wouldn't even consider it... Claudia because of her more
advanced experience in the United States was now saying
– because we now had busmen working on the buses and
things like that – and she said what about being made
inspectors? Which we had not even foreseen because we
thought we'd achieved a hell of a lot by just getting
a job on London Transport!
```

Claudia Jones was a natural leader and successfully lobbied for black people to get jobs in senior positions in London Transport and other institutions where there was a colour bar. She also campaigned against racist immigration controls such as the 1962 Commonwealth Immigration Act, which restricted migration from black Commonwealth countries such as Jamaica but not from white Commonwealth countries such as Canada.

Claudia Jones was so famous for her anti-racist activities that the American civil rights leader, Martin Luther King, stopped in London to meet her when travelling to collect his Nobel Peace Prize in 1964.

Source D

From 'The Caribbean Community in Britain', an essay by Claudia Jones published in the African-American journal *Freedomways*, Summer 1964. She writes about the impact of the *West Indian Gazette*.

The newspaper has served as a catalyst [a start of something], quickening the awareness, socially and politically, of West Indians, Afro-Asians and their friends. Its editorial stand is for a united, independent West Indies, full economic, social and political equality and respect for human dignity for West Indians and Afro-Asians in Britain, and for peace and friendship between all Commonwealth and world peoples.

Extend your knowledge

Colonial News

A Jamaican RAF veteran, Laurie Philpott, produced a newspaper named the *Colonial News* in 1957. It had national distribution as he used his ex-military contacts to ship and sell it all over the country.

Exam-style question, Section A

Describe **two** features of the *West Indian Gazette*.

(4 marks)

Exam tip

Make sure that you develop each feature you identify with some supporting information. You could first identify one thing the *West Indian Gazette* did and then add information on how it helped black people in the community.

Claudia Jones and the development of the Notting Hill Carnival

The Caribbean Carnival 1959

As a direct response to the 1958 riots, Claudia Jones wanted to celebrate African-Caribbean culture and help bring the community together. She said the community 'needed to wash the taste of [the] Notting Hill and Nottingham [riots] out of our mouths'.

The first carnival, sponsored by the *West Indian Gazette*, took place at St Pancras Town Hall, Kings Cross, on 30 January 1959. In Trinidad carnival always takes place in February: the weather is hot there, so it is always outdoors. Obviously in Britain it is very cold in February so it had to be held indoors!

The event was televised on the BBC and leading British black artists, such as Cleo Laine, performed. A beauty show was part of the carnival, to help challenge white beauty standards that defined black women as unattractive. Some of the money raised was used to help pay the bail of young black men unfairly arrested by the police after the riots.

Activities ?

1 Study Source A (page 179) and sources B and D. Describe the main features (characteristics) of the *West Indian Gazette*.

2 What can you learn from the *West Indian Gazette* about the different forms of discrimination experienced by Caribbeans in Notting Hill?

3 With a partner, discuss the importance and impact of the *West Indian Gazette* in helping black people fight against discrimination in Britain. What other sources would help?

Source E

The first Caribbean Carnival, published in the *Daily Mirror*, 31 January 1959.

Claudia was determined that the carnival would become an annual event. She moved the venue around so that the event would get more exposure and even took it to Manchester. Her carnival ran from 1959 until 1964, when she died.

From Caribbean Carnival to Notting Hill Carnival

In 1966, Rhaune Leslet, President of the London Free School, planned an outdoor event in August to promote cultural unity. Thanks to Claudia Jones' work, she found there was a network of artists – and an excited audience – from the indoor carnivals to help make this event a success.

Extend your knowledge

Leslie Palmer

One of the people who was part of the 1966 carnival was a Trinidadian migrant called Leslie Palmer. He became the director of the carnival from 1973 to 1975. He worked to bring representatives from the whole Caribbean community together to be part of the carnival. He installed more sound systems and recruited more steel bands and reggae groups to join the carnival. By 1976, 150,000 people – black and white – were attending the carnival.

In the 21st century Notting Hill Carnival is the biggest street festival in Europe, attracting over a million people and generating millions of pounds. Most of the attendees have no idea about the roots of the carnival.

Source F

Interview with Victor Crichlow in July 2001. Victor worked with Claudia Jones on the early carnivals and later became Treasurer of the Notting Hill Carnival.

The spirit of carnival is the bringing together of people, all kinds of people, the harmony that it generates, it is something that the whole world would like to have... I would like to see that same spirit going into everyday life... Carnival is a teacher, tells us how to live; living means living with people, you can't live on your own that's not living, that's existing.

Activities

1 Why did Claudia Jones decide to introduce the Carnival following the Notting Hill and Nottingham riots?

2 Look at Sources E and F. How far do these sources show that Carnival has been successful in making Caribbean culture part of mainstream British culture?

The British Black Panthers (BBP)

With no legislation to prevent racial harassment or discrimination, black people in Britain needed to campaign to protect their rights. Many groups campaigned for racial equality and civil rights. In 1968 the British Black Panthers (BPP) were founded.

The BPP:

- were inspired by the Black Panther Party* in the USA; the BPP was the first Black Panther organisation outside America
- campaigned against police brutality and in favour of civil rights; they helped black people with legal aid

- worked to educate black people about their history, to build a sense of pride in their community
- campaigned on several social issues, looking to help black people find better jobs, housing and healthcare
- had several leaders, including Darcus Howe, Altheia Jones-LeCointe and housing campaigner Olive Morris. Howe and Jones-LeCointe were later part of the Mangrove Nine.

Source G

Altheia Jones-LeCointe spoke to the BBC documentary *Mangrove 9* broadcast in 1973.

We've complained to the police about the police and nothings been done. We've complained to magistrates about magistrates and nothings been done. We've complained to judges about judges and nothing has been done. Now it's time to do something ourselves. That represents the essence of black people's experience in Britain. Since we've come here we've suffered a long train of abuses by the police, with the active support of the British state. And those abuses have been able to be carried out under the pretext that black people are criminals... That is a myth that has been created about us.

Source H

Darcus Howe spoke to an oral historian in 2001 about his experiences arriving in Britain from Trinidad.

The first thing that struck me like a thunderbolt was that people made decisions about people based on the colour of skin, which was completely outside my world of reason... that disturbed me greatly and I was determined to fight it and I continued to do so.

Source I

Black Power activist Stokely Carmichael speaking in London, 1967. Photograph by Horace Ove of US civil rights.

Extend your knowledge

Darcus Howe

Darcus Howe would go on to be one of the organisers for the biggest ever black protest march, when approximately 20,000 people took part in the Black People's Day of Action on 2 March 1981. The march was arranged because of the deaths of 13 young black people in a suspected racist arson attack in New Cross in January 1981.

Activities ?

1 Study Sources H, I and J. Why do you think the Black Panthers emerged in Britain following the 1950s?

2 How useful are Sources G and H in helping identify the reasons for the emergence of the Black Panthers?

3 Make a list of other sources that would give you useful information about the problems experienced by black people in Britain from the 1950s. Compare your list with that of a partner. Decide which source would be the most useful.

Key term

Black Panther Party*

A political party founded in America by black college students Huey P. Newton and Bobby Seale in 1966. It focused both on social campaigns to support the community and on protecting the black community from police brutality.

Source J

The *Mangrove* restaurant, 10 August 1970.

Frank Crichlow and the *Mangrove* restaurant

Frank Crichlow was a Trinidadian who opened the *Mangrove* restaurant at 8 All Saints Road in Notting Hill. The restaurant served good Caribbean food and was popular with black and white celebrities. Muhammad Ali, Bob Marley, Diana Ross, Sammy Davis Junior, Vanessa Redgrave and Marvin Gaye all ate there.

- Like 9 Blenheim Crescent, the *Mangrove* was a place where people would go to get information, advice and help for their problems. The BBP frequently met there, as did the Notting Hill Carnival organisers.
- Crichlow had a lawyer in the restaurant who would give advice to young black people who had suffered from police brutality or the Sus Law*.
- Crichlow also sponsored the Mangrove Steel Band, which gave black youngsters a chance to learn a skill, preserve their culture and entertain the community.

The police were suspicious and regularly raided the venue claiming they were looking for drugs – but they never found any. The restaurant was raided nine times between January 1969 and July 1970.

Furious at this unfair harassment, the BBP helped the community to organise a march on 9 August 1970 to protest the police action. The Action Group for the Defence of the *Mangrove* sent an open letter to announce the plans for the demonstration to protect the *Mangrove* to the Home Office, the prime minister, the leader of the opposition and the high commissioners of Jamaica, Trinidad, Guyana and Barbados.

The march against police harassment of the *Mangrove* restaurant, 9 August 1970. The photo was taken on All Saints Road – the *Mangrove* is on the left-hand side of the street behind the crowd.

Over 150 people took part in the march. Special Branch monitored the *Mangrove* and its customers, as well as the BPP. The police made a number of arrests. Among those arrested were Frank Crichlow, Darcus Howe and Altheia Jones-LeCointe. Among the charges was a claim under the Race Relations Act that the marchers had been trying to incite racial violence.

Activities ?

1 Why do you think the police actions against the *Mangrove* were seen as racist?
2 Read Source K. What does this source tell us about the reasons behind the march?

The Mangrove Nine

The defendants

At first magistrates threw the charges out. However, the Director of Public Prosecutions decided to press charges against nine of the marchers. They became known as the Mangrove Nine. They were:

- Frank Crichlow, the owner of the *Mangrove*
- Altheia Jones-LeCointe, Darcus Howe and Barbara Beese, leaders of the BBP
- Rhodan Gordon (who later founded organisations to help the black community with legal advice)
- Rothwell Kentish (who later campaigned for improved housing for the black community and for greater training for the young unemployed)
- Activists Rupert Boyce, Anthony Innis and Godfrey Millett.

Open letter, sent by Anthony Mohipp, barrister and secretary of the Black Improvement Organisation, 12 August 1970, announcing plans for the march.

We, the Black People of London have called this demonstration in protest against constant police harassment which is being carried out against us, and which is condoned by the legal system.

These deliberate raids, harassments and provocations [of the Mangrove] have been reported to the Home Office on many occasions. So too has the mounting list of grievances such as raids on West Indian parties, Wedding Receptions and other places where Black People lawfully gather.

We feel this protest is necessary as all other methods have failed to bring about any change in the manner the police have chosen to deal with Black People. We shall continue to protest until Black People are treated with justice by the Police and Law Courts.

Source M

In an interview published in *The Guardian* on 10 November 2020, Barbara Beese talked about the trial.

Such interference from the Director of Public Prosecutions was most unusual and, as far as we were concerned, reflected a determination to paint us as criminals rather than as citizens exercising our legitimate right to demonstrate against the repeated police harassment of the Mangrove.

Source N

A flyer produced during the trial by supporters of the Mangrove Nine.

They were accused of inciting a riot. If found guilty they would face long prison sentences. The home secretary insisted the trial took place at the Old Bailey, the court where only the most serious crimes were heard.

The trial

During the trial, the defendants argued that if they were going to be tried 'by their peers' (as British law demands) then the jury should be all black. They managed to get 63 jurors rejected, although the final jury had only two black people on it.

Source O

Report of Darcus Howe final speech to the jury, *Post Mercury*, 17 December 1971.

Howe said... he did not care if he was sent to prison. 'I don't care because history is on my side. If they put me in prison, they do not take away my liberty but reduce what little liberty I have. Every time I stand up to ask a question or cross examine its not because I'm seeking a verdict of not guilty but because I'm speaking for the people I represent.'

Howe told the jury the reaction of black people in North Kensington to the Mangrove Trial placed a tremendous responsibility on them. He defined the 'race riots' in 1958 as 'white people attacking black people because they believe we shouldn't be here' and said that as a result of them the black community of Notting Hill had been born to resist such attacks.

'When [The Mangrove] was attacked, people stopped coming. The restaurant started falling and the community organised itself to subsidise it. The Mangrove is ours not Frank's. Frank has lost it to the community.'

The trial focused on accusations of police brutality and racism. Howe and Jones defended themselves in court and they identified a number of damaging holes in the prosecution case. The police evidence was challenged and shown in some cases to be false or exaggerated. This also helped the jury to see the Mangrove Nine as victims, not the dangerous revolutionaries the prosecution wanted to suggest they were. The trial attracted a huge amount of public interest and coverage in the media.

The verdict

After the trial, all the defendants were acquitted of the most serious charges. Four of the nine were given suspended sentences for minor offences.

In his summing up the Judge ruled that 'What this trial has shown is that there is clearly evidence of racial hatred on both sides.' This admission that there was racism in the police was hugely important as it confirmed what the black community knew had been the case for decades. The home secretary asked the judge to take back this statement, but the judge refused.

Fighting institutional racism took a huge toll on all those involved. Normal, everyday people had to take on the entire justice system with money the activists did not have. The fact that they won is remarkable and was a landmark achievement in black British civil rights. The trial was seen as a great victory for the black community and inspired many people to organise against institutional racism.

Source P

From an interview with Frank Crichlow in the documentary film *Britain's Black Legacy* (1991).

I think I suffered very badly for what has happened in the '70s when we won that trial. I've been arrested nearly every year in the 70s I was on bail, you can easily say I was on bail for ten years, one case after the other. Don't ask me what kept me going. I think that I was standing up for my rights and that is where I got my strength from.

Source Q

From an interview in *The Guardian* 15 September 2018. Frank Crichlow remembers what the trial meant to the black community.

It was a turning point for black people. It put on trial the attitudes of the police, the Home Office, of everyone towards the black community. We took a stand and I am proud of what we achieved – we forced them to sit down and rethink harassment. It was decided there must be more law centres and more places to help people with their problems.

Activities

1 Look at Sources M, N, O and P. How useful are these sources in identifying how important the Mangrove Nine were to the black British civil rights movement?

2 Read through sources A–Q and list the different forms of discrimination faced by the African Caribbean community in the Notting Hill area.

3 Look at Sources P and Q. In them Frank Crichlow remembers the trial at two different points in his life. What can these two sources tell us about how people's views of events in their life change over time?

Exam-style question, Section A

How could you follow up Source Q to find out more about the importance of the Mangrove Nine case to the black community in Britain? In your answer, you must give the question you would ask and the type of source you could use. Copy and complete the table.

Details in Source Q that I would follow up	
Question I would ask	
What types of sources I could use	
How this might help answer my question	

(4 marks)

Exam tip

This question involves a four-stage process. The example shows you what to do at each stage.

1 *Pick a detail*: e.g. It was a turning point for black people'
2 *Choose a question*: e.g. How far did the Mangrove Nine case help to improve racism and policing for black people in Britain?
3 *Suggest the type of source to use*: e.g. The records of the Metropolitan Police Department for Notting Hill in 1971.
4 *Explain how this would help answer the question*: e.g. The data would show whether the numbers of arrests of Afro-Caribbeans in the Notting Hill area increased, remained steady or decreased and this would allow the words 'it was a turning point for black people' to be quantified.

5.5 Summary

- Claudia Jones set up the *West Indian Gazette* in 1958 in response to the many challenges faced by the black community in Britain. Her Caribbean Carnival laid the groundwork for the Notting Hill Carnival.
- In the 1960s, several groups emerged to fight for civil rights, for example the British Black Panthers (BPP). They focused on police brutality, jobs, housing, education, healthcare and legal support.
- The *Mangrove* restaurant was a cultural and community centre for black people in the West London area of Notting Hill. The police often raided the restaurant.
- After a protest march, nine people were arrested and charged with riot. The defendants used the trial to focus on wider issues of institutional racism in Britain. The trial became a major symbol of success for the black community fighting against institutional racism in Britain.

Checkpoint

Strengthen

S1 Why was the Notting Hill Carnival so successful?
S2 What were the most important reasons for the growth of black activism in Britain?
S3 Why was the Mangrove Nine case so significant in the fight for black people's civil rights in Britain?

Challenge

C1 How do the Notting Hill Carnival, the British Black Panthers and the Mangrove Nine case link together in the fight for black people's civil rights in Britain?
C2 How much progress have we made as a society regarding the civil rights of black people in Britain? Discuss the similarities or differences between the *Mangrove* protest march of the 1970s compared to the Black Lives Matter marches of 2020.

Asking questions: The *Mangrove* march

Historians ask themselves three types of questions:

- What about the content?
- What about the provenance?
- What about the context?

Look at Source A.

Source A

Black Power march protesting police harassment of the *Mangrove* restaurant, West London, 9 August 1970. Here, 150 protesters are flanked by 200 police officers, who later charged the Mangrove Nine with inciting a riot at the march.

Content questions: What are you looking at? You have some important help from the caption, but even without that, you can see Source A shows the police response to this protest.

Provenance questions: Now you need the caption! Remember, for provenance, you need to break things down into nature, origin and purpose.

- *Nature* – it's a photograph.
- *Origin* comes from the caption – National Archives catalogue. It captures the response of the police to the *Mangrove* restaurant protest; it was considered valuable (it was stored in the National Archives).

- *Purpose* can be hard for a photograph such as this. Does it look like it was set up specially? Might it be used as propaganda? Perhaps it was selected to make the point that the policing of Caribbeans in Notting Hill was excessive and discriminatory. Or perhaps the police wanted to show how many officers were needed to control the march.

Context questions: You know several things that are relevant to Source A, including the following:

- the attitude of the police and their practices were evidence of institutional racism
- Frank Crichlow was the owner of the *Mangrove* restaurant in Notting Hill, which was a place for the black community to eat, discuss social and welfare issues, and gain advice for housing problems
- the police viewed these meetings as a threat and led a series of raids on the *Mangrove*, which were justified on the grounds that the restaurant was selling drugs
- after this photo was taken, the Mangrove Nine were taken to court accused of inciting a riot and were found innocent.

So, if you were asked how useful Source A is as evidence about an enquiry into the policing of Frank Crichlow and the *Mangrove* restaurant, you could say something like this, covering content, provenance and context:

'Source A is useful as evidence about the policing of Frank Crichlow and the *Mangrove* restaurant because it shows the excessive methods deployed against the black community: there are a disproportionate number of police officers monitoring a peaceful protest march.

We know that the police held racist attitudes towards the black community and so led a series of raids on the restaurant on the grounds of alleged drug sales.

It's possible that the photograph was taken to show excessive policing – it's been taken from the front and shows the police more prominently than it shows the marchers.'

What this does (and what you can do) is explain why Source A is useful, using criteria based on the three types of question.

Source B

Some of the marchers at the Black Power protest against police harassment of the *Mangrove* restaurant, West London, 9 August 1970. In this image, the signs read 'Leave Mangrove Alone' and 'The Pigs. The Pigs, We Got to Get Rid of The Pigs'. The police stated that they believed these signs showed the marchers were planning violence.

Source C

Statement made by Frank Crichlow to the Race Relations Board, 23 December 1969.

I received on 23 December 1969 a letter from Mr John Weir of the Kensington Council, refusing to renew my licence to operate as an All Night Cafe. My restaurant is patronised by respectable people, has never had a case with the Police before – although they have unlawfully raided the premises on two occasions.

One of the grounds of refusal of the licence was that people with criminal records, prostitutes and convicted persons use the premises and the manager allows them to have meals. This power they claim is vested by the New Act [Greater Powers Act] of the GLC [Greater London Council].

I am the first person test case under the New Act – I object to the entire incident. Because I know it is because I am a Black citizen of Britain that I am discriminated against.

The **content** of Source B is fairly easy to understand, but the **provenance** makes it a little more difficult to **assess**. It preserves a moment in time from the past. We don't know all we might like to know about its **origin**, but it is taken during a peaceful protest and its purpose is probably to show the support for the campaign against racist policing. We must be cautious, however, as such photographs may have been set up to promote the argument of the Mangrove Nine that the march was completely peaceful.

Something similar might be happening with Source E. The police planted photographers in the crowd and ordered them to photograph anything that could be used to incriminate the marchers. This photo was taken by the police and was meant to support their case against the Mangrove Nine. This could mean the photo was staged so it does not give a fair picture of what was happening on the march.

Source C is a statement from Frank Crichlow, capturing his personal thoughts about his treatment at the hands of the Metropolitan Police. We know it was written to complain about his treatment and belief that the police were racist – this helps us to gain an understanding of treatment of Frank Crichlow by the police. However, it might be highly emotive, which we have to assess carefully.

Source D needs careful analysis. PC Pulley was one of the officers involved in policing the march and he was accused by the Mangrove Nine of leading the prosecution against them. PC Pulley held racist views and may have exaggerated his statement about the Mangrove Nine to protect himself and his colleagues from dismissal. No photographs could be found to support PC Pulley's statements. This source could tell us how Pulley and other officers twisted what they reported to justify their actions.

Source D

PC Frank Pulley, one of the police officers, made a key witness statement at the trial that claimed the banners showed violent intent. However photos showed only signs saying 'hands off us pigs'.

[They] read 'kill the pigs', 'slavery is still here' and 'the pigs are gonna get your mama'.

Source E

Black Power protest against police harassment of the *Mangrove* restaurant, West London, 9 August 1970. (Photograph taken by a police photographer.)

All five of these sources are only partially useful for answering the big question: What was the treatment of Frank Crichlow and the Mangrove Nine by the police?

So the historian looks for other sources: for example, oral interviews, witness statements and newspaper reports about the treatment of Frank Crichlow and the Mangrove Nine. This adds detail: the reasons, the individuals involved and the reaction of the local community.

This leads to another question: was this treatment of black people in Britain by the police typical? So, historians then compare the records for Notting Hill with other areas in Britain with a high number of Asians and black people living there.

Asking questions in the exam

The exam gives you a start by asking questions. The best way to do well is to ask some more questions – to establish the criteria you will use to make and explain your judgements, and to help you work out the best answers. The criteria you use as the reasons for your answer are one of the main things you will get marks for. So:

- ask yourself the questions
- use the questions to help you decide the best criteria
- use the criteria to explain your answer.

Activities ?

1   Look at the provenance of Source D. What might be a particular strength of this source as evidence about police treatment of the black community?

2   Now look at Source E. It was taken by the police to implicate [accuse] the Mangrove Nine. How much value would a source like this have for the enquiry?

THINKING HISTORICALLY Evidence (3a)

The value of evidence

Look at Source C, then work through the tasks that follow.

1   Write down at least two ways in which the account is useful for finding out about the treatment of Frank Crichlow and the *Mangrove* restaurant at the hands of the Metropolitan Police.

2   Compare your answers with those of a partner, then try to come up with at least one limitation of the source for explaining the treatment of Frank Crichlow and the *Mangrove* restaurant at the hands of the Metropolitan Police.

3   With your partner, decide how useful this source is for explaining the treatment of Frank Crichlow and the *Mangrove* restaurant at the hands of the Metropolitan Police on a scale of 1 to 10 (10 being very useful).

4   What if the source was used to answer the question: 'How did the black community respond to the treatment of the *Mangrove* restaurant?'

   a   Write down any ways in which the source is useful for answering this new question.

   b   Write down any limitations for answering the new question.

   c   Can you think of another enquiry about the Mangrove Nine for which this would be a useful source? Write it down and score the source on a scale of 1 to 10.

5   Compare your scores out of 10. How does the question being asked affect how useful a source is? Explain your answer.

6   Can you think of any other factors that might affect the usefulness of the source?

Using the range of sources

In the examination, you are asked to suggest a possible question and a type of source that you could use to follow up another source. As an example, this is what you might do if asked this about Source D. The framework of the question helps you through the four-stage process.

1   The detail you might follow up could be one of the problems listed, e.g. racism and policing in the Notting Hill area.

2   The question you might ask is: 'How problematic was racism within the police force?'

3   There are many different types of source in this unit. You could suggest any one of these:
   – evidence presented to Parliament
   – newspapers (local and national)
   – official records of employment of police officers in the area (where did the majority of police officers come from)?

4   Lastly, you have to explain the reason for your choice:
   – oral interviews (because they provide first-hand reports of the treatment of those the police were supposed to protect)
   – official records (because police boards have records, including lists of all the problems detailing the arrests and the demographic of the people who were arrested).

Activities ?

Using the range of sources

How useful a source is depends on the question being asked. Look at all of the sources in this chapter, and then decide which sources would be most useful to answer the following enquiry questions:

1   Why did the police and black community in Notting Hill have such a fractured relationship?

2   What was policing like in Notting Hill?

3   Why was there so much tension between the white British and Caribbean communities in the 1950s to 1970s?

4   What problems were faced by Frank Crichlow and the Mangrove Nine?

Preparing for your GCSE Paper 1 exam

Paper 1 overview

Your Paper 1 is in two sections that examine the Historic Environment and the Thematic Depth Study. Together they count for 30% of your History assessment. The questions on the Historic Environment: Notting Hill, 1948–c1970 are in Section A and are worth 10% of your History assessment. Allow about a third of the examination time for Section A, making sure you leave enough time for Section B.

History Paper 1	Historic Environment and Thematic Depth Study			Time 1 hour 15 minutes
Section A	Historic Environment	Answer 3 questions	16 marks	25 mins
Section B	Thematic Depth Study	Answer 3 questions	32 marks + 4 SPaG marks	50 mins

Historic Environment: Notting Hill c1948–c1970

You will answer Question 1 and Question 2, which is in two parts.

Q1 Describe two features of... (4 marks)

You are given a few lines to write about each feature. Allow 5 minutes to write your answer. It is worth 4 marks, so keep the answer brief.

Q2(a) How useful are Sources A and B...? (8 marks)

You are given two sources to make judgements about. They are in a separate sources booklet, so you can keep them in front of you while you write your answer. Allow 15 minutes for this question, to give yourself time to read both sources carefully. Make sure your answer refers to both sources.

You should **ask yourself the following questions about the sources**:

- What useful information do they give? What do they say or show? Check the question and only give details that are directly relevant to that topic.
- What can you infer? What do they suggest?

You must also **evaluate the sources**.

- Use contextual knowledge – for example, to evaluate accuracy or how typical they are.
- Use the provenance (nature, origin, purpose of the source) to weigh up the strengths and limitations of each source.
- Make **judgements** about the usefulness of each source, giving clear reasons. These could be based on the accuracy of the content, judged against your knowledge, and on the provenance of the source.

Analyse
- Useful information
- What does it suggest?

+

Evaluate
- Contextual knowledge
- Its strengths and limitations

Q2(b) Study Source... How could you follow up Source... to find out more about...? (4 marks)

You are given a table to complete when you answer this question. It has four parts to it:

- the detail you would follow up
- the question you would ask
- the type of source you could use to find the information
- your explanation of how this information would help answer the question.

Allow 5 minutes to write your answer. You should keep your answer brief and not try to fill extra lines. The question is worth 4 marks. Plan your answer so that all the parts link. Your answer will not be strong if you choose a detail to follow up, but then cannot think of a question or type of source that would help you follow it up.

Paper 1, Question 1

Describe **two** features of discrimination faced by the Caribbean community during the 1950s.

(4 marks)

Basic answer

Feature 1:
Black people faced discrimination in employment.

Feature 2:
Black people faced problems with housing.

The answer has identified two features, but with no supporting information.

Verdict

This is a basic answer because two valid features are given, but there is no supporting information. Use the feedback to rewrite this answer, making as many improvements as you can.

Good answer

Feature 1:
Black people faced discrimination within employment. Black employees were paid less than white people for doing the same job.

Feature 2:
Black people faced problems with housing. Many landlords were not happy about letting black people rent their properties, with signs like 'No Blacks' being common.

The answer has identified two features and describes them in more detail. There is a description of the discrimination faced by Caribbean people during the 1950s.

Verdict

This is a good answer because it gives two clear features of 'discrimination' faced by Caribbean people in the 1950s and gives extra detail to clarify the features.

Sources for use with Section A

Source A

Extract from the novel *The Lonely Londoners*, by Samuel Selvon (born in Trinidad and later migrated to Notting Hill), published in 1956. Here Selvon writes about what life was like in the Notting Hill area in the 1950s, using the slang that the Caribbean community in Notting Hill used at the time.

This is the real world, where men know what it is to hustle a pound to pay the rent when Friday come. The houses around here old and grey and weatherbeaten, the walls cracking like the last days of Pompeii, it ain't have no hot water, and… none of the houses have bath. You had to buy one of them big basins and boil the water and fill it up, or else go to the public bath. Some of the houses still had gas light, which is to tell you how old they was. All the houses in a row in the street, on both sides, they build like one long house with walls separating them in parts, so your house jam-up between two neighbours… The street does be always dirty except if rain fall…

Note: Pompeii was an ancient Roman city, which was destroyed by a volcano in AD 79.

Source B

A young black man looks for housing in London in 1958.

Paper 1, Question 2a

Study Sources A and B in the Sources Booklet (see page 195).

Study Sources A and B. How useful are Sources A and B for an enquiry into the problems of housing in Notting Hill?

Explain your answer, using Sources A and B and your own knowledge of the historical context. **(8 marks)**

Exam tip

Consider the strengths and weaknesses of the evidence. Your evaluation must link to the enquiry and use contextual knowledge. Your reasons (criteria) for judgement should be clear. Include points about:

- What information is relevant and what can you infer from the source?
- How does the provenance (nature, origin, purpose) of each source affect its usefulness?

Basic answer

Source A is useful because we can learn from it that the houses were not in good condition. This can be shown from the quote 'walls cracking like the last days of Pompeii'.

Source B is useful because it gives us a first-hand insight into the experience of Caribbean migrants in Notting Hill. We know that many landlords in Notting Hill refused to rent to black people.

Some useful information is taken from the source. The answer suggests an inference – 'walls cracking like the last days of Pompeii', but does not really explain or develop this regarding housing problems.

Verdict

This is a basic answer because:

- it has taken relevant information from both sources and shown some analysis by beginning to make an inference
- it has added in some relevant contextual knowledge and used it for some evaluation of one of the sources, but knowledge needs to be used for both
- it does not explain criteria for judgement clearly enough to be a strong answer. The evaluation using the provenance of the sources should be more developed.

Use the feedback to rewrite this answer, making as many improvements as you can.

Paper 1, Question 2a

Study Sources A and B in the Sources Booklet (see page 195).

Study Sources A and B. How useful are Sources A and B for an enquiry into the problems of housing in Notting Hill?

Explain your answer, using Sources A and B and your own knowledge of the historical context. **(8 marks)**

Good answer

Source A is also useful because we can learn about the problems that Caribbean people experienced in housing. The quote 'walls cracking like the last days of Pompeii' indicates to us that landlords did not take care of the accommodation. Many landlords chose not to spend money on improving their houses and overcharged Caribbean migrants rent. The source gives us a useful insight into accommodation. However, as the source is a novel the author may have exaggerated or overplayed the problems with housing in order to entertain his audience. Nevertheless, it was written by someone who lived during this period so gives us an accurate insight into housing conditions and this is supported by my own knowledge.

Source B is useful for learning about the housing problems in Notting Hill because we can infer that the landlords didn't want any Caribbean tenants. Many landlords had signs up saying they didn't want any black people as tenants, such as in the source. The houses of landlords who did let out were often run-down properties with mould and draughts. They would charge Caribbean tenants three times what they would charge white tenants but avoided spending any money to improve the homes because it would affect their profits. However, we are not certain whether the source captures life in just Notting Hill or the UK for Caribbean migrants in general.

> Strengths and limitations of the source are shown and contextual knowledge is used in the evaluation, which also comments on the nature of each source, using details.

Verdict

This is a good answer because:

- it has analysed both sources, making inferences from them
- it has used contextual knowledge in the evaluation of both sources
- the evaluation takes provenance into account and explains criteria clearly when making judgements.

Paper 1, Question 2b

Study Source A (see page 195).

How could you follow up Source A to find out more about the problems of housing in Notting Hill?

In your answer, you must give the question you would ask and the type of source you would use.

Complete the table below.

(4 marks)

Basic answer

Detail in Source A I would follow up:

None of the houses have baths.

Question I would ask:

How did Caribbean people respond to the poor housing conditions in Notting Hill?

What type of source I would use:

Oral testimonies.

How this might help answer my question:

They would provide first-hand information on the responses of Caribbean people to the housing problems.

The question is linked to the detail to be followed up.

The choice of source is not specific and the explanation does not show how the source would help answer the question.

Verdict

This is a basic answer because the explanation of the choice of source is not developed. The candidate needs to be more specific about what type of oral interviews would be useful, and why.

Use the feedback to rewrite this answer, making as many improvements as you can.

Good answer

Detail in Source A I would follow up:

The new Caribbean community started to form its own cultural identity to solve this problem.

Question I would ask:

How important was it for the Caribbean community to form its own cultural identity to survive in the UK?

What type of source I would use:

The West Indian Gazette showing articles and reports of the new initiatives formed by the Caribbean community.

How this might help answer my question:

The West Indian Gazette would inform on regular events and organisations that were formed by the black community. The origins of initiatives like pardner schemes and a judgement on the impact can be reached based on the number of Caribbean people who attended, the types of programmes that were on offer and the legacies of the initiatives.

The answer has given a question directly linked to the issue identified.

The explanation is linked back to the question for follow-up and the type of source chosen.

Verdict

This is a good answer because connections between the source details, the question and the source chosen for follow-up are securely linked.

Index